Edmund Wilson
A Critic for our Time

Edmund Wilson
A Critic for our Time

BY JANET GROTH

Ohio University Press Athens

Ohio University Press books are printed on acid-free paper ∞

Library of Congress Cataloging-in-Publication Data

Groth, Janet, 1936-
    Edmund Wilson : a critic for our time / by Janet Groth.
        p.   cm.
    Bibliography: p.
    Includes index.
    ISBN 0-8214-0919-0
    1. Wilson, Edmund, 1895-1972 – Criticism and interpretation. 2. Criticism –
United States – History – 20th century.   I. Title.
PS3545.I6245Z67   1989
818'.5209 – dc 19   88-32467   CIP

For A. L.

TABLE OF CONTENTS

So rich is the legacy from Edmund Wilson's long critical career that one hardly knows where to begin to elucidate it. Ranging quickly through some of the high points of that career may be as good a way as any to start, then, though with no pretense of being comprehensive.

It is particularly striking to note how often Wilson was in the forefront of critical appreciation of authors both foreign and domestic. His first book of criticism, *Axel's Castle* (1931), for example, was instrumental in furthering the understanding and appreciation of such poets of the Symbolist movement as W. B. Yeats, T. S. Eliot, and Paul Valéry.

The book not only gave a coherent account of the Symbolist movement itself, of which it was conceived as a study, but it also provided a major boost to the appreciation in America of such then little-known and scarcely understood prose writers as Marcel Proust and James Joyce. Even though Symbolism was a movement largely associated with poetry, Wilson identified Symbolist techniques used by Proust and Joyce, and his essays on each did a great deal to make *Remembrance of Things Past* and *Ulysses* accessible to readers in this country.

As the contributor of one of the major essays in the famous 1934 Henry James issue of *Hound and Horn*, Wilson may be said to have participated in a significant way in the James *risorgimento*. His reference in that essay to the ghosts in *The Turn of the Screw* as hallucinations of the governess started a critical hare that is still leading graduate students a merry chase.

Fitzgerald and Hemingway both were given important status as serious writers as a result of early and discerning praise from Wilson. His was the first serious look, too, at several new literary genres – or subgenres, if you will. The phenomenon of West Coast writing in general – the detective novel and the Hollywood novel in particular – are areas of the canon that are only now getting full-fledged scholarly attention. His precedent also began the modern enthusiasms for Nathanael West, John Berryman, and Edward Gorey.

As for women writers, Wilson, though by no means entirely free of sexism, was nevertheless a pioneer in the renewed attention now being paid to the novels of Harriet Beecher Stowe, Edith Wharton, and Kate Chopin and to the diaries of Mary Chestnut and Anais Nin.

Wilson always saw it as one of his chief goals to function as a "cross-fertilizer" between Anglo-American culture and that of the European countries. As witness to the success of that aspiration, we have his essays on Proust and Malraux, Pushkin, Turgenev, and Pasternak. One significant entry in the list of his labors to bring Russian and American culture together must not be left out of this account. Although their later relationship was to be stormy, Wilson gave very considerable momentum to the American career of Vladimir Nabokov by virtue of the favorable critical attention he brought to Nabokov's early novels (which he himself disliked and so refrained from reviewing.)

Perhaps the crowning achievement of Wilson's work as a literary critic is his essay on "Dickens: The Two Scrooges," a landmark of Dickens criticism of which Denis Donoghue has written: "It is hardly too much to say that we think of Dickens largely in Wilson's terms. . . . [as] an artist of modern fears and divisions. . . . [H]e is of the modern dispensation now, a tragic hero. . . . [A] major artist, companion of Shakespeare, George Eliot, James, Dostoevsky, Tolstoy."[1]

With accomplishments like these to his credit, why do I feel an impulse to defend my decision to produce a major study of Wilson as literary critic? The answer, surely, lies in the sort of criticism he practiced.

Throughout his long career, the feature that most clearly distinguishes Edmund Wilson's work as a critic is its persistent relation of literature to life and of life to history. It need hardly be said that such criticism is distinctly out of fashion. Indeed, in the context of structuralism, deconstruction, semiotics, and theories of the reading act – modes characterized chiefly by their rigorous expulsion of any reference beyond the *text qua text* – such an approach seems hopelessly diffuse.

Yet, it is an approach that fits well with older notions of what might constitute an ideal or comprehensive criticism; with Kenneth Burke's contention, for example, that the critic should use "all that there is to use"[2] or with R. S. Crane's description of criticism "in the grand line of Longinus, Coleridge and Matthew Arnold." (Had Crane taken into account the continuation of that line among the French, he might have added Sainte-Beuve, Taine, Michelet, and Renan.) Such criticism, he says, "mirrors the souls of writers" and attempts "to replace the works we study in the circumstances and temper of their times and see them as expressions and forces as well as subjects of art."[3]

Working in that tradition, Wilson found a way to make the tradition answerable to twentieth-century critical needs. He did so by incorporating into it elements based on the work of Marx and Freud – elements not so very different, I might add, from those used by such neo-Marxist and neo-Freudian critics as Lukacs, Eagleton, and Lacan.

These, then, are the key elements and underlying aims of Wilson's work, as will be attested to by a look at any of his major essays, such as those on Yeats, Proust, James, Dickens, and Stowe. In them, Wilson manifests characteristics of both the sympathetic critic (the Neoptolemus figure) and the suffering artist (the Philoctetes figure) of his retold Greek myth, "The Wound and the Bow." Seen from another point of view, this essay is his paradigm for the fate of the artistic act in society, a fate that is likely to fail or lack completeness unless the skills of both artist and critic are brought to bear.

The very breadth of Wilson's approach makes boundaries difficult to come by. But this is exactly the kind of critic Wilson elected to be. Others took the elements of Freudian thought or, conversely, Marxian thought in his work as occasions to call him a Freudian critic or a Marxist critic; he himself called the criticism he practiced "the historical interpretation of literature." For me the permanent value of Wilson's work resides in that single though unwieldy principle I have identified as its relation to life.

I say nothing here of Wilson the man – although a late chapter of this book looks briefly at Wilson's life in the course of some psychological speculation about unconscious sources of his criticism. Wilson the critic, however, garnered rich rewards of recognition in his lifetime. Among the honors heaped upon him were a National Book Award, a MacDowell prize, and the Medal of Freedom. But he was not without *his* critics, too, notably Stanley Edgar Hyman.

Perhaps because he had been persuaded of its evident imbalance, Hyman chose not to include his largely negative chapter on Wilson in later editions of his influential book, *The Armed Vision*. But, in the first edition, he takes Wilson to task on a number of points and finally dismisses him as a mere "translator," an introducer or popularizer of literature. In a more reasoned, and telling, study, Delmore Schwartz sounds a recurrent complaint when he notices – and deplores – the invariable emphasis Wilson gives to content over form.

The question arises, Does it constitute a defect of critical ability to concentrate on the social and biographical aspects of a work to the relative exclusion of specific details of formal technique? To a very great extent, it seems to me, the answer depends upon an understanding of the kind of criticism being practiced. In Wilson's case, it depends on an understanding of the fact that he is writing literary criticism in the tradition of Matthew Arnold and Sainte-Beuve; that is, as an art form, not as a form of academic scholarship. Judging from the bleak remarks recently made by Alfred Kazin and Jacques Barzun regarding the repellent aspects of professionalism and obscurity in current academic criticism, a return to the form of criticism that habitually links literature to life may be on the horizon.[4]

If so, Edmund Wilson is a model to emulate, ready to hand. This criticism, as Crane says, has the merit of being able to display "those general qualities of writing. . . . for the sake of which most of us read or at any rate return to what we have read."[5] It is not the only form of criticism needed, of course, but I believe it will be of increasing importance as we move into a postprint culture, an essential counterweight, as it were, to the nihilism of so much postmodernist criticism. For this reason, I call my book *Edmund Wilson: A Critic for Our Time.*

ACKNOWLEDGMENTS

I am grateful to friends, colleagues, and members of the professional staffs at the following institutions for their assistance in many ways during the preparation of this book for publication: The New Yorker Magazine, The Graduate School of Arts and Sciences at New York University, The University of Cincinnati, and the State University of New York at Plattsburgh.

Particular thanks must go to Dr. Austin Wright of the University of Cincinnati, Dr. Barbara Eckstein of Tulane University, Dr. John Gery of the University of New Orleans, Dr. Herbert Bowman, Professor Emeritus of the University of Toronto, Dr. Norman Vance of the University of Sussex, Dr. Edgar Burde, Dr. Peter Corodimas and Dr. John Shout of the State University of New York at Plattsburgh and Paul Johnston, doctoral candidate at the University of Michigan, each of whom read the manuscript, whole or in part, and made useful suggestions.

Dr. Raney Ellis, Helen Rock, James Holland and Tanvir Ahmed lent their computer expertise to the project; Gretchen Shine, Elizabeth Bowman, Evangeline Mandel, Dr. Ben Morreale and Linda Coffey Morreale, Albert Lazar, Eric Anderson, Dr. Carl Engelhart and Margaret Engelhart all provided vital space and shelter in which to work.

Laurie Curtis and Jennifer Carlson of the Special Collections, McFarlin Library, at the University of Tulsa, and Lisa Phillipson of Utica College were helpful in providing photographs of Edmund Wilson.

For these and a multitude of other kindnesses, my thanks.

J. G.
Plattsburgh, N.Y.
September 1988

All selections are reprinted by permission of Farrar, Straus and Giroux, Inc.

Excerpts from *The Bit Between My Teeth* by Edmund Wilson. Copyright © 1939, 1940, 1947, 1950, 1951, 1952, 1953, 1956, 1957, 1958, 1959, 1960, 1961, 1962, 1963, 1965 by Edmund Wilson.

Excerpts from *Classics and Commercials* by Edmund Wilson. Copyright © 1950 by Edmund Wilson.

Excerpts from *Letters on Literature and Politics* by Edmund Wilson. Copyright © 1956 by Edmund Wilson.

Excerpts from *The Shores of Light* by Edmund Wilson. Copyright © 1980 by Helen Miranda Wilson.

Excerpts from *To the Finland Station* by Edmund Wilson. Copyright © 1968 by Edmund Wilson.

Excerpts from *The Twenties* by Edmund Wilson. Copyright © 1975 by Elena Wilson, Executrix of the Estate of Edmund Wilson.

Excerpts from *A Window on Russia* by Edmund Wilson. Copyright © 1943, 1944, 1952, 1957, 1965, 1969, 1970, 1971, 1972 by Edmund Wilson, Copyright renewed © 1971, 1972 by Edmund Wilson.

Excerpts from *Upstate* by Edmund Wilson. Copyright © 1971 by Edmund Wilson.

Excerpts from *The Wound and the Bow* by Edmund Wilson. Copyright © 1929, 1932, 1938, 1940, and 1941 by Edmund Wilson.

Excerpts from *Patriotic Gore* by Edmund Wilson. Copyright © 1962 by Edmund Wilson.

Excerpts from *The Triple Thinkers* by Edmund Wilson. Copyright © 1938, 1948 by Edmund Wilson. Copyright renewed © 1956, 1971 by Edmund Wilson and 1976 by Elena Wilson, Executrix of the Estate of Edmund Wilson.

Reprinted with permission of Charles Scribner's Sons, an imprint of Macmillan Publishing Company from *Axel's Castle* by Edmund Wilson. Copyright © 1931 Charles Schribner's Sons; Copyright renewed © 1959 Edmund Wilson.

*E*dmund Wilson was born in 1895 and died in 1972. In the course of a professional career that spanned five decades, his literary output was impressive. In addition to the volumes of letters and journals now being brought out posthumously, Wilson left us five volumes of verse, two of fiction, thirteen plays, and more than twenty volumes of social commentary on travel, politics, history, religion, anthropology, and economics. All these volumes fall outside the scope of the present study, yet it is important not to forget them, for it is a vital part of seeing Wilson in the round to see him in his full dimension as a "universal literatus." (So the *Times Literary Supplement* has characterized him, stating that "only the European panoptic scholars come near matching Wilson for learning, and for sheer range of critical occupation there is no modern man to match him, not even Croce.")[1] An enormous body of work is to be borne in mind, then, even though the part of Wilson's career under assessment here is confined to one area, his contribution as a literary critic.

A good deal of commentary has already been written about Wilson's work, but surprisingly little of it has concentrated in any satisfactory way on the criticism itself. At the time this study was undertaken, four books had appeared on Wilson: Leonard Kriegel's *Edmund Wilson*, for Harry T. Moore's series, Crosscurrents/Modern Critiques, which is good on Wilson's political thought but weak on the criticism; Charles P. Frank's *Edmund Wilson*, for Twayne's United States Authors Series, which emphasizes Wilson's fiction while rather slighting the criticism; and Sherman Paul's *Edmund Wilson: A Study of Literary Vocation in Our Time*, which attempts a more comprehensive, personal approach. Paul's study, the first to be published on Wilson, contains no detailed analysis of Wilson's critical essays. It nevertheless provides some astute insights into Wilson and remains a useful discussion of his career up to 1965. More recently, there was *Edmund Wilson: The Man and His Work*, edited by John Wain. It is in the nature of a festschrift, containing celebratory essays by a number of contributors, some of which concern themselves – but only in a very general way – with the criticism.[2]

Since 1980, there have been a number of additions to the field: Richard Costa, a neighbor of Wilson's in Talcottville, supplies a volume of personal reminiscence; George H. Douglas, in *Edmund Wilson's America*, traces Wilson's thought in an intellectual history that concentrates on Wilson as an incisively correct analyst of American society; Philip French gathers in one volume materials from several BBC programs in *Three Honest Men: Edmund Wilson, F. R. Leavis, and Lionel Trilling;* and David Castronovo's *Edmund Wilson* provides an admirable brief critical biography, which does not, however, pretend to any intensive look into the tradition, method, or ultimate placing of Wilson as a literary critic, such as attempted here.[3]

Kriegel's and Frank's studies were originally doctoral dissertations – on Wilson's political thought and on his fiction, respectively. Other dissertations of which Wilson is the sole or partial subject now number twelve.[4] In addition, numerous articles make use of the occasion of reviewing specific Wilson books to discuss his work in general. Outstanding among these are the contributions of R. J. Kaufman, Norman Podhoretz, and Frank Kermode.[5]

Only two studies deal extensively with Wilson's critical contribution per se: James Morris Rodgers's "Dynamics of Creation: The Literary Criticism of Edmund Wilson" and Warner Berthoff's *Edmund Wilson*. Rodgers's 1967 study, a dissertation for the University of Rochester, is admirably thorough in summarizing Wilson's critical works, describing their reception, and demonstrating Wilson's personality-oriented approach and his dramatic method. However, it suffers from an unconvincing and arbitrary insistence that the most illuminating vantage point from which to understand Wilson's achievement is to view him as an eighteenth-century French philosophe.

Berthoff's study was written for the University of Minnesota Pamphlets on American Writers. His pamphlet represents the most authoritative attempt to "place" Wilson as a critic since Stanley Edgar Hyman made his determined assault on Wilson's critical reputation in the first edition of *The Armed Vision* (see Preface).

Although it is both more appreciative and more temperate, Berthoff's critique, like Hyman's, is weakened by a tendency to be reductionist in his view of Wilson and by an attempt to discredit Wilson's work as a critic because he was a journalist rather than an academic. For instance, although maintaining that "at no point . . . does Edmund Wilson strike us as profound or original" he notes that Wilson "from his earliest reviews . . . had known how to make his subjects interesting – the *sine qua non* of effective journalism."[6]

Berthoff proves somewhat unreliable, too, in his picture of Wilson the man: he follows his description of Wilson's characteristic vices (impatience, irritability) with the observation that

> the point to be made about them is that they are not merely personal failings but the intellectual expedients of a whole identifiable class. His postures as a critic are those of the privileged and established old resident, American style . . . beset by uneasiness at some of the changes taking place before him but not compelled to add them up and arrive at a genuinely new sum.[7]

This point of view does not take into account the fact that Wilson was considered a radical and bohemian thinker throughout the early part of his career. Also, it seems impossible to think of such books as *Axel's Castle, To the Finland Station,* or *Memoirs of Hecate County* as the work of the person Berthoff describes. Berthoff's position is revealing but incomplete. Certain passages in Wilson's autobiographical writings – particularly the journal of his late years, *Upstate* – attest that on occasion he was given to characterizing himself in a similar vein, but his work actually presents a more complex approach.

As I have indicated, the present study deals specifically with the *literary* criticism of Edmund Wilson. It is organized in four major parts in twelve chapters. The first part is devoted to a brief survey of Wilson's critical stance; it features a catalogue of Wilson's critical preoccupations, his style, method, aims, and the progress of his critical career. The next part goes on to describe the humanistic background from which his work sprang.

The third part offers documentation of Wilson's critical practice in terms of analyses of key essays, such as those on Proust, Dickens, James, and Nabokov. Among them they cover the early, middle, and late phases of his critical writing. In the cases of James and Nabokov they encompass special issues of controversy. The former reviews the difference of critical opinion that arose regarding Wilson's interpretation of Henry James's story, "The Turn of the Screw." This discussion grew out of Wilson's essay, "The Ambiguity of Henry James," in *The Triple Thinkers* (1938). The latter includes a resume of Wilson's prolonged disagreement, in print, with his distinguished contemporary and friend, Vladimir Nabokov, over Nabokov's translation of *Eugene Onegin*. It is covered here in terms of Wilson's essay on Nabokov and Pushkin, from *A Window on Russia*, a collection of Wilson's Russian pieces brought out in 1972.

The fourth, and final, part consists of two chapters. The first, Chapter 11, examines certain serious criticisms of Wilson's work put forward by earlier commentators in addition to those by Hyman and Berthoff.

The second chapter of the fourth section, Chapter 12, offers a more psychologically oriented analysis of Wilson's critical personality. It involves an examination of his art-myth, "Philoctetes: The Wound and the Bow," as a projection of his own situation. Called "The Two Wilsons" in conscious recollection of his own title, "The Two Scrooges," this chapter seeks to establish that Wilson was both the sympathetic critic (the Neoptolemus figure) and the suffering artist (the Philoctetes figure) of his retold Greek myth. The first vantage point affords a means of setting forth the strengths and weaknesses of Wilson's position as a critic. The second provides an opportunity for some psychological speculation about the unconscious sources of Wilson's criticism and the chance to draw upon the autobiographical material that has now begun to be published in the form of Wilson journals – material that, for the most part, was unavailable to writers of previous studies.

Finally – and it is hoped, within just proportions – Wilson's genuine achievements as a critic are celebrated. Wilson, like Arnold, actively promoted the use of literature for educating and humanizing the culture at large. The benefits he attributed to literature extended to the realm of the psychological, the private person as well. He believed that literature has the power to relieve the "worried intelligence and the balked emotions" of both the artist as he creates it and the reader as he sympathetically receives it."[8] When there is some hindrance to that sympathetic reception, the critic, in Wilson's view, exercises yet another function of literature – to remove the barriers of misunderstanding that might exist between a work of art and the society that both needs and resists its vision.

Like Arnold's, Wilson's importance rests upon his prominence as an exemplar of the humanist type, almost more than on his criticism itself. Often called *men of letters*, representatives of this breed have a special significance today as bearers of humanist values into a postprint culture.

As Lionel Trilling has pointed out, "anyone who has any sensitivity at all to the temper of our own time . . must see that our intellectual and emotional temper is anything but cordial to humanism – has not, really, been cordial to humanism for some decades."[9] In Wilson's lifetime, that tradition boasted precious few remnants to bear the humanist banner into the second half of the twentieth century. In America in the field of criticism, Edmund Wilson himself, along with Lionel Trilling and Kenneth Burke, was surely among the most noteworthy. His criticism brought modernists and traditionalists into fruitful dialogue, helped American novelists of the 1930s and 1940s hold to the highest literary standards, and attempted always to see beyond national and cultural borders to the universal aspects of art.

Edmund Wilson
A Critic for our Time

I.
A Brief Survey of
Wilson's Critical Stance

CHAPTER ONE

Wilson's
Critical Preoccupations

As the Preface makes clear, Edmund Wilson's lifelong critical preoccupation was the relation of literature to life and of life to history. This critical preoccupation is evident in *Axel's Castle* (1931), Wilson's first book of criticism, in his introduction to us of the Symbolist movement, literally personified in the guests who came to sit in the modest, smoke-filled Parisian living quarters of Stéphane Mallarmé.

He describes the "calm and almost religious" atmosphere in the combined sitting room and dining room, where the poet's wife sat embroidering and his daughter opened the door to Huysmans, Whistler, Degas, Laforgue, Vielé-Griffin, Valéry, (Wilson's catalogue lists no fewer than sixteen callers). They came, he suggests, to sit at the feet of Mallarmé, "a true saint of literature," because they knew him to be engaged in (and here Wilson recalls the words of Albert Thibaudet), "a distinguished experiment on the confines of poetry, at a limit where other lungs would find the air unbreathable."[1]

The same keenly human, even domestic, focus is evident in *The Wound and the Bow* (1941) when Wilson suggests that the artistic genesis of "the two Scrooges" in Dickens's *A Christmas Carol* is to be found in the author's own tendencies toward manic-depression. He does so by portraying the Dickens family dining room as recorded in the recollections of two of Dickens's

3

daughters. In one account, it is a jolly, festive room presided over by a father as benevolent as the hero in one of Dickens's own *Christmas Books*. In the other, the atmosphere is grim and laden, burdened by the harsh and unpredictable temper of Dickens—a father beloved but recalled as a family tyrant, "a wicked man—a very wicked man."[2]

In *Patriotic Gore* (1962) Wilson continues to pursue the historical and biographical context of each literary event he studies. In his account of the work of Harriet Beecher Stowe, he writes of the 1830s and the racial violence that then raged in the vicinity of the Calvin Stowe residence in Cincinnati, Ohio. Noting that Cincinnati was at that time a rowdy pork-packing center ("the streets were obstructed with pigs . . . and the bar-rooms were full of bad characters"), he portrays the river traffic (which was also the border traffic between the free state of Ohio and the slave-owning state of Kentucky) as "a constant source of disturbance." He gives evidence of the racial component in all the violence by reporting that the press of an Abolitionist paper was wrecked by a mob in the summer of 1836. And he goes on to tell the riveting story of Harriet Beecher Stowe walking into her kitchen one day that summer to find her brother, Henry Ward Beecher, at the stove melting hot lead. "When she asked, 'What on earth are you doing, Henry?' he answered, 'Making bullets to kill men with.' " Another testimony to the activism of the Beecher-Stowes at this period was their taking into their home a young black woman "who said she was free but who was presently claimed by her master; Calvin Stowe and Henry Beecher, armed with pistols, arranged her escape at night." The literary point of all this becomes clear only when Wilson tells us that "this girl was the original of Eliza Harris [the black heroine of Mrs. Stowe's novel, *Uncle Tom's Cabin*]."[3]

As these scattered quotations attest, the very breadth of Wilson's approach makes boundaries difficult to come by; *life* and *history* after all are terms that encompass virtually every aspect of a work, including its biographical genesis, its social milieu, its political and philosophical ramifications, as well as its aesthetic qualities and the ground of its appeal to the reader.

In its very diffuseness, however, Wilson's approach sub-scribes to Matthew Arnold's precept that letting the mind play freely around a subject is the best way of gaining a perspective on it. Inasmuch as the mind that Wilson brought into play on his subjects was of a high order of intelligence, unusually well-trained in languages and literature, and well-stocked with information from the other main departments of human thought, the results he obtained are often brilliant and penetrating. But inasmuch as a completely satisfactory critical approach remains ideal and nonexistent, and inasmuch as Wilson's preferred method of work – within the prescribed limits of journalism rather than of scholarship – meant that it was invariably briefer, more casual, and less rigorous than the work of the academic critic, the results he obtained are sometimes open to the charge of superficiality.

Whatever strengths and weaknesses resulted from Wilson's choice of critical approach, his preoccupation with that in literature which is most vital, most human, most "lifelike" was no accident. This will become evident when we look at him from a more private angle in a later portion of this study. I do not mean merely that Wilson was working within the tradition of his day – being traditional, he was in fact bucking the trend of the "new" criticism, both of his day and, until very recently, of ours. I mean, rather, that Wilson was disposed to write the kind of criticism he did because it alone answered the deepest conscious and unconscious needs of his mind and personality.

Murray Krieger has suggested that when we consider this aspect of a critic's work "we are talking about what has been termed 'the metaphysical pathos' behind the literary theory."[4] In a later chapter, when we pursue the matter further, such considerations may help us understand a dichotomy noted by some of Wilson's contemporaries: a certain coldness he manifested in his response to life at the same time he was manifesting warm and sympathetic responses to literature."[5] These questions are more appropriately set aside for the moment, however.

In this chapter I concentrate on tracing the overall outlines of Wilson's stance. My concentration begins with a more detailed look at his critical preoccupations, specifically, his historical consciousness. Regarding this "historical consciousness," it is natural to think first, perhaps, of his most overtly historical books, *To the Finland Station* and *The Dead Sea Scrolls*. Yet, an interest in the past is evident in Wilson's literary criticism as well; when, for example, in his essay "Proust," he takes great care to set nearly every observation within the historical frame of *fin de siècle* Paris or, again, to set his essay on Kipling within the era of the British Raj. Indeed, throughout his critical writings Wilson makes an effort to place each literary figure and each literary work within its historical time and place.

This is not to suggest, however, that Wilson wrote literary history in any formal sense. The one book of Wilson's criticism that may be said to conform to conventional notions of a literary history is his first, *Axel's Castle*. According to R. S. Crane, "the possibility of constructing a literary history . . depends, in the first place on the discovery, in any succession of works . . of a continuing subject of change that can be stated in more or less specific and literal terms."[5]

Wilson's statement of his purpose in *Axel's Castle* is "to trace the origins of certain tendencies in contemporary literature and to show their development in the work of six contemporary writers . . . W. B. Yeats, James Joyce, T. S. Eliot, Gertrude Stein, Marcel Proust, and Paul Valéry" who, he says, "represent the culmination of a self-conscious and very important literary movement."[6]

The movement is Symbolism, of course, which, says Wilson, "may be defined as an attempt by carefully studied means – a complicated association of ideas represented by a medley of metaphors – to communicate unique personal feelings."

Even in this, his most formally historical work of literary criticism, however, Wilson's application of the "principles" of literary history (as defined by Crane) are by no means systematic, for Wilson follows no recognizable methodology. If we attempt to apply Crane's categories, we find Wilson moving all over the map – now following an approach Crane defines as dialectic, now one he describes as narrative-causal; now concentrating on the history of a change in literary form, now on the literary figures behind the change; now assessing the aesthetic, now the social implications of that change for the artist and for society.

But it is characteristic of Wilson to be loose and unsystematic – it is part and parcel of the comprehensiveness implied in his notion (stated in the dedication to *Axel's Castle*) of what literary criticism "ought to be – a *history* [emphasis mine] of man's ideas and imaginings in the setting of the conditions which have shaped them."[7]

Brian Gallagher, in his dissertation "The Historical Consciousness of Edmund Wilson," says that

> to the extent Edmund Wilson is a historian, he is a romantic historian, who approaches history as an art rather than a science, who relies heavily upon narration to convey the importance and complexity of the historical events with which he deals, and who has not only clung to a romantic belief in the efficacy of individuals over the abstract workings of historical laws, but who has also produced a body of work that testifies to the continuance of the spirit of individualism in American letters.[8]

I think Gallagher's description is sound as far as it goes but too narrow in its emphasis on romanticism and Americanism. When we look at Wilson's own most complete statement on the subject – his essay in *The Triple Thinkers*, "The Historical Interpretation of Literature" – we find a critical stance that is more complex than romanticism (though it certainly contains romantic elements) and more deeply attached to roots in European tradition than is conveyed in the portrait of him as an American individualist.

As Wilson sees it, the historical tradition dates from the beginning of the eighteenth century, when the Neopolitan philosopher, Vico, wrote *La Scienza Nuova*, which Wilson calls "the first social interpretation of a work of literature."[9]

The key assumption behind this approach is that the social world is the work of humanity (i.e., no supernatural interpretation applies) and "that human arts and institutions are to be studied and elucidated as the products of the geographical and climatic conditions in which the people who created them live, and of the phase of social development through which they are passing at the moment."[10]

Wilson sees traces of the same approach in Dr. Johnson and even more clearly in Herder, but he finds that its first complete flowering occurs in the mid-nineteenth century in France, with the critic, Hippolyte Taine. Of the school of historian-critics to which Taine belonged – Michelet, Renan, Sainte-Beuve – Wilson points out that Taine was the first to apply the Viconian principle "systematically and on a large scale in a work devoted exclusively to literature." Wilson interchangeably refers to this approach as "the social interpretation of literature" or "the historical interpretation of literature"; and it should be noted that, as his essay makes clear, he regards it, by whichever name, as the kind he himself practices. As will be demonstrated later on in this section, it is an approach closely identified with the aims and ideals of humanism. Wilson tells us that his own acquaintance with it was indeed through Taine. It came early and it was decisive. He writes in "A Modest Self-Tribute": "I suppose that the primary key in my reading to my work as a literary critic is my finding in my father's library, at some point when I was about fifteen, the brilliant translation by H. Van Laun of Taine's *History of English Literature*."[11]

It is significant that what Wilson singles out as having particularly thrilled him about Taine was not so much Taine using his famous method, sketching in the historical origins of a work – that is, its *"race, moment, milieu"* – but Taine dramatically portraying Swift in quest of his bachelor's degree,

> a singular spectacle: a poor scholar, awkward and queer, with hard blue eyes, an orphan without friends, who depended on the charity of an uncle and had barely enough to live on, and who had already been refused his degree on account of his ignorance of logic, present[ing] himself for a second time without having condescended to read the subject up.[12]

The passage makes an interesting comparison with Wilson's description, in *Axel's Castle*, of an early symbolist poet, Tristan Corbiere:

> he was the son of a sea captain who had also written sea stories and he had an excellent education, but he chose for himself the life of an outlaw. . . . Melancholy, with a feverishly active mind, full of groanings and vulgar jokes, he used to amuse himself by going about in convict's clothes and by firing guns and revolvers out the window in protest against the singing of the village choir.[13]

It would seem that perhaps even more influential as a molder of Wilson's future work than Taine's *"race, moment, milieu"* formula was the trick Wilson learned from him of presenting in dramatic, vivid terms the literary personality of the artist. Wilson says as much when he writes: "my whole point of view about literature was affected by Taine's methods of presentation and interpretation. He had created the creators themselves as characters in a larger drama of cultural and social history."[14]

Here, in Wilson's (and Taine's) bias toward literary biography, we see the romantic element in the tradition they work in. One cannot help noticing, too, a reinforcement of Gallagher's idea that for Wilson literary history – indeed, all history – is properly approached as an art rather than a science. In the same passage Wilson goes on to state that "writing about literature, for me, has always meant narrative and drama as well as the discussion of comparative values."[15]

Of course, Wilson's formation as a critic did not stop at the age of fifteen. He goes on in the same essay to tell of others whose critical precepts and examples helped to shape his work, including Sainte-Beuve and Matthew Arnold, of whom more will be said later in this section.

In fact, Taine's passage about Swift contains the germs of still more of Wilson's later method – his preoccupation with the sociological as well as the psychological implications to be found in a writer's life and work. Taine, with his artist's instinct (the instinct that, Wilson maintains, saves him from being the mechanist he thought he was) has given us a good deal more than mere physical description in that passage. He has given us a glimpse of Swift's economic situation (poor), his social class (the dependent relative of a member of the *petit bourgeoisie*), and his psychological makeup (antisocial, defiant) as well.

To Taine's instinctive knowledge of the forces that shape human life – and literature – Wilson was to add the more formalized knowledge of Marx and Freud. Let us turn, first, to look at how he incorporated some of the thinking of Marx into his criticism. Because Marx's theory of the relation of the (material) base of society to its (immaterial) superstructure so permeates Wilson's view of the relation of literature to life, perhaps it would be well to quote here the key passage from *The German Ideology*:

> Men are the producers of their conceptions, ideas, etc. – real, active men, as they are conditioned by a definite development of their productive forces and of the intercourse corresponding to these, up to its furthest forms. Consciousness can never be anything else than conscious existence, and the existence of men is their actual life-process.... Life is not determined by consciousness, but consciousness by life.[16]

In the Marxist concept of society, therefore, the writer is a producer of intellectual commodities (i.e., books), who not only gets his living from the economic base of society but also his religious ideas, philosophy, and view of the world – what Marx calls the "superstructure."

As Wilson puts it, "Marx showed, I suppose for the first time – how people's theories of society and economics, no matter how well-reasoned or sober – have a way of turning out to be defenses of their class position and financial interests."[17] It is important to note that, both for Marx and for Wilson in his use of Marx, the relationship between base and superstructure is diverse and complex; not static but dynamic.

In "The Literary Class War," Wilson cites a doctrine of dissociation between ideology and poetic vision put forward by Marx's associate, Frederich Engels, to resolve a seeming contradiction in Marx's construct of the base and the superstructure. He begins by noting that "even the art of each period is bound up with the interests of the dominating classes." Explaining that this is because his products are a part of the Marxist superstructure, which rests on the methods of production, Wilson continues: "The writer nine times out of ten gets his principal characters from that class; and even if he steps outside it, his point of view will still be colored by the point of view of the class. His images, his rhythms, his technique, all will be affected by its habits."[18] Yet he goes on to maintain that art, because it purports to give "not a simple message" but "a complex vision of things," can, in fact, implicitly condemn a society with which its author may believe himself to be in accord.[19]

Just as Engels noted that, although in life Balzac defended

the King, the Church, and the dynasty, in the depths of his works he exhibits an undisguised admiration for "the republican heroes of the Cloitre-Saint Merri."[20] By the same token, Wilson notes that a

> really first-rate book by an agonizing bourgeois may have more human value, more revolutionary power, than second-rate Marxists who attack it. A really great spirit does not lie though its letter killeth. Personally I can testify that the writer who has made me feel most overwhelmingly that bourgeois society was ripe for burial was none of our American Marxist journalists but Proust.[21]

"The artist," says Wilson, "belongs to two worlds: a classless supernational one which does not exist yet, but which the mind can partially apprehend, and a real one of which he is part."[22] This recognition of the possibility of a dialectical conflict between a writer's thesis and his or her actual vision of things is a distinction of signal importance in allying Wilson with the essential Marx rather than with the orthodox Marxist critics of the 1930s.

Rather than apply Marxist ideas in any rigid or oversimplified way, Wilson makes use of Marx's insights in his criticism by attempting to show the correlation between the class of a writer, the way a writer makes his living, and his vision of life.

In later essays, particularly those on Dickens and Proust, we shall see Wilson actively engaged in making such correlations. In "The Case of the Author," he turned the attempt upon himself. Stating that "it is probably true that in order to be able to value people's opinions properly, you ought to know who they are, what their income is, and where they got it from," Wilson goes on to say, "I shall accordingly supply to Marxist criticism the economic facts about myself at the same time that I offer myself as a specimen of the current American bourgeoisie."[23]

After identifying himself as the product of several generations of upper-middle class professionals and a person who has a comfortable income from a job as a literary editor, Wilson admits that these facts of his life have undoubtedly conditioned his thinking. At the same time, he suggests that his readings in Marx have provided him with a more enlightened view:

That vision was naive that I had during the war: of science and poetry as great independent entities superior to social institutions – it was the product of having come to know them in the isolation of school and college. I did not understand then how science and art are always entangled with the institutions of the particular social world which, for its good reasons, provides them with leisure.[24]

Wilson clearly believes that not only writers but literary critics, too, are "bound up with the interests of the dominating classes." And, in an essay called "The Literary Class War II" he maintains that

nothing provides plainer evidence of the class bias of the bourgeois critic than his continual lamentations over the fact that the works of contemporary writers have no central faith or system to sustain them, and his simultaneous rejection as propaganda of all these works which depend on Marxism.[25]

Wilson's reference here is to the greater ease with which critics of the period were able to swallow what he terms Eliot's "gropes for a faith and a system among the shadows of Anglo-Catholicism" as against the works of Dos Passos and Shaw. Wilson accuses the critics of tending to bar out these works "as not genuine literature at all."

Wilson, of course, disagrees with such critics and argues that "if anything is characteristic of those two writers it is their careful thinking out of their material in terms of their fundamental philosophy, the precision of their design and its close relation to their central point of view."[26]

But, if Wilson is critical of an anti-Marxist bias on the part of the bourgeois critics of his day (the examples he cites seem to indicate he is thinking here especially of the "new critics" who were, in fact, much more receptive to Eliot than to Dos Passos or Shaw), he is certainly not "pro" the so-called Marxist critics of his day either. Key figures among the latter were Granville Hicks and Michael Gold, who, as editors of *The New Masses*, were formulators of the orthodox critical position, going so far as to suggest that the working class provided the only really satisfactory subject for a writer.

Disagreeing sharply in an essay he contributed to a symposium held by *The New Masses*, Wilson argued that "all artistic forms must be successful, not in terms of political or social institutions, but in terms of their own particular crafts." From this point of view, says Wilson, "there can be no such thing as proletarian literature anymore than there can be proletarian chemistry or proletarian engineering." Finally, he points out, "the work of say, a proletarian poet, however different in vocabulary or form, must in the end meet the same requirements as the poetry of a conservative courtier like Horace or Racine."[27]

An example of the detachment Wilson maintained throughout these critics' wars that raged over Marxism in the 1930s is to be found in an article he wrote for *The Nation*. He announces that he finds both Marxists and anti-Marxists full of depressing inaccuracies always assuming that the view of the Marxist critic is simply to explain the work of art in terms of "crude economic determinism." He goes on:

> Real dialectical materialism is of course a much more complicated affair, which allows man to make his own history, though, "not just as he pleases," but conditioned by, "circumstances as he finds them," which allows works of art and ideas to influence economic conditions as well as economic conditions to mold ideas and art, and which conceives the various departments of human thought as continually straining to set themselves free from the entanglements of class relations and to establish professional classes of their own.[28]

In addition to Wilson's more complex application of "real dialectical materialism," James Y. Dayananda, in a dissertation on the subject, isolates three other elements in Wilson's criticism that he designates as Marxist. One of these we have already looked at – the tendency of the literary establishment to be bound up with the interests of the dominating class – and we have discovered that Wilson was well aware of this tendency and consciously fought against it.

A third Marxist element in Wilson's criticism, in Dayananda's view, is his awareness of the "dialectical relationship between form and content in literature." It is an awareness, says Dayananda, that distinguishes Wilson "from those orthodox Marxists who do not care much for form; their chief concern is with the content of a work of literature." Whereas Wilson, he goes on to maintain, "is aware that form is conditioned by content and that content is conditioned by form. . . . In short, [Wilson's] criticism is concerned with the literary work as a whole."29

In point of fact, Wilson's critical method, too, tends to emphasize content over form. Nevertheless, Dayananda rightly acknowledges Wilson's recognition that the two are related mutually and complexly. He is right, too, to insist that Wilson was influenced in his thinking about them by the Marxist idea of the complex relation of base and superstructure. Yet, here, I think Dayananda is finding a Marxist element in an attitude that much predates Marxism; an insistence upon the mutual importance and interdependence of form and content, after all, is an aesthetic concept going back at least as far as Aristotle.

Wilson's view that criticism most properly treats the work of art as a whole – in its ideas as well as its technique – certainly distinguishes his criticism from that of the agrarian or "new" critics of the period, who were aggressively attempting to isolate the literary from the social aspects of art; but in doing so it allies him not with specifically Marxist doctrine but with a much older humanist tradition of which both he and Marx are heirs.

The same is true of the remaining two elements in Wilson's criticism that Dayananda designates as Marxist: his "reverence for the priesthood of literature"30 and his "sense of the need to relate the practice of literature with the effort to change society."31

Although on the latter point, certainly, the influence of Marx *is* noticeable, not only in the writing of Wilson but in writers from Malraux to Koestler and Sartre; it is manifest more as an intensifying and quickening of what was basically an old humanist position.

Dayananda concludes that Wilson is not after all a Marxist critic – and here there is an echo of Gallagher's finding that Wilson is not after all a historian. Rather, Dayananda suggests, Wilson's "pragmatic and imaginative version of Marxism" is at best summed up by the term *para-Marxist*.32

Marxist or not, one of the aspects of Wilson's critical preoccupation with the relations between literature and life was certainly an interest in those relations as they concern politics.

As his battles with the Marxist party-liners made clear, in Wilson's opinion, no state, under whatever type of government (including communism), has the right to interfere in the direction of literature. On the other hand, Wilson is convinced, art that takes no interest in social or political realities stands in danger of becoming a mere elitist game. He is inclined to feel that both politically directed art (e.g., the strike novels of the 1930s) and ivory tower art for art's sake (e.g., the work of Villiers de L'Isle-Adam) results in severe aesthetic limitations.

In his essay, "The Historical Interpretation of Literature" and elsewhere, Wilson states his belief that the most artistically successful approach was that adopted by the writers of czarist Russia who, from Pushkin on, conducted a full-scale criticism of society, but only by implication. In this way he may be said to be subscribing to a critical dictum of Frederich Engels, who wrote in a letter to Margaret Harkness: "I am far from finding fault with you for not having written a point-blank socialist novel. . . . The more the opinions of the author remain hidden, the better for the work of art."[33]

This is not to say that Wilson, with his historical consciousness, ignored the propaganda content of literature: he simply refused to be alarmed about it. "There is no reason why propaganda should not be good or even great literature," says Wilson, pointing out that "Much of the stuff we are fed in school as classics of the rarest quality – Cicero's orations against Catiline, Burke on the French Revolution . . . Dante . . . and Shakespeare [is] patriotic propaganda."[34]

Moreover Wilson displays none of the antagonism to politics generally associated with American intellectuals. He asks us to "suppose even that some of our American writers became professional politicians – suppose they chose to use their literary gifts exclusively for political ends." Then, rather impishly, he conjures up a vision sure to set off alarm bells aplenty:

> Suppose Dreiser, for example, by some freak, were to turn into a great Communist Statesman? Why on earth should anyone regret it? Is not Statesmanship as important as literature? Doesn't it require as much imagination, as much in-

tellect, as much will? Is it not one of the major activities of humanity?[34]

In the long run, however, Wilson clearly supports the value of indirection over against "point-blank" politics in art. We have seen his remark on the effectiveness of Proust as a social critic, and elsewhere he says: "It is true that art may be a weapon: but in the case of some of the greatest works of art . . . it is difficult to see that any important part of this value is due to their function as weapons."[36]

Finally, he comes to a distinctly Arnoldian view of the social and political and cultural value of art residing in the fact that art is, by its very nature, a "criticism of life":

> in works of the highest order . . . the purport is not a simple message, but a complex vision of things, which itself is not explicit but implicit; and the reader who does not grasp them artistically, but is merely looking for simple social morals, is certain to be hopelessly confused.[37]

As to whether the *critic* should play a political role *per se*, I think it is fair to say that Wilson believed the critic should be alert to the political implications of a work of art and should involve himself in explicating the socio-political morals implied in it, whether consciously (as in Pushkin) or unconsciously (as in Proust). But if we are to take into account Wilson's own stance vis-à-vis open political affiliation with any of the political factions raging for his commitment at the time he began to write, his answer would seem to be that the critic performs his function best from a position of detachment.

Daniel Aaron sums up Wilson's position of nonalignment well. Pointing out that Wilson denied advocating either a proletarian culture or a proletarian literature, he goes on to say "He did believe, however, that socialism could and should profoundly modify American culture 'in form and style . . . as well as in point of view.' " Ultimately, says Aaron, "he took his stand between those who thought that intellectual, moral, and aesthetic activity operated in a social vacuum, and those who thought of human conduct solely in terms of economic appetite."[38]

[*Note:* I mean to turn now to the other major aspect of the relation between literature and life that preoccupies Wilson — the psychological. For this purpose it will be necessary to look more closely at some elements of Freud's thinking that bear on the matter of psychoanalysis and its relation to literature. For some years now, there has been a brisk traffic in revision, not only in this area of Freudian scholarship but in terms of Freud's life, his character, his reputation, and indeed of the value of his basic theory of the unconscious. The result has been to introduce a whole new vocabulary of terms into the discussion, terms derived from structuralism by way of Russian formalism and the science of semiotics. I employ no such terms. Readers of Lacan, for example, will undoubtedly find much of the following presentation naive. In this respect I am grateful for two recent books, each of which I have found helpful in validating my decision to retain a traditional approach. For a thorough review — and a rigorous questioning — of the current status of the "Revised Version" in all its aspects, I am grateful for the recent appearance of the collected papers of a special issue of *Critical Inquiry* edited by Francoise Meltzer under the title *The Trials of Psychoanalysis*. Especially helpful in this collection is Peter Brooks's "The Idea of a Psychoanalytic Criticism." I am grateful, too, to the recent appearance of Peter Gay's widely — and justly — acclaimed biography for restoring to us the historical Freud with most, if not all, of his familiar contours intact, thereby making it possible to present traditional interpretations and summarizations of his major concepts without apology. Moreover, the Freud I present here, being of the older dispensation, is the Freud Wilson understood and knew.]

It may be well to begin by reminding ourselves, briefly, of the general significance to literary criticism of Freud's work. According to Herbert J. Muller,

> for the literary critic, aside from the obvious biographical clues, psychoanalysis has illuminated the whole province of imagery and symbolism. It has not only discovered a wealth of unsuspected meanings but made clear their importance as unconscious revelations of the artist's mind and

character. . . . Freud's whole analysis of dream phantasy bears on the materials and methods of imaginative action. The necessity of sensory images, the indifference to strict logic and literal realism, the substitutions and displacements, the remarkable condensation of material, the frequent ambivalence – all that he discovered in dreams elucidates . . . their power of "concealment yet revelation."[39]

Frederick Crews, too, offers a catalogue of the uses of psychoanalysis to criticism:

Using psychoanalytic assumptions, a critic can show how a writer's public intention was evidently deflected by a private obsession. He can deal with blatant or subtle appeals to fantasy, as in the habitual practice of a genre like science fiction or the Gothic novel. He can reveal a hidden consistency behind shifts of tone or characterization, or make a new approach to a puzzle that has resisted commonsense solutions. Or again, he can draw biographical inferences on the basis of certain recurrent themes that the author hadn't consciously meant to display.[40]

Although this is helpful in designating some of the territory illuminated by Freud, several areas of potential misunderstanding still must be cleared up before going further. First, it is important to distinguish between Freud's own use of his principles in his studies of artists and the use of those principles on the part of the literary critic.

Wilson, in a reference to Freud's study of Leonardo da Vinci, notes that it "has little critical interest: it is an attempt to construct a case history."[41] We can see this distinction more clearly in the following passage from Frederick Crews:

Freud was not interested in art but in the latent meaning of art, and then only for illustrative purposes. . . . The artist, Freud tells us, has "an introverted disposition and has not far to go to become neurotic. He is one who is urged on by instinctual needs which are too clamorous; he longs to attain to honour, power, riches, fame, and the love of women: but he lacks the means of achieving these gratifications. So . . . he turns away from reality and transfers all his interest, and all his libido too, on to the creation of his wishes in the life of phantasy, from which the way might readily lead to neurosis."[42]

In partial mitigation of Freud, Muller reminds us that

> Freud's later theories allow a more adequate treatment . . .
> [of] the motives of phantasy and art. In *Beyond the Pleasure
> Principle* he went beyond the wish fulfillment, as he had
> found that some dreams do not evade the unpleasant sensa-
> tion but go through it, seek to master it on its own ground –
> come to grips with it, that is to say, as tragedy does with the
> most fearful realities of human life.[43]

Crews, too, notes that "Freud's own views lead us beyond
the static 'museum piece' criticism he usually practiced," and
points out that, in literary criticism, "We are free to use Freud's
interpretive techniques without endorsing his competitive and
ambivalent remarks about artists."[44]

Second, it is important to note the various differences of
focus to be found in psychoanalytic criticism: on the psychology
of the author; on the psychology of the characters the author
has created; or, too recently to have been part of the context in
which Wilson applied Freudian precepts, on the psychology of
the reader.

In Wilson's own criticism, his essay on Kipling, with its
heavy concentration on biographical data, would provide an example of the first type and his criticism of "The Turn of the
Screw," with its concentration on the psychological makeup of
the governess, would provide one of the second type. Sometimes, a critic will focus on the psychology of an author's literary
characters exclusively for the purpose of finding clues to the
psychology of the author himself. This borders on psychohistory
and is represented in criticism by such works as Ernst Jones's
study of Hamlet and Leslie Fiedler's *Love and Death in the
American Novel*. To some extent it is the focus of Wilson's
criticism also – though not of his most successful. (I am thinking,
especially, of his essay on Ben Jonson.)

There is yet another possibility of focus in Freudian
criticism: a combination of the first two. Wilson's usual – and
sounder – practice was in this vein, in which he sought to
preserve a more dialectical movement back and forth between
an author's biography and his fictional characters, using the
work to illuminate the artist and the artist, the work.

But the complexities of the subject make it essential to pause once again, to try to be more specific about just what we mean when we speak of "Freudian" elements in criticism. Here again, Frederick Crews is helpful, reminding us that the man, in the Freudian view, "is the animal destined to be overimpressed by his parents." That is, subject to a superego, he is prey to the promptings of guilt. From this point of view, says Crews, "neurosis is comprehensible as 'abnormal attachment to the past.' " He goes on to elucidate Freud's key discovery "that human beings can neither freely accept nor freely deny the parental demand that sexual and aggressive urges be tamed. All men, he saw, struggle not only against unregenerate impulses but also against their guilt for continuing to harbor those impulses."[45]

Crews notes that, "individually and in the mass . . men, tormented by the persistence of what they have foresworn, necessarily *regress together*." A "pooling of fantasies" is the result, says Crews. It is engaged in "to impose bearable contours on the world" and it "seems to be a minimal requisite for all human achievement, even the achievement of those who work alone."

This brings us to the role of the artist in society. Here, Crews draws upon the insights of Ernst Kris to locate the origins of art

> in a "regression in the service of the ego," . . . [which] uses symbolic manipulations to reconcile competing pressures. The artist is someone who provisionally relaxes the censorship regnant in waking life, foregoes some of his society's characteristic defenses, and allows the repressed a measure of representation, though (as in strictly unconscious symptom formation) only in disguised and compromised form.

Crews goes on to explain that, under such circumstances, the artist's "social role and his own equilibrium dictate a sign of victory for the ego, if not in 'happy endings' then in the triumph of form over chaos, meaning over panic, mediated claims over naked conflict, purposeful action over sheer psychic spillage." "In this sense," says Crews, "the making and the apprehension of art works reenact the entire human project of making a tenuous cultural order where none existed before."[46]

The view that this perspective indicates of the primary

function of art bears a striking resemblance to Wilson's as he presents it in the form of a retelling of the classical myth of Philoctetes, which he calls "The Wound and the Bow." Unfortunately, its length precludes quoting it here in full. What follows is a brief paraphrase in aid of our discussion of the psychological elements in Wilson's criticism, to which it is very germane:

Philoctetes (the artist-figure in Wilson's metaphor) is a Greek archer, said to possess an invincible bow. He is pictured by Wilson as an outsider, shunned and in exile from the community. His fellows, though impressed by his extraordinary gifts, nevertheless resist the unpleasantness to which his presence among them invariably gives rise. This is symbolized in the myth by the festering wound on Philoctetes' foot that periodically erupts, emitting an offensive odor as it does so.

When the Greeks find that they must have Philoctetes' dauntless bow to defeat the armies of Troy, they send Neoptolemus, the son of Achilles, to lure it away from Philoctetes and bring it back for their use. But Neoptolemus finds himself genuinely touched by Philoctetes' plight and refuses to trick him or take away his bow; instead, he pleads with Philoctetes to accompany him back and swears to him "that the sons of Aesclepius will cure you if you let us take you to Troy."

Philoctetes is incredulous at first, but, as Wilson puts it, "now Heracles suddenly appears from the skies and declares to Philoctetes that what the young man says is true and that it is right for him to go to Troy. He and the son of Achilles shall stand together like lions and shall gloriously carry the day."

Wilson interrupts himself at this point (he has been giving us *his* version of Sophocles' version of the myth) to say that "The *deus ex machina* here may of course figure a change of heart which has taken place in Philoctetes as the result of having found a man who recognizes the wrong that has been done him." The upshot is that "The long hatred is finally exorcised" and Philoctetes sails with the rest to Troy.[47]

The entire myth is generally taken as Wilson's metaphorical way of saying that great gifts and great suffering go hand in hand in the formation of the artist. What has not always been seen so clearly is that the essay may also stand as Wilson's metaphorical statement of the artist's and the critic's relation to and function in society. The general failure to recognize this may be attributable to the general failure to recognize that Neoptolemus is the critic-figure in Wilson's version of the tale.

Yet, the importance Wilson ascribes to Neoptolemus is unmistakable, as his concluding paragraph shows, when he asks "How then is the gulf to be got over between the ineffective plight of the bowman and his proper use of his bow, between his ignominy and his destined glory?"

His answer is most instructive in its suggestion of a paradigm for sympathetic criticism. "Only by the intervention," Wilson tells us, "of one who is guileless enough and human enough to treat him, not as a monster, nor yet as a magical property which is wanted for accomplishing some end, but simply as another man, whose sufferings elicit his sympathy and whose courage and pride he admires." By taking the risk, involving himself, and keeping faith with Philoctetes, Neoptolemus, says Wilson, "dissolves Philoctetes' stubbornness, and thus cures him and sets him free, and saves the campaign as well."[48]

Not until Leon Edel, in his introductory portrait of Edmund Wilson in *The Twenties*, identified Neoptolemus with Wilson himself did the full implications of Wilson's essay become evident. Edel points out that "Neoptolemus, in this recreation, becomes a kind of archetypal critic, as Philoctetes represents the archetypal artist; he reflects, even more than the archer, the image and vocation of Edmund Wilson."[49]

Returning to the myth from this perspective we can imagine Wilson making the point, through the artist-figure Philoctetes, not only that genius and suffering may be inextricably entwined but also that the artist must remain engaged or run the risk of losing, at least to a degree, some of his artistic power. We can also see Wilson's suggestion, by means of Neoptolemus, that the critic's function is twofold: one, to treat the artist with "sympathetic imagination" (Edel's phrase, incidentally, for Wilson's critical approach), while holding him always to his highest abilities; and two, to become his champion and mediator with the rest of society.

To the extent, then, that art can assist in the "human project of making a tenuous cultural order where none existed before," by helping the populace to triumph over its dark demons of ignorance and intolerance, "the long hatred is exorcised," Troy is vanquished, and the promise of the myth is fulfilled. It is fulfilled, for example, whenever a critic succeeds in bringing an artist of transcendent yet difficult, and in some ways repellent, works, such as Proust's *Remembrance of Things Past*, into the public consciousness.

Perhaps, because such an explicit interpretation of the myth could so easily seem to be self-serving – calling up as it does distinct echoes of his own critical efforts – Wilson never put it forward himself. The result, though, is that his essay has been almost universally misread in a distortion that takes only the Philoctetes figure as its focus. According to this reading, the myth's meaning is that the artist (the archer) works out his neurosis (the wound) in the exercise of his art (the bow). The objection to such a view is the same as that raised by the whole issue of the connection between art and neurosis. There can be no necessary connection, it is argued, because it explains nothing; after all, there are plenty of people with neuroses who are not artists. And the hostility to such a connection among literary people is understandable. As Crews acknowledges: "Such an emphasis is insulting to the artist."[50]

In response to a rhetorically conceived objection that "The psychoanalytic view of the writer as neurotic is presumptuous and condescending," Crews answers, in part: "It cannot be too strongly affirmed that psychoanalytic theory . . . finds no necessary connection – at the most a useful analogy – between artistic production and the production of neurotic symptoms." Crews goes on to point out that, wherever it occurs, "This analogy rests on the supposition that both art and neurosis originate in conflict and may be conceived as ways of managing it." He then goes on to make the signal distinction between art and neurosis:

> But whereas the neurotic's solution is the helplessly regressive and primitive one of allowing repressed ideas to break into a disguised expression which is satisfying neither to the neurotic himself nor to others, the artist has the power to sublimate and neutralize conflict, to give it logical and social coherence through conscious elaboration, and to . . . reach and communicate a sense of catharsis.

Crews goes on to note that "The artist may, of course, be impelled by a certain degree of neurotic conflict to submit himself to unconscious dictates; this corresponds to the undeniable observation that great numbers of artists *are* neurotic." However, Crews notes – and here again the distinction is crucial – "neurosis alone cannot produce art and is inimical to the preconscious elaboration and the sublimation that make art possible."

It is worth noting that there is nothing in the criticism of Wilson (whom Crews describes as a "first rate critic") to indicate that he would differ with this view.[51] At the same time, there is much to indicate that he would subscribe to Crews's amplification of it:

> But the literary work which is completely free from its biographical determinants [it's maker's personal conflicts] is not to be found, and in many of the greatest works . . . unresolved emotion and latent contradiction are irreducibly involved in the aesthetic effect. To appreciate why there are gaps in the surface we must be prepared to inspect what lies beneath them.[52]

As we shall see in the ensuing "cases in point" from Wilson's essay on Dickens, this squares very well with Wilson's complex view of the matter.

What it comes down to, roughly, is the point of view that both the content and the form of art emerge out of the artist's life struggles. Sometimes these struggles are psychological, sometimes social and economic. One of the implications of this insight but only one is that to understand and appreciate the artist's work fully we need a sense of what his or her struggles were. Wilson felt strongly that the biographical material leading to the revelation of such struggles can, in a case like Dickens's, for example, increase our understanding of the artist's comparative failure in some areas – his lapses into sentimentality or melodrama and our sympathy for his problems.

Thus, Wilson is able to say of the Dickens family penury and of Charles's childhood humiliations that they are biographical data

> worth knowing and bearing in mind, because they help us to understand what Dickens was trying to say. He was less

given to false moral attitudes or to fear of respectable opinion than most of the great Victorians; but . . the meaning of Dickens' work has been obscured by that element of the conventional which Dickens himself never quite outgrew.

And Wilson goes on to insist that "it is necessary to see him as a man in order to appreciate him as an artist – to exorcise the spell which has bewitched him into a stuffy piece of household furniture and to give him his proper rank as the poet of that portiered and upholstered world who saw clearest through the coverings and the curtains."[53]

Of course, when the artistic effort is successful, as in *Bleak House*, the same biographical material that helped us to understand the artist's conflicts can help us to see him triumph over them. As Wilson suggests, further, if literature is properly studied – that is, studied by a sensitive, thorough, historically conscious, responsible, and sympathetic critic – "the attitudes, the compulsions, the emotional 'patterns' that recur in the work of a writer" can yield up illumination not only of the writer and the work, but also of the writer's time and place, for "these attitudes and patterns are embedded in the community and the historical moment and they may indicate its ideals and its diseases as the cell shows the condition of the tissue."[54]

Still, one is inclined to ask, in all of this attention to the personality of the artist, to the historical background and the political and social foreground and the psychological underground of literary works, what becomes of the works themselves? Does Wilson in fact criticize them in any serious meaning of the term? Do the purely aesthetic aspects of a work of art, such as form, style, unity, structure, and imagery, figure at all among Wilson's critical preoccupations? A number of Wilson's critics charge him with slighting form or leaving it out of his criticism altogether. This study provides some evidence to the contrary, however.

Wilson was acutely aware of the importance of aesthetic values in any criticism worthy of the name. He shows his awareness in "The Historical Interpretation of Literature," when he tells us that "the problems of comparative artistic value still remain after we have given attention to the Freudian psychological factor just as they do after we have given attention to the

Marxist economic factor and to the racial and geographic factors." He goes on to say that "no matter how thoroughly and searchingly we may have scrutinized works of literature from the historical and biographical points of view," it is still incumbent upon the "historical" critic to arrive at some evaluation of their success in the manner of such more aesthetically oriented critics as Eliot and Saintsbury. Finally, says Wilson,

> we must be able to tell good from bad, the first-rate from the second-rate. We shall not otherwise write literary criticism at all, but merely social or political history as reflected in literary texts, or psychological case histories from past eras, or, to take the historical point of view, in its simplest and most academic form, merely chronologies of books that have been published.[55]

Even so, there is no denying the fact that Wilson pays little attention to literary form. He assumes that a first-rate work is formally accomplished, but what interests him most about a work, nearly always, is the progress and ramifications of its argument.

Thus, when Joyce's elaborate schema of bodily organs, senses, arts, and sciences tends to get in the way of that progress in *Ulysses*, Wilson protests that

> it was these organs and arts and sciences and Homeric correspondences which sometimes so discouraged our interest. We had been climbing over these obstacles without knowing it, in our attempts to follow Dedalus and Bloom. The trouble was that, beyond the ostensible subject and, as it were, beneath the surface of the narrative, too many other subjects and too many different orders of subjects were being proposed to our attention.[56]

And, in spite of the sensitivity Wilson displays, from time to time, about such matters as structure and rhythm, symbol and metaphor, his criticism is mainly centered in matters of content: the theme, the actual *meaning* of a work, its psychological truth, its power to illuminate life in a vivid and persuasive way – these tend to be the aesthetic questions that engage him.

As will become evident in the historical discussion to follow, Wilson's candid appeal to such extraliterary values as the author's psychology is a common feature of the critical tradition he is working in, however alien it may be to most modern, academic critical practice. As Wilson notes in his "Historical Interpretation of Literature" essay, the psycho-biographical element has been present in criticism since long before Freud. It is a clear facet of Dr. Johnson's *Lives of the Poets*, for instance, as well as of the literary portraits of Sainte-Beuve.

Freud's work, of course, added tremendously to the possibilities for its more sophisticated use in criticism. Not, as Wilson warns, as a psychoanalytic case history but, rather, as Van Wyck Brooks uses it in *The Ordeal of Mark Twain* (clearly a work that was a model for Wilson's own "Dickens: The Two Scrooges").

The important thing, notes Wilson, is to make sure that such criticism is based on sufficient evidence and sticks close to the facts, and the documents of the writer's life and work. Under such circumstances, he says, a crucial happening, of typical significance to an artist's psychology in general, can be used as a key to a whole career. This is, of course, the way Wilson uses the incident of Dickens's childhood incarceration in the blacking factory. Out of the psychological and, it must not be forgotten, the social matrix of that incident, Wilson is able to make a number of essentially literary critical points.

He finds in it the clue to Dickens's motivation as an artist, for, he tells us, "The work of Dickens' whole career was an attempt to digest these early shocks and hardships, to explain them to himself, to justify himself in relation to them, to give an intelligible and tolerable picture of a world in which such things could occur."[57]

He finds in it the clue to Dickens's construction of certain of his characters when he notes that "his interest in the fate of prisoners thus went a good deal farther than simple memories of the debtors' prison or notes of a court reporter. He identified himself readily with the thief, and even more readily with the murderer." The reason for this he says—and this is vintage Wilson—is both psychological and sociological, for, "the man of powerful will who finds himself opposed to society must, if he cannot upset it or if his impulse to do so is blocked, feel a compulsion to commit what society regards as one of the capital crimes against itself. With the antisocial heroes of Dostoevsky, this crime is usually murder or rape; with Dickens, it is usually murder."[58]

He finds in it the key to Dickens's social attitudes, and to the view of Victorian society contained in his novels. Although, he notes, "Dickens had at first imagined that he was pillorying abstract faults in the manner of the comedy of humors . . . the truth was that he had already begun an indictment against a specific society; the self-important and moralizing middle class." Their rise, as Dickens recognized and as Wilson reports, ushered in a new age that "had brought a new kind of virtue to cover up the flourishing vices of cold avarice and harsh exploitation and Dickens detested these virtues."[59]

The connection between Wilson's aesthetic and psychological preoccupations becomes still clearer in the fascinating dictum he embeds in his essay (in *Axel's Castle*) on Proust. Wilson there maintains that "the real elements . . . of any work of fiction, are the elements of the author's personality" – that the author's imagination embodies the fundamental conflicts of his or her nature, and that the author's personages are personifications of his or her own impulses and emotions. The relations between the characters in the stories, then, are reflections of the relations between these impulses and emotions in their author.[60]

In Wilson's conception, the imagination operates in a fashion very similar to Freud's conception of the dreaming mind. It may be well to pause here to remind ourselves that this view is not held by Wilson alone. "Of all mental systems," Lionel Trilling has written, "the Freudian psychology is the one which makes poetry indigenous to the very constitution of the mind. Indeed, the mind, as Freud sees it, is in the greater part of its tendency exactly a poetry-making organ."[61]

And Peter Brooks, citing Jack Spector's *The Aesthetics of Freud*, to the effect that "Neither Freud nor his followers . . . have ever shown concretely how specific formal techniques correspond to the process of the unconscious," speaks of his own

> flat-footed (and unfashionable) [belief] that the persistence, against all odds, of psychoanalytic perspectives in literary study must ultimately derive from our conviction that the materials on which psychoanalysis and literary critics exer-

cise their powers are in some basic sense the same: that the structure of literature is in some sense the structure of mind.

He goes on to suggest that

we continue to dream of a convergence of psychoanalysis and literary criticism because we sense that there ought to be, that there must be, some correspondence between literary and psychic process, that aesthetic structure and form, including literary tropes, must somehow coincide with the psychic structures and operations they both evoke and appeal to.[62]

Wilson stresses that what makes for our greater or lesser satisfaction in different works is the superior thoroughness and candor with which the author presents such "dangerous psychic materials," that is, his or her own conflicting emotions. As these are embodied in characters, Wilson says, they should, ideally, make up what we can recognize as an organic whole rather than, as happens sometimes in even so great an artist as Dickens, mere conventional elements of virtue and villainy in whom the author has scarcely projected himself at all.

Indeed, Wilson feels that the characters are more or less artistically satisfactory just to the degree that they *are* such personifications – or, in the Freudian term, *projections* – of the author. What is more, authenticity, validity, psychological truth – all of these matters are understood by Wilson to be the result of the degree of honesty the artist is able to bring to the exploration of his or her own consciousness.

We have already looked at the amplification of that point – Crews's view that "in many of the greatest works . . . unresolved emotion and latent contradiction are irreducibly involved in the aesthetic effect. To appreciate why there are gaps in the surface we must be prepared to inspect what lies beneath them."[63] Thus, it would appear that Wilson's inquiries into the psychological components of a work and its author has revelations to offer that are not only psychological and sociological in their purport but literary and aesthetic as well.

Before leaving the subject of Wilson's Freudianism it is important to note that, like his Marxism, it never consists in the application to his criticism of an ideological or scientific ortho-doxy; rather, he uses both as instruments of insight into the rela-tion of the work to life and history. Wilson ruefully comments, in "The Historical Interpretation of Literature," that the problem of analyzing literary works grows ever more complex with the addition to Taine's *race, moment, milieu* of this new combina-tion of Marxist and Freudian elements—with the methods of anthropology sometimes brought to bear as well. However, as I have suggested in the Preface, Wilson found a way to use that complexity, using every resource of the developing disciplines, and especially those based upon the work of Marx and Freud, to bring freshness to the great works of the past and to make the nineteenth-century critical tradition of which he was a part truly answerable to twentieth-century needs.

CHAPTER TWO

Wilson's Critical Style, Method, Aims, and the Progress of his Critical Career

*B*efore going on to describe the humanist critical tradition in greater detail, however, it may be well to look at Wilson's critical style and method to understand more fully how he arrived at his critical achievements. We may begin by noting the chief characteristics of his prose style. It differs from more academic critical styles by exhibiting a lesser degree of formality. As he put it in his self-conducted "Interview With Edmund Wilson": "I can't write the jargon of the critical quarterlies."[1]

In the same interview he only half-jocularly attributes his success as a writer to his use of the periodic sentence, his use of the colon, his use of the semicolon, and his "invariable habit of writing in pencil on those legal-size yellow pads." The latter is an apparent consequence of his belief that "composing on the typewriter has probably done more than anything else to deteriorate English prose."[2]

Wilson's ideals in prose are that it be "well written, intensely felt, pungent, terse"; that it have "color and rhythm"; that it be "highly personal"; and that it bear the eighteenth-century qualities of "lucidity, force, and ease." These last three, Wilson praises as "the great Trinity" and tells us that he was himself trained in that style by an Englishman who taught him at the Hill School in Pennsylvania.[3]

Wilson's tone (he credits Voltaire as his model) is an essential part of his strategy as a critic.[4] It is intended to provide a nondidactic, neutral medium that will allow the free play of the intellect over the subject at hand. The resulting fluidity, sometimes starting trains of thought without necessarily arriving at conclusions, is of course reflected in the structure, which often unfolds organically in Wilson's work, proceeding by a process of association of ideas.

When Wilson *does* wish to argue a point to a particular conclusion (which is likely to remain implicit) the structure of his essay tightens correspondingly into the formal lineaments of argument or debate. On these occasions Wilson marshals his evidence rather like a lawyer preparing a brief. Both methods have their origins in biographical models: the former, looser style from his mentor at Princeton, Christian Gauss; the latter from his father, a well-known attorney.

Wilson devised his own method of carrying out his literary endeavors while remaining a member of the working press, a method perhaps inspired by the example of the French (Sainte-Beuve's *Causeries*, for instance) but brought to complete realization by his own special needs. These he has expounded in an essay, "Thoughts on Being Bibliographed":

> To write what you are interested in writing and to succeed in getting editors to pay for it, is a feat that may require pretty close calculation and a good deal of ingenuity. . . . My own strategy . . . has usually been, first to get books for review or reporting assignments to cover on subjects in which I happen to be interested; then, later, to use the scattered articles for writing general studies of these subjects; then, finally, to bring out a book in which groups of these essays are combined. There are usually to be distinguished . . . at least two or three stages; and it is of course by the books that I want to stand, since the preliminary sketches quite often show my subjects in a different light and in some cases, perhaps, are contradicted by my final conclusions about them.[5]

Wilson's willingness to change his mind in print was often misunderstood. For example, J. A. Clark's article of 1938, "The Sad Case of Edmund Wilson," roundly deplores the tendency: "Wilson's career has been blighted by his unwillingness (or inability) to take a definite critical position and hold it long enough for everybody concerned to get his second wind."[6] In truth, however, this unabashed readiness of Wilson to change his position has deep and valid philosophic roots in humanist thought; it is part of his effort to see all around a subject in a nondidactic, disinterested way, and as such it represents a vital intellectual principle. As Wilson puts it:

> This method of working out in print one's treatment of something one is studying involves a certain amount of extra writing and consequently of energy wasted; but it does have the advantage of allowing one's ideas first to appear in a tentative form, so that they are exposed to correction and criticism.[7]

That the exigencies of this working method were not all positive is borne out in Chapter 8, when the structural form of Wilson's otherwise exemplary Dickens essay is seen to have been blurred in the course of its conversion from five magazine articles into a single essay.

In a broader sense, Wilson's criticism follows (sometimes simultaneously) two major methods, which may be designated as the historical-comparative and the biographical-narrative. To some extent Wilson's choice between them is dictated by his choice of subject matter. When dealing with contemporary figures Wilson eschews the biographical-narrative form. He does make use of whatever facts are publicly available regarding the figure's racial, religious, and social background – such as Eliot's New England ancestry, for example, or Yeats's term in the Irish parliament. Both men were alive at the time Wilson wrote about them in *Axel's Castle*. With living authors, although the notable exception is Hemingway, he is more likely to avoid any overt psycho-biographical points and stick to a close analysis of the text, noting in a comparative way its literary forebears and its relation to the current literary scene. Meanwhile, he pays special attention to the way in which the work bears upon the contemporary social and political situation.

When dealing with figures from the past, however, Wilson often displays a simultaneous interest in the artist's life and his work. Such a full-scale treatment as his essay on Dickens, for example, is biographical and narrative as well as historical and comparative. One should make the further stipulation that, for Wilson, as he himself has suggested, the term *narrative* tends to embrace a dramatic method of presentation.

At this point it is instructive to look at Wilson's praise of Van Wyck Brooks's *Indian Summer* because it elucidates several other aspects of Wilson's own method:

> Mr. Brooks has now mastered the whole art of this histor-
> ical-biographical narrative – an art which has its special
> difficulties unknown to the teller of invented fables. To
> reduce this kind of actual material to a story which will carry
> the reader along, to find a scale and provide a variety which
> will make it possible to hold his attention becomes a species
> of obstacle race, in which the writer has made a wager to
> play a graceful and entertaining role while hampered by the
> necessity of sticking to texts, of assembling scattered data
> and of organizing a complicated unity.

The important keys here to Wilson's own work are: "the necessity of sticking to texts" and "the organization of data from scattered sources." Wilson stresses that there is, first, the necessity to *collect* such data – diaries, letters, papers, and memorabilia of all sorts, together with any unpublished work by the subject that may be available.

Then, there is the necessity of "reading the subject up" – and Wilson certainly did so tirelessly. In preparation for his essay on Proust, for example, he was not content to stop with the massive work itself, in its original French. He also sniffed out and digested Proust's letters, his early volume of stories, *Les Plaisirs et les Jours*, the memoirs of one Mme. Pouquet, who belonged to the Bibesco social set so important to Proust, and commentaries by other French contemporaries, among them Lucien Daudet. Add to this Wilson's already extensive familiarity with the *fin de siècle* world – with the papers pertaining to the Dreyfus case, the writings of Anatole France, the journals of the Goncourts, and so on – and one gets some idea of what Wilson means by "materials from scattered sources" and "reading a subject up."

Rarely is there an instance in Wilson's formal criticism that finds him less than completely prepared. By his own admission, however, his essay on Edith Wharton represents such an instance.[8] In her case, he tells us, he had not even read all of her work. The essay, ironically, is called "Justice to Edith Wharton." That it is one of Wilson's less satisfactory efforts is, at least in part, attributable to this departure by Wilson from his own established practice.

As to his method of getting into the literary texts themselves, Wilson's almost invariable procedure is to synopsize them. This method has called forth both praise and blame from evaluators of his work – and both will be examined in Chapter 11. Quite simply, he uses his synopses to set immediately before us the symbols, themes, structure, as well as the characters and plot, of the texts he wishes to discuss. It is actually a very efficient way to get at these important matters. One wonders if the reason this method is often neglected may not be the difficulty of doing it well. To condense imaginative material without distortion means, first of all, to have utterly at one's command the whole of the work as well as its different parts. Second, it requires one to grasp the relationship of one part to another and, third, to be ready accurately and sensitively to interpret its meaning. This may prove no great challenge in the case of a writer like Kipling, but it becomes a task of enormous complexity in the case of Proust or Joyce.

Recalling the other key item in Wilson's paragraph on Van Wyck Brooks, let us examine for a moment "the necessity of sticking to texts." A strong point in favor of Wilson's method of synopsis is to be found just here; that is, in the fidelity to the text to which it holds the critic who uses it. The method tends to ensure that any analytic point or generalization the critic makes about the literary subject is grounded in the concrete. For instance, Wilson desires to overthrow the received idea of Dickens as a jolly popular novelist by reference to the prevalence of gloom in Dickens' work. He does so by recounting the plots of the interpolated tales in *Pickwick Papers* – plots that invariably revolve around such gloomy subjects as madness, murder, betrayal, and revenge.

Not only Wilson's use of synopsis, but all of the aspects of his critical method noted here will be seen in more detail in the discussions of individual essays which follow.

Of Wilson's critical aims, we have already said that the overriding aim of his critical effort was to explore the relation of literature to life and of both to history. In "The Historical Interpretation of Literature," he suggests some of the components of that overriding aim when he tells us of his interest in "the origins of works of literature" and of "finding therein a key to an artist's whole career."[10] But later he suggests that the genesis study itself is only a means to a larger end: the discovery of the "attitudes and patterns embedded in the community and the historical moment" as these are discernible in the literary work.[11] All the components seem to combine in his statement, in the dedication to *Axel's Castle*, "of what literary criticism ought to be – a history of man's ideas and imaginings in the setting of the conditions which have shaped them."

Ultimately, Wilson suggests, the aim of not just literary criticism but "all our intellectual activity, in whatever field it takes place, is an attempt to give a meaning to our experience – that is, to make life more practicable; for by understanding things we make it easier to survive and get around among them.[12]

Art and, in particular, literature has, in Wilson's view, the power to "make life more practicable," because through its cathartic aspects it has the effect of relieving "our worried intelligence and . . . our balked emotions."[13] "This relief" says Wilson, "brings the sense of power, and with the sense of power, joy." This "positive emotion," he maintains, "tells us that we have encountered a first-rate piece of literature."[14]

Although Wilson persists in identifying this view of the purpose of art and of all mental activity with "the historical point of view," fundamentally, it is a humanist attitude. He sets it forth rather explicitly in the following passage:

> The experience of mankind on earth is always changing as man develops and has to deal with new combinations of elements; and the writer who is to be anything more than an echo of his predecessors must always find expression for something which has never yet been expressed, must master a new set of phenomena which has never yet been mastered. With each such victory of the human intellect, whether in history, in philosophy or in poetry, we experience a deep satisfaction: we have been cured of some ache or disorder, relived of some oppressive burden of uncomprehended events.[15]

But to return from Wilson's thoughts about the general aim of art to his ideas on the function and aim of criticism, we find that he further saw criticism as a means toward the cross-fertilization of ideas from one literature to another, one discipline to another, one culture to another. He writes in "A Modest Self-Tribute":

> I may claim for myself that I have tried to contribute a little to the general cross-fertilization, to make it possible for our literate public to appreciate and understand both our own Anglo-American culture and those of the European countries in relation to one another, to arrive at a point of view from which we may be able to deal with systems of art and thought that have previously seemed inaccessible or incompatible with one another."[16]

The number of essays Wilson has left us on Russian literature alone would substantiate this claim.

Wilson's urge to cross-fertilize even extends to a concern that one area of literature should not be divorced from another – poetry from the novel, the novel from drama, and so on – and that the literary concerns of one social class should not be remote from other classes nor those of one area of the country from those of another. The former is exemplified in Wilson's essay, "Is Verse a Dying Technique?" the latter is present in both its social and regional aspects in Wilson's essays on writers of the western United States, collected under the title "The Boys in the Back Room."[17]

Throughout his criticism, Wilson brings to his discussions an insistence upon the wholeness of literature. His work abounds in comparative points as he shows the relationship between works of different genres, languages, and cultures. To take just one example, Wilson's essay on Yeats compares Yeats not only to Waller, Keats, Shelley, and the Pre-Raphaelites, but to Mallarmé, Dante, and Flaubert.[18]

Wilson speaks of a related critical aim in "Thoughts on Being Bibliographed," when he tells us of a youthful ambition to carry on "that work of 'Enlightenment' of which the flame had been so fanned by Voltaire. I suppose that I, too, wanted to prove myself a 'soldier in the Liberation War of humanity' and to speak for the 'younger generation' who were 'knocking at the door.' " He then goes on to describe the road, which he saw as the literary road that "had still to be broken: the road to the understanding of the most recent literary events in the larger international world – Joyce, Eliot, Proust, etc. – which were already out of the range of readers the limits of whose taste had been fixed by *Egoists* and *The Quintessence of Ibsenism*."[19]

The principal instrument through which Wilson attempted to achieve this aim in his own work was *Axel's Castle*. In this book, within a historical frame that somehow made them seem less maverick and more acceptable to the public, Wilson presented such then startling writers as Valéry, Rimbaud, Yeats, Eliot, Proust, Joyce, and Gertrude Stein. In doing so he became the critic who, perhaps more than any other, prepared America for the works of a distinctly modern sensibility that were being produced in Britain and on the Continent in the 1920s and 1930s.

All through his work of the 1930s and 1940s Wilson went on giving candid and astonishingly durable assessments of such writers on the contemporary scene as Hemingway, Faulkner, Fitzgerald, and Malraux. Only in the 1950s and 1960s did a shift in Wilson's critical attention become really apparent. Recognizably literary concerns were increasingly less prevalent in his work. So much was this the case that in 1963 it was possible for Richard Gilman to describe Wilson as a critic who had, for some time, ceased altogether to criticize. The matter is complicated and explication must, for the moment, be deferred.

Leaving aside, then, questions of the wisdom or propriety of the changes discernible in Wilson's criticism, what follows is a brief description of the course his work did in fact follow over the years. This may be summed up as the progressive shift in emphasis of the elements in Wilson's 1931 statement regarding what he thought literary criticism should be: "A history of man's ideas and imaginings in the setting of the conditions which have shaped them."

A more descriptive gloss of that statement might look something like this: criticism should be a historical "placing" and a biographical "profile" of the artist, accompanied by an analysis and evaluation of the moral and political ideas, as well as the aesthetic vision, contained in his or her art – this to be rendered along with a description of the cultural setting of the work and a probing of the psychosocial conditions out of which it sprang.

When we look at Wilson's critical books in chronological order, we can see that in *Axel's Castle*, at any rate in the chapters on individual writers, the imaginative work itself – the element of the artist's aesthetic vision – remains the center of his concern. *The Triple Thinkers*, although it does contain some aesthetic evaluations, of Pushkin, Housman, and Henry James – is concerned with humanism, Marxism, the future of verse, and the teaching of the humanities. That is, it deals with moral, political, and cultural considerations, and these not so much in terms of imaginative works but in terms of criticism and education.

In *The Wound and the Bow* the psychological conditions shaping art and artist predominate, whereas in *Patriotic Gore* the concern is the social conditions – specifically of the North and South in the period of the American Civil War. In Wilson's book, *O Canada*, the setting itself has assumed the dominant position, Wilson being particularly concerned with seeing in that country's literature a picture of a national culture.

In order to see that this shift in emphasis is part of a continuous critical effort and not a discontinuous one, it will be necessary to come to a clearer understanding than has been reached by earlier Wilson commentators of just what sort of criticism Wilson is actually practicing.

Depending on which aspect of this description of Wilson's critical stance one focuses upon – or which of the critical preoccupations – the commentators on Wilson's work may arrive (and indeed have arrived) at a variety of labels for it. Leon Edel, focusing on Wilson's unusual ability to identify with the artist, his frequent habit of helping to expound, interpret, and gain appreciation for the artist's work, has called him a "sympathetic" critic.[20] Northrop Frye, focusing on his unusual powers of anticipating and empathizing with the responses of the average literate reader, calls him a "public critic," a man "who represents the reading public at its most expert and judicious."[21] Warner Berthoff, perhaps remembering Wilson's method of working first in terms of magazine articles, calls him, rather disparagingly, a writer of "critical journalism"; and Stanley Edgar Hyman, along similar and still more reductive lines, labels him a "popularizer,"

a "translator" for the literarily nonadept.[22] To Charles Glicksberg he is (in 1937 at any rate) a Marxist critic, though a recalci-
trant one.[23] To Robert Heilman he is, at least when he is discussing "The Turn of the Screw," Freudian.[24] Donald Stauffer's label
is "historical critic."[25] To any number of others he is a
biographical critic. Clive James (surfacing as the author of the
Times Literary Supplement review noted elsewhere), calls him
a "metropolitan critic." Most recently, Giles Gunn has designated him by two rubrics – he calls him "a critic of moral imagination" and a "culture critic."[26] As the present brief survey has
hoped to show, all of these descriptions are, at least partly, true.
What is missing is the single all-encompassing term that would
suggest the enormous range Wilson's criticism actually does
take in.

The quest for such a term is more than a mere impulse to
pigeonhole; it is of the first importance in securing for Wilson in
the future the place that his achievement argues he should
have – and which the very difficulty of classifying him threatens
to obscure. The significance of proper classification in any field
is well stated by Stephen Jay Gould in his description of the importance to taxonomists of deciding, once and for all, upon the
proper classification for the mushroom; whether it is one plant
among many or a whole new kingdom (the Fungi) separate
from both plants and animals. Gould suggests that taxonomists
invest so much energy in the decision for good reason. "They
understand better than most scholars that classifications do not
merely provide convenient and neutral pigeonholes for arranging information: they represent structures of thought that
largely determine both the status and the content of a subject.[27]

In aid, then, of finding the term by which to make such a
classification in Wilson's case, let me review. I have said that the
single feature that most clearly distinguishes Edmund Wilson's
literary criticism is his persistent relation of literature to life and
of life to history. As I have noted, perhaps with tiresome insistence, the very broadness, not to mention vagueness, of such a
distinction makes it difficult to approach Wilson's work in any
systematic way. When one tries to break down the area of his
critical concerns, for example, one is confronted with all of the
component parts of "life" and "history"; that is, with all of the

concerns of humankind – excepting perhaps only the purely
mathematical and formulaic ones of the pure scientist. In short,
one is confronted with Wilson's humanism.

But identifying Wilson's approach as humanistic and his
criticism as representative of the humanist tradition scarcely
solves the problem. For, in doing so, we have not only failed to
narrow our subject and thus simplify our problems of analysis,
we have tapped into the largest, most complex intellectual tradition there is.

In the face of such complications, only my conviction that
any other approach to Wilson's work has proved too partial, too
incomplete to render him justice prompts me to go on. For what
one sees in the other studies of Wilson's work is reminiscent of
the story of the blind man and the elephant. We have already
seen the variety of descriptions – all to some extent true – that
have been applied to his criticism. In dissertations alone,
scholars have attempted to find the single most useful principle
for their analyses in the following Wilson traits: his historical
consciousness, his political and social concern, his sympathetic
identification with the artist as a modern symbol of alienation,
his incorporation into his criticism of certain elements of Marxism, and in one study, in the deep ambivalences – "the violent
contraries" – in Wilson's unconscious.

Wilson the man has proved as elusive as Wilson the critic.
He has been viewed as an American patrician, an eighteenth-
century French philosophe, the American Sainte-Beuve, the
American Dr. Johnson, and the American Plutarch. He has
been located politically in every sort of description, from
communist-bohemian-radical to conservative-reactionary; from
liberal to elitist.

Numerous questions have arisen in the minds of the writers
who have turned their attention to Wilson. What, for example is
one to make of his extensive use of the personal biographical
sketch in *Axel's Castle*, a work purportedly the historical
account of a theoretical movement? Why did he write so little on
"black humor" or modern absurdist literature in general? What
was he doing, writing about Indians, and Zulus, and the Dead
Sea scrolls?

Finally, there is the problem of trying to see Wilson whole

and finding a coherent way to assess his accomplishment. In sum, a way of answering the question asked by Clive James in his unsigned *Times Literary Supplement* review of *Upstate*, "What does Wilson's effort amount to?" The review, which becomes in fact an overview of Wilson's whole career, goes on: "We need to decide whether critical work which has plainly done so much to influence its time vanishes with its time or continues." James suggests that it can continue only if it is seen to have "embodied, not just recommended, a permanent literary value." And he concludes that Wilson's work does, but he notes that the nature of that value has proved very difficult to define. Citing Trilling's view that an interest in ideas is the very essence of Wilson's criticism, James contrasts it with Kazin's remark that Wilson is not at home with ideas. He concludes that the permanent literary value embodied in Wilson's work "must perforce reside in whatever is left after opposing . . . estimations of Wilson have cancelled each other out."[28]

I am already on record that the permanent value of Wilson's work resides in that single, though unwieldy, principle I have identified as its relation of literature to life. I will now assert, further, that the most comprehensive and coherent analytic approach to Wilson's criticism is to see it as a representative modern example of the tradition of humanism.

II.
Humanistic
Backgrounds of
Wilson's Criticism

CHAPTER THREE

Arnold and Sainte-Beuve

*A*s a term, *humanism* has proved to be every bit as troublesome – and as indispensable – to intellectual historians as *romanticism* or *classicism*. Like them, it has had a variety of meanings, acquiring new ones over the years. Indeed, its changing meanings are the inevitable consequence of its focus: on the living principle, the human being, rather than on an aesthetic tenet or an ideology.

The humanist position can embrace Christian humanism as well as secular humanism. It incorporates – in Matthew Arnold's terms – Hebraism as well as Hellenism. It can be brought to bear on the sciences as well as on the arts. Humanism can be flexible within new historical situations, can incorporate new thought and can grow, but its very dynamism makes it difficult to give it a specific definition.

Within the single focus of the human, however, there is a dual aspect of humanism that remains constant throughout its many guises, whether classical, Renaissance, or modern. On the one hand, humanism is always characterized by its insistence that learning – in whatever field or discipline it takes place – be seen in terms of its application to human life. On the other, humanism is always characterized (whether in its Christian or its secular guise) by a separation of the human and the divine or supernatural.

Beyond defining humanism in this way, the term must take into account at least four different aspects of humanism: humanism as it is associated with a specific movement in intellectual history; humanism as it is associated with a specific part of the educational curriculum (i.e., the study of the humanities); humanism as a personal philosophy; and humanism as it is associated with a specific type of critical approach. For a clearer picture of the aspect of humanism I have undertaken to discuss here – humanism as it represents a specific critical approach – it will be helpful always to keep in mind the classical historical background out of which it grew.

The seeds of humanism are to be found in Greece in the fifth century B.C. with the first recorded systematic inquiry into the source of virtue and the good life. Both the inquiry itself and the results of the inquiry – locating both virtue and happiness in the acquisition of knowledge – form the foundation of humanism. To associate learning with the most intimate connections to personal and communal life is thus one of the cornerstones of the humanist tradition.[1]

The humanist spirit is manifest in Socrates' dictum "The unexamined life is not worth living," in the Delphic Oracle's injunction to "Know thyself," and in Protagoras' view of man as "the measure of all things." But, it is the Latin poet Terence who has provided perhaps the single most constant watchword of humanism in his *Nihil humanum alienum puto* – "I am human, and nothing that is human is alien to me."

With the Romans, the idea of linking learning and life – indeed, of seeing the former as a prerequisite for the "life worth living" – became more organized. Such linkage is to be found, for example, in the rhetoric of Cicero and Quintillian. And the idea finds elaborate codification in a work of Cicero called "Tully's Offices," a treatise on ethics that he wrote for the instruction of his son. It was, in effect, a complete humanist curriculum and was widely used by Western educators for centuries thereafter, both as a means of instructing the young in Latin and as the best practical guide to life produced by the ancient world.

The phenomenon of Renaissance humanism took place from the fourteenth to the seventeenth centuries. It began in Italy with the poet Petrarch and such writers, teachers, and thinkers as Bruni, Salutati, Piccolomini, and Vives. Humanism was represented in Germany by Philip Melancthon and in

England by the Dutch-born theologian Erasmus, John Colet, and Thomas More. Even though we are all familiar with the dramatic upsurge in learning and discovery that accompanied the phenomenon of Renaissance humanism, the interesting factor to note, for our purposes, is the degree to which the whole regalia of new mental life followed from a reintroduction into the school curricula of those old principles of linkage between learning and life, words and matter, represented in the work of Cicero and Quintillian.

Walter J. Ong points out that, in the Middle Ages, the schools had fallen under the domination of the scholastics. The young were taught the principles of scholastic logic (very like the formal symbolic logic of modern times) and almost their whole curriculum involved the discipline of disputation – not, it must be kept in mind, over anything that corresponded to reality but merely a drill in the method. It was, says Ong, "a policy which fitted them for only one thing – becoming themselves teachers of scholastic logic." Moreover, it was not, he notes, "suitable for anyone interested in living."[2]

So the Renaissance was first and foremost a movement of educational reformers, designed to liberate learning once more into some vital connection with life. The spectacular degree to which they succeeded is to be found in the glories of the Renaissance itself, as well as in the seeds that, planted there, blossomed forth into the modern world, both in terms of the science and technology of the industrial age and of the developments in the arts. With the spread of humanism beyond the Renaissance, the problem of defining it becomes more complicated, however.

The sense of the term by which one might call Wilson a humanist, a *literatus*, or man of letters, for example, is quite different from that by which one might refer to all educators who teach in the humanities as humanists. To make the distinction clear it will be necessary once again to take a look at the matter from a historical point of view.

It was a second century Latin grammarian who first designated a portion of the educational curriculum as the humanities; that is, as *literatus humanitas* or "humane letters." In his conception, it referred to the study of those things that made one most human. Unlike this branch of the modern curriculum – where it is a designation used to distinguish between the sciences on one hand and all other subjects on the other – in the classical curriculum "humane letters" was understood to contain both grammar and philosophy; that is, both manner and matter, words and things, form and content.

Further, in those days philosophy consisted of both moral and natural philosophy – subject matters we would recognize as encompassing both arts and sciences (the *natural* in natural philosophy having reference to the physical sciences).

This more comprehensive meaning of the term humanism continued to have wide currency up to the Victorian Age. Hence, those who shared and practiced the scientific spirit in the eighteenth century, characterized by its combined program of emancipation and enlightenment, may be said to have been participants in a golden age of humanism. In France, humanists of this type were represented by Diderot and a group of Encyclopedists who came to be known (by virtue of that older meaning of philosophy) as *les philosophes*; in America they were represented in men like Benjamin Franklin, Thomas Jefferson, and many others among the founding fathers.

The critical turning point away from the association of the arts and sciences conceived of as a joint humanistic enterprise – at least insofar as the school curriculum was concerned – became a matter of record in England in the 1880s. It came in the form of a quarrel between two men, each of whom was himself an educator and a representative humanist – Matthew Arnold and Thomas Huxley.

The crisis was precipitated by Huxley's address on "Science and Culture," in 1881, which seemed to pit the two terms against each other and to argue for the greater importance of science. It evoked a reply from Arnold in a lecture called "Literature and Science." As Arnold announces at its start, "Literature and Science" is an inquiry into the future of the humanities conceived of as a field of study separate from the sciences. "I am going to ask," says Arnold:

> Whether the present movement for ousting letters from their old predominance in education, and for transferring the predominance in education to the natural sciences,

whether this brisk and flourishing movement ought to prevail, and whether it is likely that in the end it really will prevail.[3]

History must be said to have replied in the affirmative, although Arnold makes a memorable case. He argues for retaining the old view of the relation between the arts and sciences, correcting and expanding Huxley's definition of literature by stating that the humanities for him do not include merely works of polite literature. They include the whole range of ancient and modern writings: Greek science and mathematics as well as poetry, and in modern times, the writings of men like Copernicus, Galileo, Newton, and Darwin, as well as Shakespeare and Goethe.

Thus, Arnold asserts the same principle of the organic unity of human nature that underlies both the old humanist definition of the humanities and his own earlier definition of culture. By doing so, he reduces the only issue remaining between him and Huxley to the question of whether training in the methods or processes of natural science, and instruction in terms of scientific fact, ought to form the main part of education for the majority of humankind. Granting that such subjects ought to form *some* part of education, Arnold argues that it ought not to form the predominant part.

Arnold, by the force of his own eloquence and influence, may have staved off total domination of the sciences over the humanities in English and American education for a time. Nevertheless, with the increased importance of science in the twentieth century, the sharp separation between the two areas of the curriculum grew steadily until, in the 1950s, C. P. Snow pointed out that the result was, in effect, "two cultures."

One consequence of the defensive posture into which the humanities were thrown was the entry into the study of literature, especially in America, of a spirit distinctly alien to the spirit of humanism as we have been defining it. Scholars and literary critics became increasingly concerned to make the study of literature more like a science, or at any rate more of a discipline exclusive unto itself. Form and method took precedence over content. The trend became predominant with the advent, in the 1940s and 1950s, of the "new criticism," and of such influential books as Brooks and Warren's *Understanding Poetry*, Wellek's *Theory of Literature*, and Frye's *Anatomy of Criticism* – all of which advocated narrowing the study of literature to its purely literary components.

This uneasiness over the introduction into the study of literature of any extraliterary content still largely prevails. Indeed, since the advent of Russian formalism, French structuralism, and deconstruction at Yale, it has dominated academic critical thought. This has not occurred, however, without a certain wrenching, or deconstruction, of terms. Critical theory grounded in philosophical opposition to any referential relation between "text" and "world" is quite frequently taught in departments of the humanities, and strictly textual or structuralist scholar-critics are often called humanists by virtue of the fact that they teach in a branch of the modern curricula designated as the humanities. The philosophical principles underlying their criticism, however, would have little in common with those of humanists in the more general sense such as Matthew Arnold or Edmund Wilson.

Giles Gunn, in a recent book called *The Culture of Criticism and the Criticism of Culture*, has discussed most cogently this historic split and its ramifications, which he points out go far beyond matters of educational curricula.[4]

One more aspect of the term *humanism* remains to be clarified: that is, humanism as a personal philosophy. Even though it is characteristic of humanism to evince a repugnance for dogma and to be reluctant to adhere to any strict or easily classified tenets, Corliss Lamont has, in fact, been able to isolate ten "central propositions of the humanist philosophy." Although not incompatible in its idealism with Christian tenets, the humanism Lamont systematizes will be seen to be distinctly the secular variety. I propose to look at his propositions here, in slightly paraphrased form, with interpolated comments citing like-minded positions taken by Wilson in his writings.

According to Lamont, then, humanism as a personal philosophy is characterized by, first, a naturalistic attitude toward the universe that considers (1) all forms of the supernatural as myth, (2) Nature as the totality of being, and (3) humankind as the evolutionary product of Nature with no consciousness after death.

Wilson came by his understanding of the physical universe largely through his reading in the work of Alfred North Whitehead. Although, in his later years, Wilson admitted to being a little envious of friends who possessed a religious faith, there is throughout his life a definite self-proclaimed stamp of secularism on him. In *A Piece of My Mind* he writes:

> As we come to understand more and more about the processes of "life" and "matter," we discover that it is less and less easy to differentiate clearly between them. As we probe into the happenings in the universe – electrical and cerebral phenomena, the transit of light waves and sound waves, the multiplication of cells in organisms, the inherited combinations of genes – we find them, to be sure, less amenable to the "laws" of the old-fashioned scientist who thought in mechanical terms. But we do not find a God.[5]

Lamont makes the further point that, having its ultimate faith in people, humanism believes that human beings possess the power or potentiality to solve their own problems through reliance, primarily, upon reason and scientific method, applied with vision and courage. Clearly, although he disdained faith in the supernatural, Wilson could be downright visionary in the faith he placed in artists and scientists. We recall his statement in *Axel's Castle*:

> And who can say that, as science and art look more and more deeply into experience and achieve a wider and wider range, and as they come to apply themselves more and more directly and expertly to the needs of human life, they may not arrive at a way of thinking, a technique of dealing with our perceptions, which will make art and science one?[6]

As for resistance to deterministic thinking and a belief that, although conditioned by the past and constrained by other objective limits, human beings possess genuine freedom of action and are masters of their fate (which Lamont isolates as a fourth element in humanism), Wilson's tacit approval shows through in his concern to get at this element in Marx. "Real dialectical materialism" he was at pains to remind the so-called Marxist critics of the 1930s, "allows man to make his own history."

Lamont goes on to note that humanism believes in a thoroughly ethical, moral, and democratic value system that grounds all this worldly happiness in the freedom and progress "of all mankind, irrespective of nation, race, or religion." And he makes clear that the humanist feels duty-bound to be active in pursuit of such goals, both nationally and internationally. In view of Wilson's socialist tendencies this insistence upon "democratic values" may seem, at first glance, to rule out his inclusion in the humanist camp.

Writing, in the 1930s, of Marxism – still untainted by the Stalinist horrors to come – as "something new in the world," Wilson displays the intensity of his hopes for it, precisely because "it is a philosophical system which leads directly to programs of action." He quotes Vincent Sheean to the effect that Lenin's Marxist vision "has in its completeness and its compelling force a good deal in common with the vision of Dante."

Still, the socialism Wilson to some extent embraced in the 1930s was always democratic socialism at heart, as is evident in his essay of the period, "An Appeal to Progressives."[7] And his strong adherence to democratic principles is apparent in the following letter written to his friend John Dos Passos in 1964:

> You seem to mistake my point of view. I am not "between for and against Marxism." The Marxism of the so-called Communist countries is today mostly mere cant to cover their exploitation by the Russians. But the problem in these countries as well as here at home is to prevent the apparently inevitable tendency toward centralization and nationalization from crushing individual initiative and any leeway for minority groups.[8]

Moving on to another aspect of humanism as a personal philosophy, Lamont firmly aligns it to an appreciation of natural beauty. As for Wilson's appreciation of Nature, many passages in his journals demonstrate just that. The following entry from *Upstate* is an example:

> This afternoon, July 6, I saw out between two trees on the lawn, reading and watching, from my deck chair, the sky and the tops of the trees. Everything was so beautiful and interesting that I stayed out till 8:15. There were chipmunks or small squirrels chasing one another across the back roof,

and through the trees swallows and other birds, a butterfly
as high as the top of the elm, which looked a bright red when
the sinking sun shone through its wings. I had never felt so
much before that I had the freedom of that realm of treetop,
roof and sky.[9]

Lamont also aligns humanism with a strong advocacy of
the arts and an appreciation of their life-enhancing properties.
Of the "transcendent" powers of the human spirit evident in
literature, Wilson was acutely aware, as we have seen. He
states his view most explicitly in this dialogue from *Discordant
Encounters*: "That is the great thing about a classical education:
it enables us to know the worst early, yet encourages us to maintain our dignity in presence of it. The classical writers allow us
no illusions; yet they make it possible for us to do without them."

Lamont's tenth – and final – point regarding the tenets of
humanism emphasizes the importance of a scientific attitude,
especially its disinterestedness and openness in the pursuit of
truth, a position we have found Wilson taking often. The
matter-of-factness with which Wilson refers to this attitude in
his "Thoughts on Being Bibliographed" illustrates how much it
was, for him, an ingrained habit of mind: "This method of working out in print one's treatment of something one is studying involves a certain amount of energy wasted; but it does have the
advantage of allowing one's ideas first to appear in tentative
form, so that they are exposed to correction and criticism."[10]

In addition to the philosophical positions given by Lamont,
it is interesting to note the moral positions – the concepts of virtue – apposite to humanism as a personal philosophy. One of the
most curious but prominent features of later humanism is the
way it embraces not only classical learning but also classical
values, Stoic and Epicurean values in particular.

Walter Lippmann, a slightly older contemporary of
Wilson's and a colleague at the *New Republic*, listed these values
and described their properties as the ethical basis for his book, *A
Preface to Morals*.[11] Since the book was widely regarded as a
model humanist document, it may be said to provide our most
complete idea yet of what a humanist like Arnold or Wilson
means by such terms as *intellectual conscience* and *intellectual
heroism*.

Lippmann names and defines courage, honor, veracity and magnanimity as the central humanistic virtues. (I give his definitions in paraphrase.)

1. courage: embodies the principle of all virtue, which is to transcend the immediacy of desire and live for ends that are transpersonal.

2. honor: the faithful holding of oneself to an ideal of conduct though it is inconvenient, unprofitable, or dangerous to do so.

3. veracity: saying and believing what one thinks is true, even though it would be easier to deceive oneself and others.

4. magnanimity: caring more, as Aristotle says, "for truth than for opinion," speaking and acting openly, not living at the will of another "except it be a friend," not recollecting injuries, not caring that one should be praised or others blamed, and not complaining or asking for help in unavoidable or trifling calamities.

Few people, Lippmann acknowledges, possess these virtues in all their varieties or are wholly matured to the core of their being. Yet, he maintains, the more closely one attains to their achievement, the closer one will be to happiness, for they "stand as the accumulated wisdom of the race."[12]

Wilson, who reviewed *A Preface to Morals* when it came out in 1929 and whose review appears in the 1960 edition as an Introduction, calls it "far and away" Lippmann's best book, "beautifully organized, beautifully clear." He says that in it Lippmann "has not merely, as other writers have done, shown us the picture of our own confusion, with our ancient sanctions and authorities gone and obliged to stand on our own feet: he gives us the assurance that we shall be able to do so, that we have begun to do so already."[13]

Ironically, although he finds much to praise, the fault Wilson finds with the book is, in humanist terms, fundamental: a failure, on Lippmann's part, to inject the work with the vital principle of life. The result, says Wilson, is that "we are not so ardently responsive as we should like to be, because the point of view which Lippmann commends seems to exclude intense feelings of any kind, and even to err a little on the side of complacency."

Wilson is objecting to a suggestion of quietism in the book; Lippmann, for example, describes the wise man as one who can look on the tragic aspects of life and yet enjoy it. "Why should he enjoy it," asks Wilson, "if it is a tragedy?"[14] This bias of Wilson in favor of intense feelings is reminiscent of Arnold's insistence that humanism calls for "full-bloodedness" as well as reason.

Perhaps the best way to conclude this overview of humanism in all its guises would be to reiterate the two constants in humanism over the ages: the insistence upon the organic link between literature and human life, and the insistence upon separation of the human and the divine, focusing on the social world as the work of humanity.

Aristotle and Longinus may be said to have manifested this approach among classical critics, and in the related field of rhetoric, it may be noted as characteristic of Cicero and Quintillian; it passes into the post-Renaissance world in the work of historians such as Vico and Herder and literary critics such as Dr. Johnson. But, as for identifying it with a specific critical approach, the difficulty once again is the all-encompassing nature of humanism itself.

So persuasive was the humanist point of view in Western culture from the seventeenth to the twentieth centuries that, in truth, it may be said with some justice that virtually all learned writing not specifically connected with the church was humanist.

Nevertheless, a specific critical approach may be seen to emerge, in France in the nineteenth century, in the writings of Charles Augustin Sainte-Beuve. It is composed of the self-conscious and consistent adherence to a set of principles best described as those of classical humanism, combined with a conscientious attempt to incorporate the new learning of the sciences. In a somewhat adulterated form it was advanced by the work of Hippolyte Taine, and it reached its fullest flowering up to the modern era in England in the criticism of Matthew Arnold.

True, two or three practitioners of criticism in the same vein do not a tradition make. However, it must be kept in mind that each of these figures had numerous epigones and that a number of noted critics on either side of the Atlantic are recognizably practitioners of the same approach. It is simply beyond the scope of this study to deal with them.

It is, however, a major proposition of this study that in Edmund Wilson the tradition finds a major adherent. To get a more specific picture of this tradition, therefore, I propose to look briefly at the work of Sainte-Beuve, Taine, and Arnold, paying special attention to the ways in which the practice of each relates to the critical practice of Edmund Wilson.

Beginning, then, with a look at Charles Augustin Sainte-Beuve (1804-1869), we find that (as Matthew Arnold describes him in an appreciative essay written at the time of his death), he exhibits many traits that have come to be recognized as humanistic. He was a student and lover of classical Greece; an indefatigable, conscientious, and disinterested toiler in the profession of letters, ever engaged in the pursuit of excellence and in working toward the advancement of culture.

Although at one time he held the chair of poetry at the College of France, like Wilson, Sainte-Beuve was more journalist-critic than teacher. For most of his adult life he worked feverishly, six days a week, to bring forth, on the seventh, one of his carefully wrought reviews. These came to be collected in more than twenty-eight volumes, principally in two series, *Causeries du Lundis* and *Nouveaux Lundis*.

His critical focus was not so much on the literary qualities of a work as on the relation of the literary work to life. "Literary opinions occupy very little place in my life and my thoughts," he wrote. "What does occupy me seriously is life itself and the object of it."[15]

By the time he reached maturity, Arnold says of him: "he had become the perfect critic – a critic of measure, not exuberant; of the centre, not provincial; of keen industry and curiosity, with 'truth' (the word engraved in English on his seal) for his motto."[16]

When Arnold describes that "industry and curiosity" in greater detail, by quoting a passage from Sainte-Beuve's notes, we are reminded of Wilson and his idea of "reading a subject up."

Today I set to work on Grimm. . . . I have . . . the edition of his *Correspondence* by M. Taschreau. I have also the *Memoirs* of Madame d'Epinay, where there are letters of his. But it is possible that there may be notices of him mentioned in the bibliographical book of that German whose name I have forgotten. I should like, too, to have the first editions of his *Correspondence*; they came out in successive parts.

"Thus he prepared himself," comments Arnold, "not for a grand review article once a quarter, but for a newspaper review once a week."[17]

According to Arnold's description of Sainte-Beuve, Wilson shares with him still other habits of mind associated with humanism: an ideal of magnanimity of spirit and an adherence to the principle of intellectual conscience that Arnold calls "truth" in this essay but that he has described better elsewhere by the former phrase.

Sainte-Beuve's magnanimity of spirit as it manifests itself as an ideal in his criticism, Arnold calls "amiability" and Trilling refers to it as his "grave, imperturbable amenity."[18] It is evidenced in Sainte-Beuve's distaste for the work of a more violent colleague, whose reviews he calls the work of "a gladiator and a desperado." Referring to this colleague's article on Condorcet as "odious and false," Sainte-Beuve explains his own critical code by stating that "one may be severe upon Condorcet, but not in that tone or in that note."[19]

The same spirit is evident in Wilson's criticism, in the following passage from *Axel's Castle*. In it, Wilson displays *his* distaste for the "tone" and "note" in which Paul Valéry has criticized Anatole France:

Valéry adopts the general tone of desiring in a patronizing way to say something kindly and appreciative about France, but everything that he says turns out to sound disparaging. . . .

Now one would naturally not expect Paul Valéry to go against his convictions. . . . Furthermore, with Valéry's criticisms of France it is possible partly to agree. . . . [Y]et . . . as one reads this patronizing and feline paper one cannot help rebelling.[20]

Intellectual conscience, the other humanist trait shared by Sainte-Beuve and Wilson, is not easy to define, even bearing in mind Lippmann's *Preface to Morals*. Matthew Arnold nevertheless cites Sainte-Beuve's attempt to do so in this passage from an earlier essay:

> "In France," says M. Sainte-Beuve, "the first consideration for us is not whether we are amused and pleased by a work of art or mind, nor is it whether we are touched by it. What we seek above all to learn is, whether *we were right* in being amused with it, and in applauding it, and in being moved by it." Those are very remarkable words, and they are, I believe, in the main quite true. . . .
> All the world has, or professes to have, this conscience in moral matters.
> A Frenchman has, to a considerable degree, what one may call a conscience in intellectual matters.[21]

Wilson finds, and applauds, something of the same quality in Proust:

> When Proust, in his wonderful chapter on the death of the novelist Bergotte, speaks of those moral obligations which impose themselves in spite of everything and which seem to come through to humanity from some source outside its wretched self (obligations 'invisible only to fools – and are they really to them?') . . . he speaks for every moral, esthetic or intellectual passion which holds the expediencies of the world in contempt.[22]

This elusive trait is not, of course – as both Arnold and Wilson knew very well – the exclusive property of the French; it comes into Western culture from classical humanist sources. However, having noted these common bonds between Wilson and Sainte-Beuve in terms of shared humanist ideals – and even having shown that these have had an influence on their critical production – the crucial task remains of isolating, in the work of each, the principles that form a common critical approach.

George Saintsbury, in his introduction to a selection of Sainte-Beuve's *Causeries du Lundis*, points out that the central maxim they espouse is that what the critic "has to do is to discover, display in an orderly fashion, and illustrate as best he can, what his author has done."[23]

Looking further into the work of Sainte-Beuve, it develops that his conception of the proper display of "what his author has done" was that it must reveal the author himself as well as his surrounding milieu: "For me, " he writes, "literature, the production of an author, is not distinct or at any rate not separable from the rest of the man and his make-up."[24]

How like Wilson's praise of Taine that sounds: "[He] created the creators themselves as characters in a larger drama of cultural and social history." Wilson goes on to say that "writing about literature, for me, has always meant narrative and drama as well as the discussion of comparative values."[25]

In the same passage Wilson remarks that his criticism has been influenced – indirectly, at least – by Sainte-Beuve as well. Confessing that he has read only a dozen or so of Sainte-Beuve's essays, he writes: "I have undoubtedly been influenced by writers – such as Arnold and Henry James – who were influenced by Sainte-Beuve."[26]

Certainly he was in agreement with Sainte-Beuve's conviction that "nothing relating to the life, experience, and art of the writer is alien to the critic."

More interesting still, in its implications for the author of *The Wound and the Bow*, is Sainte-Beuve's view that if he will "merely let [his literary subjects] disclose themselves in a free way, without hurrying them," he will at last "seize the familiar trick, the telltale smile; the indefatigable wrinkle, the secret line of pain hidden in vain beneath the already scanty hair."[27]

So Walter Jackson Bate describes Sainte-Beuve's critical approach. In the relevance given to a writer's biography we can see the precursor of Wilson's "historical consciousness." In the relevance claimed for personal revelations we can see some precedent for the interest Wilson took in probing (by the more sophisticated means of psychoanalysis) what he came to call a writer's "wound" and what Sainte-Beuve here calls his "secret line of pain."[28]

Describing his own method, Sainte-Beuve said, "I analyse. I botanize; I am a naturalist of minds. What I should like to establish is the natural history of literature."[29] He was not, however, advocating any rigid categorization, such as is possible in the case of animals or plants. For, he notes dryly, "Human nature is more complex, endowed with what we call *liberty*, which in each case admits of a great variety of possible combinations."[30]

He seems, finally, to have had no intention of turning literary criticism into a science in any literal sense. According to Bate, he was trying, rather, to introduce a more objective and detached position for the critic than that to which he had been exposed in the circle of Victor Hugo. The link here to both Arnold and Wilson is in just such disinterestedness; that is, regarding considerations of party or fashion.

Sainte-Beuve himself was to note, late in his career, that "In spite of everything, I have continued of the classical school." And indeed, as Bates points out, "the objective and open flexibility of mind urged by Sainte-Beuve may as justly be called 'classical' as 'scientific.'" It may, with equal justice, be called humanist.

In his final peroration in *Axel's Castle* we can see Wilson, too (having earlier cited a point of natural science from Alfred North Whitehead), manifest an ideal encompassing both art and science. He does so from the distinctly humanist point of view that it is the proper function of both "to apply themselves more and more directly and expertly to human life." Wilson, in this instance allows himself the vision of a future in which such efforts may "arrive at a way of thinking, a technique for dealing with our perceptions, which will make art and science one."[31]

Taine, too, adopted a quasi-scientific view of his method. And he was well aware of his own indebtedness. In his introduction to *The History of English Literature*, he states his conviction that Sainte-Beuve's method of examining the artist's surroundings, of collecting personal anecdotes about him, of inquiring into his relation to the thought, the movements, and the persons of his time constitutes "the fit work of the contemporary critic." And he goes on to acknowledge that "No one has done it so justly and grandly . . . as Sainte-Beuve," and to state that, in the matter of bringing the scientific method to bear on criticism, "we are all his pupils; his method has revolutionized, in our days . . . every kind of . . . criticism. From it we must set out in order to begin the further development."[32]

In the opinion of the "pupil's" master, however, Taine's own attempt at "further development" erred in the direction of over-simplification. Sainte-Beuve was well aware that his method might easily "degenerate into . . . [a] product-of-the-circumstance theory." And, says Saintsbury, although "he did not fall into the error himself, . . . he marked it clearly in his greatest disciple."[33]

Indeed, Sainte-Beuve charged that, in Taine's work, the idiosyncrasy of the individual writer is lost sight of, if not positively denied, in the process of explaining him. Wilson quotes Flaubert as issuing much the same complaint against Taine when he asserted that "On this system you can explain the series, the group, but never the individuality, the special fact which makes him this person and not another. This method results in leaving *talent* out of consideration."[34]

Wilson is on record as in agreement with such sentiments. In fact, his early enthusiasm for Taine underwent a considerable shift by the time he had reached maturity. In his chapter on Taine, in *To the Finland Station*, Wilson describes Taine's method as stultifyingly machinelike. Such a system, he says, "automatically sorts out the phenomena, so that all the examples of one kind of thing turn up in one section or chapter and all the examples of another kind in another, and all the things which do not easily lend themselves to Taine's large and simple generalizations do not turn up at all."[35]

Sainte-Beuve, reiterating his objection to overformulaic applications of his method, such as Taine's, makes the point that, in his own conception of it, criticism "would always be an *art*, demanding a skilled artist."[36] Here we find another link between Wilson and Sainte-Beuve – a shared emphasis on the importance of artistry in the writing of criticism. It is precisely on these grounds that Wilson is able to offer Taine a measure of defense. Had he succeeded in making it the mechanistic product he thought it to be, Taine's work, in Wilson's opinion, would have little value. Rather, Wilson came to see its essential quality as creative: "The truth was that Taine loved literature for its own sake – he was at his best himself a brilliant artist – and he had very strong moral convictions which gave his writing emotional power."

When Taine is writing well, says Wilson, the moment, the

race, and the milieu combine, but what ensues is like "the chord in Browning's poem about Abt Vogler . . . not a fourth sound, but a star."[37]

And for at least one of Taine's chapters Wilson's enthusiasm never faded. He tells us that as a young man in New York, reading Taine in French, "I became so absorbed by the *coup de théâtre* at the end of the final chapter by which Taine evokes Alfred de Musset in order to contrast him with Tennyson and leaves Musset with the moral advantage, that I continued to read it on the street all the way to some engagement."[38] Because of its signal importance to Wilson, I quote it here:

> He was not a mere dilettante; he was not content to taste and enjoy; he stamped his mark upon human thought; he told the world what man is, and love and truth and happiness. He suffered, but he imagined; he fainted, but he created. He tore forth from his entrails the idea which he had conceived, and he held it up before the eyes of all, bloody and alive. That is harder and finer than to go fondling and gazing upon the ideas of others. There is in the world only one achievement worthy of a man: the bringing forth of a truth to which we give ourselves up and in which we believe. The people who have listened to Tennyson are better than our aristocracy of bourgeois and Bohemians; . . . but I prefer Alfred de Musset to Tennyson.[39]

Many years later, writing of Taine in *To the Finland Station*, Wilson still finds it "one of his most eloquent chapters," and the end of it, "one of the passages where he seems really great." It is, says Wilson, "not merely a vindication of Musset; it is a vindication of Taine."

In addition to Taine's artistry, the thing Wilson says he admires about that passage is the quality of "intellectual heroism" it evokes. This is reminiscent of the "intellectual conscience" Arnold admires in Sainte-Beuve. The quality, by either name, incorporates several aspects of the humanist concept of virtue. Wilson displays his regard for it repeatedly. We have already seen him do so as it manifests itself in the work of other writers. He does so again in this passage of his own from *To the Finland Station*:

Whoever has known the Russian revolutionaries of these pre-War generations at their best has been impressed by the effectiveness of the tsarist regime as a training school for intellect and character in those who are engaged in opposing it . . . these men and women combine an unusual range of culture with an unusual range of social experience and, stripped of so many of the trimmings in which human beings have swathed themselves, have, in surviving, kept the sense of those things that are vital to the honor of human life.[40]

However imperfectly Taine practiced it, then, he may still be said to have passed some of the humanist values of Sainte-Beuve's critical method on to Wilson, who was already disposed to be receptive to them.

Continuing to track the course of humanism as a critical tradition, Lionel Trilling tells how it extended from the French criticism of Sainte-Beuve into England by way of Matthew Arnold. Noting that "Arnold was the most influential critic of his age," Trilling goes on to inquire into the causes of Arnold's success. For one thing, his style, Trilling suggests, was perfectly adapted to fulfill Arnold's own view of what criticism is: "the endeavor, in all branches of knowledge, theology, philosophy, art, science, to see the object as in itself it really is."[41] Arnold, he points out, further prescribes for criticism that it be patient and flexible "and know how to attach itself to things and how to withdraw from them."[42]

"Moreover," says Trilling of Arnold's success as a critic,

With this style went a biographical talent nicely suited to the critical purpose, not so brilliant and dramatic as to overshadow the literary evaluation but alert to the tone and inflection of personality, able, by reference to these, to illustrate the spiritual meaning of style.

Like Bate, Trilling cautions against taking too literally the scientific aspects of this biographical method – learned "in larger part from Sainte-Beuve":

Sainte-Beuve had called himself a naturalist of souls, and from Sainte-Beuve, his acknowledged master, Arnold learned the attitude of the "scientist" in literature. [But] the

"science" to which Sainte-Beuve subscribed was not Taine's;
it had no system, no categories; it was an attitude merely –
an insatiable curiosity and, so far as possible, the abrogation
of passion and partisanship.[43]

We can see how closely this conforms to Arnold's own words:

Real criticism is essentially the exercise of this very quality
[i.e., curiosity]; it obeys an instinct prompting it to try to
know the best that is known and thought in the world, irre-
spectively of practice, politics, and everything of the kind;
and to value knowledge and thought as they approach this
best, without the intrusions of any other consideration
whatever.[44]

Here, then, are some of the key elements that made up
Arnold's criticism. For all their unscientific looseness, we may
nevertheless discern in them the elements of a critical tradition
whose ideals and principles are closely identified with humanism. This is evident in Arnold's insistence upon broadening the
base of critical practice, extending it beyond the proscribed
realm of literary works to include virtually all of the social, political, and cultural aspects of life, just as it is evident in his insistence upon the disinterested pursuit of excellence as a critical
ideal.

We note, too, the reappearance in Arnold of that openness
and flexibility of manner, that conversational ease and amenity
of tone, that biographical emphasis on the personality of the
artist, that "sensitivity to the spiritual meaning of style" already
met in Sainte-Beuve. Yet, we may go still further. For we shall
not have explored sufficiently the humanist link that connects
Arnold to Sainte-Beuve, on the one hand, and Arnold to Wilson,
on the other, until we have looked at the philosophical and aesthetic positions their criticism implies.

As we do so, we move well beyond the "attitude merely" of
the "scientific" impulses of the tradition – move to something
educative, indeed, almost evangelical in its critical aims. "Of the
humanism that Arnold established for himself and tried to hand
on to others," says Trilling, "we must observe that it was active
and not passive, that it was never a mere attitude." And he goes

on to say of Arnold that "He had, we might say, a kind of passion for society."[45]

Commenting on the influence of Sainte-Beuve, Trilling suggests that, in his high seriousness, Arnold was going beyond the tradition he learned from Sainte-Beuve, that what we see of this in him is rather the tradition of his father (the famous Dr. Arnold, headmaster of Rugby) as it showed forth in the moral strenuousness that was strong in him. "He might use Sainte-Beuve's grave, imperturbable amenity," says Trilling, "but beneath it was the intense desire to correct the world and to make right prevail."[46]

That Arnold was strongly influenced by his father – who was, of course, also a humanist, though of the Christian variety – is undoubtedly true. Yet, when it comes to moral influences, I believe that the picture may be enlarged to include his critical master as well. Think, for example, of that pronouncement of Sainte-Beuve: "Literary opinions occupy very little place in my life and my thoughts. What does occupy me seriously is life itself and the object of it."[47] Think, too, of his view of criticism, which prompted Arnold to identify him as possessing an "intellectual conscience." Such a conscience, we recall, concerns itself not merely with whether a work has interested and amused one but with the question of whether one was right in responding so.

Clearly, "moral strenuousness" is one of the natural concomitants of the humanist focus on the social world as the work of humanity. Such a focus seems invariably to lead to the moral imperative to work for its improvement. For the humanist critic this imperative has an aesthetic component as well. This element in classical humanism led Bate to describe it as a tradition valuing that in art which promotes "moral harmony and completeness."

At a conference on the state of criticism, William Phillips included in his remarks a precis of the humanist philosophy of art. According to this view, says Phillips, art is seen to be "like history . . . an element of the movement toward a more just and rational society."

> In short, art is conceived to be a transcendent form of truth, morality, justice, progress – an instrument, as it were, of

social and intellectual liberation. . . . It assumes that there is a given knowledge of political and human truths against which art can be tested and which the highest art reflects. It also assumes that art is therapeutic and cathartic, and thus basically, moral – and wholesome – in its nature.[48]

Actually, this juncture of the philosophical and the aesthetic is just where the issue becomes complicated. The aesthetic of both Arnold and Wilson is one of complete seriousness in its regard for the importance of art and the respect it is due. Yet, when the situation arises that finds their artistic judgments in conflict with their humanist philosophy, the strain invariably shows; the high standards of artistic merit they consistently uphold sometimes give way before these pressing humanist concerns. Arnold, for example, in the course of his essay on Byron, discusses the comparative merits of Wordsworth and Leopardi this way: "Leopardi is at many points the poetic superior of Wordsworth. . . . Where, then, is Wordsworth's superiority? . . . It is in Wordsworth's sound and profound sense 'Of joy in widest commonality spread.'"[49] Thus, an underlying pessimism in an artist's work becomes for the humanist critic an aesthetic flaw.

In like manner, Wilson, in his essay on Proust in *Axel's Castle*, says of Proust's novel – for the artistry of which he has expressed profound admiration – that it is "one of the gloomiest books ever written." Complaining of "Proust's interminable, relentlessly repetitious and finally almost intolerable disquisitions on [pessimistic] themes," Wilson says that they "end by goading us to the same sort of rebellion that we make against those dialogues of Leopardi in which, in a similar insistent way, Leopardi rings the changes on a similar theme: that man is never happy, that there is no such thing as satisfaction in the present." Says Wilson, "We have finally to accept with dismay the fact that Leopardi is a sick man and that, in spite of the strength of his intellect, in spite of his exact, close, sober classical style, all his thinking is sick."[50]

By the same token, a work that is artistically flawed but that has life-enhancing properties in humanist terms can find aesthetic dispensation in this critical tradition. We have already seen Arnold forgive Wordsworth some artistic lapses. In the case of Byron, he is ready to forgive moral ones as well. "True," says Arnold, "as a man, Byron could not manage himself, could not guide his ways aright, but was all astray. . . . True, also, as a poet, he has no fine and exact sense for word and structure and rhythm. . . . Yet," he concludes, "a personality of Byron's force counts for so much in life."[51] The implication is clear that Arnold is ready to overlook imperfections in both the man and his art because of what I take to be Arnold's sense of the superior virtue of Byron's "full-bloodedness." Wilson, too, finds that he can excuse Byron much, and on similar grounds. Maintaining that he "cannot accept the opinion . . . that Byron was a 'blackguard' and a 'cad,' " Wilson suggests that "Byron's gift was for living rather than for literature."[52]

In a later article on Byron, Wilson goes on to say that: "Byron, in literature, presents a peculiar case: he was not a great literary artist, and it is only by familiarizing ourselves with his life as well as with his work that we come to appreciate his merits and understand why it was possible for Arnold to speak, as he did, in one breath, of "Goethe's sage mind and Byron's force."

The reason, says Wilson, is to be found in Byron's *engagement* with active life as well as with literature. Wilson praises Byron's "knowledge of Europe and the world, the consciousness of the stage upon which he was playing" and concludes that Byron possesses "generous ideas and impulses which counterbalance his faults and errors." Wilson goes on to compare this capacity of Byron's unfavorably to "the limitations of the typical literary man who agreeably diverts the hours of a safe and regular life by turning out novels or poems."[53]

If we are to understand the aesthetic at work here, it will be necessary to go back to a phrase of Arnold's to the effect that art is a "criticism of life" and look more closely at what he means by it.

Lionel Trilling, in his Introduction to the *Portable Matthew Arnold*, notes that the phrase, "like so many of [Arnold's] phrases" has been frequently misunderstood. But, Trilling goes on to say,

> what Arnold meant is that literature – although it does indeed, in one of its activities, say specifically what is wrong with life – characteristically discharges its critical function

by possessing in a high degree the qualities that we may properly look for in life but which we are likely to find there in all too small an amount – such qualities as coherence, energy, and brightness.

Literature for Arnold, Trilling continues, "in its possession of these qualities . . . stands as the mute measure of what life may be and is not."[54]

Arnold himself says, "It is important, therefore, to hold fast to this; that poetry is at bottom a criticism of life; that the greatness of a poet lies in his powerful and beautiful application of ideas to life, – to the question: How to live."[55]

In "The Study of Poetry," Arnold links the importance he ascribes to poetry to the general disintegration of meaning in the modern world: "There is not a creed which is not shaken, not an accredited dogma which is not shown to be questionable, not a received tradition which does not threaten to dissolve." And he predicts that "More and more mankind will discover that we have to turn to poetry to interpret life for us, to console us, to sustain us."[56] He sees it, in other words, as a humanist enterprise.

Along with such great claims, it is obvious, go great responsibilities. Already in "Preface to *Poems*, Edition of 1853," Arnold had conceived them so, as is evident in his explanation of the exclusion from that edition of his poem "Empedocles on Etna." Quoting Schiller to the effect that "All art is dedicated to Joy" and concluding with him that "The right art is that alone, which creates the highest enjoyment," Arnold goes on to ask:

What then are the situations, from the representation of which, though accurate, no poetical enjoyment can be derived? They are those in which the suffering finds no vent in action; in which a continuous state of mental distress is prolonged, unrelieved by incident, hope, or resistance; in which there is everything to be endured, nothing to be done . . .

Such situations when the occur in life, says Arnold "are painful, not tragic; the representation of them in poetry is painful also." He concludes with the identification of his own poem of Empedocles as such a work: "and I have therefore excluded the Poem from the present collection.[57]

The romantic element that entered Arnold's thought by way of Schiller's concept of Joy is echoed in Wilson as well when he links the control the poet exerts upon the raw materials of life to a sense of mastery over life's confusions. "With each such victory . . ." says Wilson, "we experience a deep satisfaction: we have been cured of some ache of disorder, relieved of some oppressive burden of uncomprehended events." He concludes with the observation that the relief accorded the reader "brings the sense of power, and, with the sense of power, joy."[58]

Thus the humanist aesthetic sees art as not cathartic only but, as Phillips suggests, therapeutic as well. The moral and philosophical basis of this position is clarified by Arnold in his essay on Wordsworth: "If what distinguished the greatest poets is their powerful and profound application of ideas to life, which surely no good critic will deny, then to prefix to the term ideas here the term moral makes hardly any difference, because human life is in so preponderating a degree moral."[59]

What Arnold has in mind here is straight out of classical humanism. In his view, "A large sense of course is to be given to the term *moral*. Whatever bears upon the question, 'how to live,' comes under it."[60]

When we turn to Arnold's expansion upon his definition of the term *moral*, in "The Function of Criticism," we are brought into direct contemplation once again of the humanist insistence upon linking literature and life: "A poetry of revolt against moral ideas" says Arnold, "is a poetry of revolt against *life*; a poetry of indifference towards moral ideas is a poetry of indifference towards *life*."[61]

Wilson, like Arnold, opts for a broad interpretation of *moral*, and he, too, is capable of the insistence that art, in order to be of the highest value, must be of value on a humanist scale as well. On the former point we recall the reproof Wilson wrote to the Marxist critics who would have art come equipped with Marxist morals. After noting art's capacities of transforming power, he reminds them that "our views and feelings may be altered as effectively . . . by a sonnet about love as by a philosophical dialogue or a modern play of social criticism"[62]

On the latter point – that in order to be first-rate a work of art must measure up on a humanist scale as well – there is

Wilson's caveat about symbolist works voiced at the end of *Axel's Castle*: "The question begins to press us again as to whether it is possible to make a practical success of human society, and whether, if we continue to fail, a few masterpieces, however profound or noble, will be able to make life worth living even for the few people in a position to enjoy them."[63]

What the humanist critic means by the term *moral*, then, is that which is life-affirming, useful to the overarching purpose to which, in this view, the artist and every social animal must subscribe – the task of building the good society.

Surely, it is this stricture that helps us to understand the motivation behind Arnold's rejection of one of his own strongest poems, his preference for a weaker over a stronger poet, and his promotion only of that art that gives a salutary interpretation of life, the better "to console us," the better "to sustain us."

But here I must pause for a moment to consider the degree to which Arnold's position has been under attack for several decades. Indeed, the article quoted earlier citing William Phillips's characterization of the humanist view of literature as containing within it transcendent or therapeutic value does so in the context of its being a thoroughly discredited view.

As Giles Gunn puts it, "The preponderance of critical schools and emphases in . . . modern Western criticism generally, from the New Critics and the neo-Aristotelians to the newest rhetoricians and post-structuralists have been curiously deaf to the moral claims of art and strangely insensible to the moral imperatives of criticism."[64]

We need look no further than the bleak pages of post-World War I history, cataloguing one disastrous failure after another that might be laid at the feet of humanism – in the sense that the "sage Goethe's" Germany gave us mustard gas, trench warfare, the *Blitzkrieg*, and the Holocaust – to find probable cause for such discrediting. It may equally well have been the toll of the cumulative hypocrisies of decades of self-proclaimed humanists, such as Walter Lippmann, exposed in biography as having been prevented not one whit by their embrace of humanism as a personal philosophy from having led scandalous private lives.

It is easy enough to grant the probable causes for skepticism, then; but I find it more difficult to account for the frequently concomitant contempt with which patently moral critics such as Arnold and Wilson are dismissed as philosophical and theoretical naifs because of their view that literature is vitally, even crucially, related to life. This contempt is usually accompanied by a tacit certainty that neither Arnold nor Wilson has ever contemplated the problem that both "literature" and "life" may be mere linguistic constructs devoid of referential meaning.

Gunn elucidates the matter by pointing out that

> in much contemporary art and thought we find ourselves confronted with a skepticism not only about the values of human expression, but also about the epistemological privileges assumed by the individual self. . . . the human self is no longer seen as earning the right to moral respect through its resistance to the interventions of culture; instead it is conceived as but the last in a long line of metaphysical self-deceptions, or "fictions," as they are called, by which human beings in the West have attempted to evade what Wallace Stevens, in his poem "The Snow Man," calls the "Nothing that is not there and the nothing that is."[65]

But such a view ignores the fact that Arnold is, in "Dover Beach," the poet of a world view every bit as unblinking as Wallace Stevens's. Indeed, the view that the "fictions" we construct of language is all that we have in the way of meaning is very like the one Wilson held. He expressed it early in his career,when he wrote in his notebooks of the 1920s of "The artists working with all their might to make life look interesting and attractive; the philosophers and historians to give it some sort of meaning," and it was a view to which he subscribed throughout his life.[66]

In fact, the concept of artists and humanist writers in other fields, working away with all their might to provide us with sustaining "fictions" from the edge of the abyss may be, finally, the key to Wilson's concept of "intellectual heroism." Two further clues from his writings reinforce this conjecture.

At the end of his later essay, "The Historical Interpretation of Literature," for example, Wilson makes a serious attempt to state his criteria of excellence in art and his idea of its function: "In my view, all our intellectual activity, in whatever field it takes place, is an attempt to give meaning to our experience."[67]

Gunn makes a still bolder claim for its importance. He says "This kind of knowledge is extremely hard to come by in an age so heavily ideological, logocentric, and monologistic as our own, but it may well prove indispensable not only to the study of human culture but also to the survival of the human species."[68]

I am inclined to let Wilson have the last word on the matter. The following is again from his own critical manifesto, "The Historical Interpretation of Literature": "The aim and function of the artist is" no less than "to make people see things in a new way, and, therefore, precisely to modify their consciousness, to make them give things new values."[69]

What values can one possibly speak about from the edge of this discredited, valueless void? Almost as if he were choosing an Arnoldian touchstone, Wilson chooses Proust's passage on the death of Bergotte. He calls it "perhaps the noblest passage in the book (i.e., the six volume, 4000 page *Remembrance of Things Past*), because it "affirms the reality of those obligations, culminating in the obligation of the writer to do his work as it ought to be done," incorporating such otherworldly values as " 'goodness, scrupulousness, sacrifice,' " and finally taking on the force of laws – "those laws to which we are brought by every profound exercise of the intelligence, and which are invisible only – and are they really? – to fools."[70]

CHAPTER FOUR

The Humanist Tradition in America

The continuity of humanist criticism extending from Matthew Arnold to Edmund Wilson that I have been implying here is not an undisputed matter of record. The influence on Wilson of Taine and Sainte-Beuve has been noted by Wilson commentators before – though I have gone farther in presenting the evidence than those making the earlier assertions. Matthew Arnold is one model for Wilson's critical approach, however, to whom I have paid much greater attention than has been customary. Warner Berthoff, as we shall discover in Chapter 11, challenges Wilson's claim even to be considered a humanist. Yet, one scholar (before Gunn) who draws a direct parallel between Arnold and Wilson does so not on the basis of their literary criticism but of their shared humanist tradition. Commenting upon Arnold's essay, "Pagan and Medieval Religious Sentiment," William Robbins has this to say: "In all its operations this principle of redress and restraint, of balance and flexibility, is in a tradition of humanistic writing which, as I suggested with reference to biblical criticism, looks back to Erasmus and forward to Edmund Wilson."[1]

With the exception of Frank Kermode and Alfred Kazin, other studies of Wilson have noted a connection to Arnold, if at all, only in the most cursory way.[2] And there is not much in Wilson's work itself to go on, beyond the mild reference, in "A

Modest Self-Tribute," to the effect that he had first read Arnold's essays in about 1922 and that, through him, he had undoubtedly been influenced by Sainte-Beuve.[3] Yet a comparison of the two critics yields striking parallels.

Beginning – as they were both likely to begin themselves – with a biographical fact, we note that both Arnold and Wilson were sons of distinguished fathers. Both came out of homes that prized education, and both remained loyal (though often critically loyal) to the idea of its importance. Both conceived an early love for the classics, for Greek classics especially, and for Homer in particular. Both read widely in other languages – Arnold more in German, Wilson more in Russian – and both openly acknowledged their debt to the French in providing them their critical models.

As for Arnold's famous touchstone method of criticizing poetry, while Wilson does not specifically subscribe to it in theory, his practice is often very similar. The manner in which he uses Dante, Flaubert, Pushkin and Joyce as standards of excellence against which to compare other writers is reminiscent of Arnold's practice in "The Study of Poetry." Indeed, in the case of Dante, the standard is the same.

Even in so superficial a way as in the "image" projected by Wilson and Arnold there is an interesting point of comparison. Although Lionel Trilling paints a picture of a dashing, even flamboyant Arnold in youth and Leon Edel tells us that Wilson was given to setting himself apart from *his* flamboyant generation by cultivating a certain air of austerity in matching socks and ties, in later life the two figures present far less contrast.[4] Arnold's positions as inspector of schools and lecturer in the Oxford Chair of Poetry, together with his own mature demeanor, leant him an air of authority; Wilson, although of necessity earning his living by writing, which meant that he was identified more with journalism than with scholarship, was always able to wear a mantle of awesome dignity. Each was destined in his own time to be thought of as a representative "man of letters."

Both Arnold and Wilson wrote poetry, though here the superiority of Arnold's poetic gift asserts itself as a sharp distinction between them. It is an important point of resemblance, nevertheless, that each knew what it was to make the imaginative, as distinct from the analytic, creative effort.

Each regarded the culture of his own country as being in a state of unhealthy isolation from the literature and thought of continental Europe, and each was interested in doing what he could to amend that situation.

Both Arnold and Wilson regarded the Christian Church (and organized religion in general, in the West) as having permanently lost its usefulness as a cohesive force in society, and both were dedicated to the proposition that the only adequate alternative was to be found in literature. Here is another difference in that Arnold, as the contemporary of Tennyson and Browning and a serious poet himself, naturally thought of that alternative in terms of poetry. But Wilson, as his essay "Is Verse a Dying Technique?" indicates, believed that in the twentieth century the amount of power poetry could be reasonably expected to wield was so drastically reduced that the medium itelf would have to be modified to fit the spirit of the age. He suggests, taking Proust and Joyce as his examples, that the symbolist novel might become the poetry of the future.

Returning again to their points of agreement, we find another similarity between Arnold and Wilson arising out of their conception of criticism as taking in a much broader field – ranging over the whole orthodox literary scene of poetry, fiction, and drama, and extending into nonfiction as well – to take much fuller account of history and politics than had been (or, indeed, still is) the usual practice. Both took very seriously the possibility for good or ill to be found in literature as a shaping force, regarding it as a significant vector in determining the form of government under which a nation would live and the degree of moral vigor it would possess.

In view of these similarities, it is surprising that no one has yet noted the numerous ways in which, whether by sympathy or design, Wilson's approach to literature followed Arnold's already established critical model. Indeed, certain of Wilson's works seem to be almost conscious exemplifications of Arnold's concepts. Wilson's studies in other cultures, for instance – *Red, Black, Blond, and Olive; Apologies to the Iroquois*; and *The Dead Sea Scrolls* – are manifestly Arnoldian in their humanist, educational function as studies in comparative values. And *Patriotic Gore*, Wilson's examination of certain little-known documents and literature written during the Civil War, certainly has as one of *its* functions that it is a definer of the zeitgeist. Wilson even undertook, in his compendium of the critical commentaries, formal and informal, of American writers in all periods – called *The Shock of Recognition: The Development of Literature in the United States Recorded by the Men Who Made It* – the kind of useful reference tool Arnold would have called the "journeyman-work" of literature and of which he would have approved heartily.[5]

Turning to the portion of Wilson's work that is the subject of this particular study, his purely *literary* criticism, we have already seen the close association between Wilson and Sainte-Beuve. We have noted, too, Wilson's own testimony that he is more likely to have absorbed Sainte-Beuve's methods from Arnold (whom he rightly judges to have been strongly influenced by them) than from any deep knowledge of Sainte-Beuve acquired on his own.

When we compare the contents of their critical volumes, still another similarity between Arnold and Wilson emerges: each had a marked tendency to choose as subjects of their critical essays little-known figures, foreign, obscure, or both. In Arnold's case, one thinks of Maurice and Eugenie de Guerin, Joubert, and Marcus Aurelius; in Wilson's of Chapman, Cabell, Casanova, and Philoctetes. Wilson, having spent so much of his early career in the introduction and explication of major figures, does not say much of his growing tendencies in this direction, though as the years passed he was subjected to increasingly querulous complaints about it, together with inquiries as to why he did not deal more with the literary mainstream. Rather, with few exceptions, he persisted in locating his literary subjects off the beaten track, explaining mildly that in his opinion the major figures were already receiving plenty of attention.

Arnold is more enlightening on the question of why he concentrates on the out-of-the-way literary subject.[6] He maintains that, in the case of foreign authors, it fills a cultural gap for his countrymen; that it is salutary to abstract from obscure geniuses their life-giving stimulus; that it is educationally sound, because we generally learn the most from what is new; and, finally, that it is a way of not getting bogged down in the controversy that so often surrounds the most prominent literary figures.

Actually, Wilson does give a reason for ranging so far afield for his subjects – and one that, interestingly, again echoes Arnold. He gives it in "A Modest Self-Tribute," where it emerges as a key factor in what he conceives to be his major contribution to criticism:

> I have been working as a practicing critic, to break down the conventional frames, to get away from the academic canons, that always tend to keep literature provincial. . . . I may claim for myself . . . that I have tried to contribute a little to the general cross-fertilization, to make it possible for our literate public to appreciate and understand both our Anglo-American culture and those of the European countries in relation to one another, to arrive at a point of view from which we may deal with systems of art and thought that have previously seemed inaccessible or incompatible with one another.[7]

In spite of the obvious compatibility between Arnold's views on the importance of comparative values and the sentiments Wilson expresses here, a number of factors may have contributed to the general tendency to overlook Arnold as a shaping influence in Wilson's work. For one thing, Wilson himself invariably led people firmly away from England and toward France when discussing his literary influences and, with a surprising meekness and consistency, all of his biographers have followed where he led, to the point of failing to note discrepancies. Thus, we are told repeatedly that Wilson's model in criticism is Sainte-Beuve, when in fact, as we have seen, by Wilson's own account, Arnold is a more likely source of influence in that direction.

Another factor is that Wilson's references to Arnold are few and usually mildly depreciating. This is not surprising if it is borne in mind that Wilson – like Eliot, Pound, the Bloomsbury group, and virtually all of the artists and intellectuals who arrived at their creative maturity after the First World War – was deeply committed to disassociating himself from the received ideas of the Victorian age. Not one was anxious to ally himself with

Arnold, a man who had cut so large a figure in so compromised a past. This, notwithstanding that every one of them had been influenced by him.

However, as I have hoped to show, the links between Wilson and Arnold are numerous and compelling. Finally, I find very suggestive the fact that in that casual reference to the year in which he first read Arnold's essays – "about 1922" – Wilson also tells us that it was the very time that he was "setting up in practice as a critic." Arnold thus became, if not the earliest, certainly the most *immediate*, and – it now seems probable – one of the most significant influences on Wilson's critical career.

The prevailing tendency has been to trace the humanist critical tradition as coming to America from Arnold by way of the New Humanism of Irving Babbitt and Paul Elmer More. However, I intend to demonstrate that the more vital link is to be found in Edmund Wilson himself.

An important distinction exists between the humanist critical positions identified with Wilson in this study and those identified with Irving Babbitt and Paul Elmer More. Walter Jackson Bate has termed the critical movement that the latter two critics led in the 1930s "the so-called 'New Humanist' movement." Bate goes on to describe it further as a movement that was "built upon the classical humanism of Matthew Arnold but applied its criteria with a far more rigid moral interpretation and with a less flexible sense of the conventions, esthetic demands, and formal qualities of art."[8]

Here are excerpts from Alfred Kazin's account of it in *On Native Grounds*:

> It was at this point [the 1930s] . . . that the counter-reformation against modern literature and thought which called itself the New Humanism made itself felt . . . the New Humanists spoke only for a few conservative critics and teachers of literature. . . . They had no share in contemporary imaginative literature, were completely out of sympathy with the modern age, contemptuous of democracy, and distrustful even of the poetic achievements of a fellow traditionalist like T. S. Eliot.

But, Kazin goes on, attempting to account for the brief but intense influence exerted by Babbitt and More:

they had a *sense* of standards . . . and it was the assurance
with which they inveighed against naturalism in literature
and impressionism in criticism . . . that gave them their importance. . . . For the movement was a summons to order of
all who were in revolt against the disorderliness of modern
life, its drift and despair.[9]

That the movement was more elitist and reactionary than
Arnoldian and humanist seems borne out by Kazin's further
description:

The materialism of American life, Babbitt and More felt,
was corrupting every last citadel of cultivation and taste;
and while the gentlemanly traditions of honor, morality,
self-control, the summom bonum of decorum, were being
destroyed from the inside [by the decline of the humanities
and the dominance of science in the universities] they were
being threatened from without by Populism and Socialism
and the new emancipation.[10]

George Santayana, himself a noted humanist, was moved to attack the new humanism in an essay titled, significantly, "The
Genteel Tradition at Bay."[11]

In 1930 Norman Foerster put together a collection of
manifesto-like essays, led off by entries from Babbitt and More,
that set forth the new humanist dogma. This inspired a counter-
collection edited by Hartley Grattan that contained essays not
only by Wilson but also by Allen Tate, Malcolm Cowley, Kenneth Burke, R. P. Blackmur, and Lewis Mumford among others.
Called *A Critique of Humanism* in response to Foerster's title,
*Humanism and America: Essays on the Outlook of Modern
Civilization*, it provides strong evidence that the more genuinely humanistic spirit is to be found among the opposition.

Grattan is only the first of a number of the contributors to
remark on Babbitt's and More's perversion of the term
humanism. He says the very fact that it "has such emotive
power and such a broad meaning makes it peculiarly distasteful
for one whose allegiance to humanism has never wavered to attack a doctrine which is known as the New Humanism." Yet,
Grattan notes, "for something like thirty years now, Professor
Irving Babbitt has been advocating this doctrine which is sec-
tarian in essence and humanistic in name only."

Among other unhumanistic elements in Babbitt's doctrine, Grattan cites these: it concentrates its press for reform on the individual, ignoring such factors as the environment, the economic system, the industrial revolution, and the mechanization of society consequent upon it. He charges further that the new humanism is unhumanistic in its resistance to science, its hospitableness toward religion, its perpetuation of the dualism between mind and body and concludes that it is, finally, a glorification of the very values that are least human – self-restraint and (a Babbitt watchword) the "inner check."[12]

How little justification there is for seeing the new humanism of Babbitt and More as a continuation of the tradition we have been examining is apparent in Bate's description of the movement's moral values: Man, in this view, is naturally weak, but by way of the inner check, "through the mental grasp of universal truths, through the control of his animal nature, through bending his imagination and his emotions to his rational hold on truth, fulfills his own nature, achieves *decorum* – that is, propriety, or a fitting in with universal law – and so becomes 'human.' "[13] This premise, Bate points out, while theoretically classical is decidedly unclassical as applied by new humanist critics. Ultimately, Bate says of Babbitt and More, "such critics looked back to some classical values, but unlike Arnold, they interpreted them with a quite unclassical dogmatism and openly didactic bias."[14]

Wilson, too, maintained that Babbitt and More, far from being inheritors of the classical humanist line, were distorting and even betraying the intentions of their classical models. In his contribution to the Grattan *Symposium*, he makes a blistering attack upon Irving Babbitt for having built his own brand of "Harvard humanism" upon what Wilson regards as a trumped-up Sophoclean principle of self-restraint that Babbitt had extracted from the phrase "law of measure" in *Antigone*. "This," writes Wilson, "seems to me a grotesque misapplication of the speech from Sophocles." And he goes on to argue that

> Where the "law of measure" comes in is certainly not in connection with the conduct of Sophocles' people . . . the "fierce child of a fierce father," Antigone; the relentless and morbid Electra, etc. – but in Sophocles' handling of his mater-

ial – the firmness of his intellectual grasp, the sureness of his sense of form, the range of psychological insight which enables him to put before us the rages, the ambitions, the loyalties, of so many passionate persons.

In the same essay, Wilson is moved to turn Babbitt's emphasis on "measure" and "decorum" against him. Noting that "As a matter of fact . . . Professor Babbitt . . . has managed to exempt his own professional activities from the law of measure, the duty to refrain," Wilson charges that Babbitt and the other new humanists "drop their ideal of decorum the moment they put pen to paper." For, he suggests,

> It is not decorous to look for nothing but mistakes in the writings of your contemporaries; it is not decorous always to call attention to these mistakes with a sneer; it is not decorous to take a word like humanism, which has formerly applied to the great scholars, philosophers, satirists, and poets of the Renaissance, and to insist that it ought to be regarded as the property of a small sect of schoolmasters . . . it is not decorous to assume that you yourselves are the only persons who have taken seriously the vices and woes of your own time and that everybody except yourselves is engaged either perversely or stupidly in trying to make them worse.[15]

Wilson is no more receptive to the ideas of Paul Elmer More, the other leader of the new humanists, on the moderns than we have seen him to be to Babbitt's on the ancients:

> one may agree with Mr. More that the artist should not be irresponsible and that he cannot dispense with humanity and nature – one may even agree that "art for art's sake" has given rise to a good deal of nonsense. . . . But in the course of the nineteenth century, they were goaded into talking this way . . . by the progress of the industrial revolution and the rise of the middle class. . . . They swore, if they had any spirit, that they were going to work at their craft even though nobody wanted their wares, and they thus arrived at the slogan that has irritated so many people. . . . But what student of literature . . . what critic aware of art in its relation to the other forces of society in which it is practiced, will assert that even the poet of the *fin de siècle* could or should have done otherwise?[16]

One comes away from such discussions of the new humanism as those offered by Kazin, Bate, and the Grattan *Critique* convinced that one of the unfortunate consequences of this whole episode is that, although Babbitt and More failed utterly to establish their reactionary reforms, they did succeed in so obscuring the real values of humanism as to substantially weaken subsequent perceptions of them.

It was Wilson, after all, who saw more clearly than Babbitt and More where the important literary movements of the 1920s were heading and exactly the nature of the crisis they posed in terms of the continuity of a literary tradition; Wilson who saw the lines of tension drawn and the questions raised – and still pending – between art and technology, between artistic isolationism and artistic involvement; and he who did his best to assess the issues in the light of comparative values – of "the best that has been thought and said" in many cultures. It was Wilson, and not the apostles of the "inner check," who more accurately transposed the Arnoldian concept of the *Zeitgeist* and the whole tradition of humanism into a modern key when he said of the symbolist writers Yeats, Eliot, Proust, Joyce, Valéry, and others at the conclusion of *Axel's Castle*:

> And though we are aware in them of things that are dying – the whole belle-lettristic tradition of Renaissance culture perhaps . . . they none the less break down the walls of the present and wake us to the hope and exaltation of the untried, unsuspected, possibilities of human thought and art.[17]

In the chapters that follow, I will be presenting further evidence of Wilson's humanism as it is manifested in his criticism.

Note: Giles Gunn's book has appeared just before going to press. It is the firmest link so far noticed in print of the direct line in criticism from Arnold to Wilson. Even though it refers to them both variously as "culture critics" and "critics of moral imagination," Mr. Gunn's book firmly sets them in the humanist tradition and as firmly distinguishes their branch of humanism from that of Babbitt and More, which he finds "the less important." [18]

III.
Wilson's Practice as a Critic: A Closer Look

CHAPTER FIVE

"W. B. Yeats"

*W*ilson's essay, "W. B. Yeats," is Chapter Two of *Axel's Castle*, published in 1931. This first book of formal literary criticism by Wilson is subtitled "A Study in the Imaginative Literature of 1870-1930." After a chapter of historical analysis of the symbolist movement and preceding the general summary of that movement at the end, the bulk of the book is given over to studies of six writers – W. B. Yeats, James Joyce, T. S. Eliot, Gertrude Stein, Marcel Proust, and Paul Valéry – who, in Wilson's view, show the development and, in some ways, represent the culmination of Symbolism, which he terms "a self-conscious and very important literary movement."[1]

The chapter on Yeats is the first on an individual writer. Perhaps because Yeats's view of the world and his rendering of it into art, so seemingly unrelated to his life as a theater administrator and member of parliament, has the effect of making Wilson's usual biographical approach all but impossible; perhaps because Yeats's "masks" and Wilson's reluctance to probe the private situation of the still-living poet combine to frustrate any very telling psychological penetration of Yeats as a subject; this essay shows neither the sure application of Marxist nor the firm grasp of Freudian principles that Wilson was to display later on. Yet, "W. B. Yeats" invites our attention here because it presents a clear instance of the humanist bias of Wilson's aesthetic – valuing most that art which gives us a criticism of life in Arnold's sense – and because its dialectical movement shows Wilson following an Arnoldian pattern in his method as well.

Frank Kermode, one of the few critics to see the close kinship to Matthew Arnold in Wilson's work, applied an Arnoldian
yardstick to Wilson in his reappraisal of *Axel's Castle*, written on
the occasion of a new edition in 1961. He begins with Arnold's
prescription for good criticism: "critics should be undulating and
diverse; their criticism should not hurry, but be 'patient' and
'flexible, and know how to attach itself to things and how to
withdraw from them.' "

Kermode goes on, in an especially cogent paragraph, to apply Arnold's points to Wilson. Noting that Wilson's is "clearly
the credo of a man with a deep theoretical hostility to Symbolism," he asks how Wilson is able to avoid treating the Symbolist
poetry under consideration "as a mere symptom of decadence."
Answering his own rhetorical question, Kermode says: "The
reason is simply that he has a powerful primary, undogmatic
response to poetry; he can attach himself and then withdraw,
and on the withdrawal feels free to disapprove." Most percep-
tively, Kermode notices that "in fact this is the whole method of
Axel's Castle: passionate identification with the work under
discussion; followed by detached appraisal; followed by historical inference which does not neglect the primary response."[2]

Wilson's chapter on Yeats offers an admirable opportunity
to trace the working out of that method. Actually, in this instance, Wilson does not begin precisely in "passionate identification" with Yeats's poetry. Part One begins, rather, with some
biographical data about Yeats, his birth at the latter part of the
nineteenth century and his parentage. (He was the son of an
Irish painter loosely allied with the Pre-Raphaelite school in
England.)

Wilson goes on to connect these beginnings with the Romantic and Pre-Raphaelite qualities to be found in Yeats's early
poetry, specifying Shelley and Keats as early models. He moves
quickly forward to cite Yeats's Symbolist associations, a period
of residence among Mallarmé's circle in Paris and a friendship
with Arthur Symons. Wilson notes, too, however, the distinc-
tively Irish character of Yeats's symbolism. All of this is
presented as but laying out the ground – the merest glance at
the historical, biographical, and literary framework out of which
Yeats emerged.

Such are Wilson's powers of compression that by the time we have reached page two of the essay we are in direct confrontation with Yeats's poem, "On a Picture of a Black Centaur." We are not yet, however, into the stage of "passionate identification." Rather, this is a look at Wilson in his comparative mode, comparing Yeats's poem about the black centaur with one of Mallarmé's about a swan, showing the heavy reliance upon verbal music in each. Significantly, in terms of identifying Wilson's critical bias, Wilson displays a preference for Yeats's poem over the French one because, in Yeats, the images "constitute a world of which one can to some extent get the hang, where one can at least partly find one's way about."[3] We recall here Wilson's – and Arnold's – prejudice in favor of poetry that stands as a criticism of life by its superior powers of coherence, energy, and brightness; poetry that, by helping us to "get the hang" of the world, consoles and sustains us.

Kermode's reference to the hostility between Wilson's credo and that of the Symbolists would be oversimplified if we were to put it in terms of the humanist's belief in art as a humanist enterprise, on the one hand, versus the Symbolist's belief in art for art's sake, on the other. Yet, there is some sense in which the humanist focus on the good of society *is* deeply hostile to the artist's – and, particularly, after Poe, to the modern artist's – insistence on the autonomy of artistic imagination. When we recall Wilson's description of the new program Mallarmé envisioned for poetry: to make an assault on "the confines of poetry, at a limit where other lungs would find the air unbreathable," we see that communicating meaning and consolation to the reader is very far from a Symbolist priority.

In the initial chapter of *Axel's Castle*, Wilson's concern surfaces in his description of the influence Poe had on the early Symbolists. He points out that it was in emulation of Poe that they introduced into their poetry a confusion between the perceptions of the different senses and attempted to make the effects of poetry approximate to those of music. Symbolist poetry, Wilson notes, is also characterized by a confusion "between the imaginary and the real, between our sensations and our fancies on the one hand, and what we actually do and see, on the other."[4]

He goes on to say that

It was the tendency of Symbolism – that second swing of the pendulum away from a mechanistic view of nature and from a social conception of man – to make poetry even more a matter of sensation and of the emotions of the individual. . . . Symbolism, indeed, sometimes had the result of making poetry so much a private concern that it turned out to be incommunicable to the reader.[5]

We find these reservations of Wilson's about the aims and methods of the Symbolist poets in general echoed in the present case. Here, with regard to the deliberate confusion in Yeats's early poems between the imaginary and the real, for example, he says with a real note of alarm that "The world of imagination is shown us in Yeats's early poetry as something infinitely delightful, infinitely seductive, as something to which one becomes addicted, with which one becomes delirious and drunken." Nevertheless, by the time he stops to examine "The Man Who Dreamed of Fairyland," Wilson has so far embraced the poet that he describes it as "one of the most beautiful of Yeats's early poems."[6]

Furthermore, he proceeds patiently – criticism should be patient and flexible – to enter the world of Yeats's fairies, the very supernatural world so antipathetic to his own personality. He perhaps does so the more willingly for having recast it "in its real aspect" as "the life of revery and imagination – and solitude."[7]

Having so far attached itself to the poetry, Wilson's method, as Kermode perceived, is to withdraw and make an historical inference. Apropos of Yeats's creation of the persona of the solitary Michael Robartes, Wilson notes, "It was characteristic of the *fin de siècle* writers to want to stand apart from the common life and live only in the imagination."[9]

He makes the further historical observation that, though Symbolism has its deepest roots in France, the English critic Walter Pater anticipated certain of its attitudes in his essay "The Renaissance," with its credo: "Not the fruit of experience, but experience itself, is the end."[9] Returning to the poet at hand, Wilson points out that "In Yeats, we find the aestheticism of

Pater carried through to its consequences" one of which is to be "thrown fatally out of key with reality." Of this consequence, Wilson maintains, Yeats, "even in this earliest period, is unceasingly aware."[10]

For the balance of Part One, Wilson remains very intensely concentrated – yes, passionately attached – to Yeats's poetry. He describes its progression from the "dim and iridescent poems of Romantic rhetoric typical of his work in 1899" to the greater concreteness of the later poems. And he equates this progression with the evolution in Yeats of a philosophy that stressed the destructive consequences of turning one's back on the responsibilities of the real world to stay in the world of pure imagination.

Wilson's humanist bias is once again evident in the tone of approval with which he notes that Yeats is "No longer content with the ice-eyed queens of fairyland," pausing to note that, although "he no longer hopes from real life any satisfaction other than the triumph of imagination through art, he applies to poetry all the vigor of his intellect and all the energy of his passion."

Henceforward, says Wilson (now in a state of passionate attachment to his subject), Yeats "would reduce his verse to something definite and hard – at the same time more severe and more passionate. Now the soap-bubble colors vanish; the music of fairyland dies away; we behold only, earthly and clear, the bare outlines of "cold Clare rock and Galway rock and thorn."[11] Of the poems in the period after 1912, Wilson notes only that Yeats "finds his subjects now in the events of his own life, no longer transposed into romantic convention, and in the public affairs of Ireland."

Withdrawing once more to make an historical inference (comparative this time), Wilson, in the ensuing evocation of Dante is reminiscent of Arnold in the employment of his touchstone technique. The Yeats of this more mature phase, says Wilson, "can even challenge comparison with Dante . . . by his ability to sustain a grand manner through sheer intensity without rhetorical heightening."[12] Anticipating Yeats's own theory of masks, Wilson refers to this manner as a "Dantesque mask," and he suggests that, when Yeats assumes it, he is like Dante in at least three other ways as well: "in the compactness and point of his two- or three-line allusions; in his epigrammatic bitterness; and in the quality of his moods of exaltation."

Although Wilson associates this quality with Dante, his description of it contains an echo of those classical values we have found to be so essential a part of Wilson's own value system. Yeats's exaltation, says Wilson, is "no longer the opium dream of fairyland, but such as life has to offer within its limits . . . the admiration for ancestor or friend, the pride in honor kept or work well done."[13]

At the beginning of Part Two we find Wilson still at a distance from his subject, this time in order to discuss the difficulty experienced by the modern poet in attaining to "the kind of dignity and distinction which have been characteristic of the poet in the past." The passage provides examples of a number of the characteristics of Wilson as a critic that we noted in Chapter 1. His historical consciousness is evident in the very conception of the subject. The Romantic element appears in his conception of the poet as a culture hero. The Marxist perspective is evident in his recognition that the change he is describing is a reflection of a change in the interaction between economic base and cultural superstructure. He alludes, for example, to the aristocratic patronage characteristic of the Elizabethan era and notes that the position of the poet "is becoming more and more impossible in our modern democratic society."

Finally, Wilson's humanist perspective shows through in his recognition of the interrelatedness – the organic linkage – of literature and life, words and matter, science and the arts. "The ascendancy of scientific ideas," says Wilson of modern times, "has made man conscious of his kinship with the other animals and of his subjection to biological and physical laws rather than of his relation to the gods."[14]

Yet the withdrawal into historical inference is not, in this case, succeeded by a new attachment to the poetry. It is, rather, the prelude to a discussion of Yeats's critical writings and his autobiographical work, *The Trembling of the Veil*. In fact, much of this section of the essay on Yeats is taken from a review he wrote of that book for *The New Republic*.[15] This is in accord with what Kermode calls Wilson's "necessary practice" as a literary journalist. And, as we have seen in our look at his method, it is a

deliberate part of that method to work up his ideas first in periodical form.

Yet, if we have come to the essay with the expectation that
the poems themselves would be its focus, the whole of Part Two
seems something of a digression. This is to forget, however, the
tradition Wilson is working in, the tradition that accepts the
proposition, as Sainte-Beuve put it, that "literature, the production of an author, is not distinct or at any rate not separable from
the rest of the man and his makeup."[16]

Wilson's stated rationale for looking at Yeats's criticism and
his autobiographical writings is that, in his view, they present "a
remarkably honest and illuminating account of the difficulties of
remaining a poet during the age in which we live." Here Wilson's
gift of sympathetic imagination asserts itself, prompting him,
Neoptolemus-like, to put himself in the poet's place, to feel his
problem: "the modern poet who would . . . deal with life in any
large way, must create for himself a special personality, must
maintain a state of mind, which shall shut out or remain indifferent to many aspects of the contemporary world."

Wilson goes on to suggest that "This accounts partly, I suppose, for Yeats's preoccupation in his prose writings with what
he calls the Mask or Anti-Self, a sort of imaginary personality,
quite antagonistic to other elements of one's nature, which the
poet must impose upon himself."[17] Such perceptions, says
Wilson, led Yeats to take up "from the beginning, in his
criticism, a definite and explicit position in regard to
Naturalism." This position Wilson characterizes as a decision to
"stand apart from the democratic, the scientific, modern world"
and to resolve that "his poetic life shall be independent of it; his
art shall owe nothing to its methods."

We know from our investigation of Wilson's personal
philosophy how alien such a rejection would be to him. He is,
nevertheless, able both to recognize that Yeats's "principles in
literature are those of the Symbolists" and also to recognize that
"he formulates them more clearly and defends them with more
vigor than anyone else has yet done in English."[18]

Wilson follows his assertions regarding Yeats's prose with a
long quotation to illustrate them from an early essay Yeats
wrote on Shelley. Again, we remember Wilson's alliance with

the French tradition that says that what the critic has to do is "to discover, display in an orderly fashion, and illustrate as best he can, what his author has done." This tradition, moreover, advocates listening to writers "long and carefully," letting them "disclose themselves in a free way, without hurrying them,"[19] a tradition that, we know, Wilson absorbed from Sainte-Beuve by way of Arnold.

Returning to Part Two and looking at it from this perspective, we see that, if we substitute the life of the poet (i.e., "the rest of the man and his make-up") for his poetry, the structure that identifies the method of *Axel's Castle* as a whole continues to hold true through this second part as well. Thus, the historical inference with which the section begins is followed by a "passionate attachment" to Yeats's life and thoughts as reflected in the autobiography and in his essay on Shelley. This is followed, in turn, by another withdrawal as, apropos of Yeats's activities in the Abbey Theatre, Wilson takes an historical look at the Symbolist drama.

He traces the ways in which the struggle between naturalism and Symbolism, which he has been following in post-Romantic poetry, is paralleled by a similar struggle in European plays of the period. We are asked to notice, among other things, the dialectic at work: the way in which, for example, the Naturalism of Ibsen is countered by the Symbolism of Strindberg. Yeats's own dramas, Wilson says, returning briefly to his subject, are not so much Symbolist in the vein of Strindberg, however, as Symbolist in the vein of Maeterlinck. "These plays," notes Wilson, "take place in the same sort of twilit world as Maeterlinck's – a world in which the characters are less often dramatic personalities than disembodied broodings and longings."

Having come so close to the work once more, in the case of these Yeatsian dramas, Wilson feels free to stand back and, not surprising in light of his description of their content, to disapprove. He says that "Yeats's plays have little dramatic importance because Yeats himself has little sense of drama, and we think of them primarily as a department of his poetry, with the same sort of interest and beauty as the rest."

Then, turning from the work back to the life of his writer, Wilson notes that, his weakness as a dramatist notwithstanding, "Yeats the director and propagandist of the Abbey Theatre does have considerable importance in the history of the modern stage."[20] He then proceeds to give us an historical overview of Yeats's part in that history, including his championing of O'Casey and Synge.

This leap from one genre to another seems scarcely less odd to the reader trained in the new critical school than did the earlier obtrusion of biographical data. Yet it is, in fact, only another manifestation of the broader, more inclusive humanist definition of "literature"; what comes under its rubric, what belongs in the discussion.

True to form, Part Two ends with Wilson once more passionately attached to Yeats's work – once again, his prose work – interweaving his appreciation of its style with comparisons drawn from music, from Butler, Walton, and Dryden, and contrasting it with that of Yeats's contemporaries: Kipling, Eliot, and Shaw. Wilson concludes that, "whereas with Kipling, Eliot or Shaw, the style seems to aim at the effect of an inflexible impersonal instrument specially designed to perform special functions," Yeats's prose is "still a garment worn in the old-fashioned personal manner with a combination of elegance and ease."[21]

Part Three calls upon all of Wilson's gifts of sympathetic imagination, patience, and flexibility as well as his skills of compression and synopsis, for he goes on in his examination of Yeats's prose writings to take account of Yeats's mystical book, *A Vision*.

One sees the necessity for his doing so, in view of the close relation this strange, theosophical work of Yeats bears to his poetry at that time. It may not be too much to say that it is not possible to read and understand the poems in this period of Yeats's work without knowledge of the book. But the strain it imposes on Wilson's sympathies is clear. Wilson comes at the subject, characteristically, from a biographical angle, telling us of Yeats's interest in the famous spiritualist, Madame Blavatsky, and he goes on – again characteristically – to draw an historical comparison, in this case, with Huysmans.

Here, it is as if Wilson is grasping at every evidence of rationality in Yeats with which he can identify. He notes that, "Just as in Huysmans's case, we always feel that the wistful student of Satanism has too much solid Dutch common sense really to deceive himself about his devils, so in Yeats . . . the Romantic amateur of Magic is always accompanied and restrained by the rationalistic modern man."[22]

Wilson goes on, patiently and flexibly, to describe the complicated theory of personality types that Yeats called the Great Wheel and that forms the principal part of *A Vision*. Setting forth the works' "unfamiliar conceptions" (as Wilson calls Yeats's paraphernalia of "*daimons, tinctures, cones, gyres, husks,* and *passionate bodies*") in a shortened, simplified, but otherwise straightforward manner must surely have represented an act of forebearance on Wilson's part, arch-enemy of "daimons" that he was.

But, having embraced the mystical *Vision*, and even having found that "Yeats has worked all this out with great care and with considerable ingenuity," Wilson feels free to withdraw and, having withdrawn, to disapprove once more. He concedes that *A Vision*, when we try to read it, makes us impatient with Yeats. And, he goes on, "one would think that to elaborate a mystical system so complicated and so tedious, it would be necessary to believe in it pretty strongly. Yet now and then . . . we are startled by an unexpected suggestion that, after all, the whole thing may be merely 'a background for my thought, a painted scene.' " Downright testily, Wilson asks, "If the whole thing . . . has been merely an invented mythology, in which Yeats himself does not believe, what right has he to bore us with it. . . ." In spite of his own negative response to Yeats's flirtation with mysticism, Wilson cannot dispense with his strong positive response to the side of Yeats that impresses him as that of a man whose "sense of reality today is inferior to that of no man alive."

In the passages that follow, Wilson makes a supreme effort to understand the coexistence in Yeats of "the world we know" and the world of his "fantastic imaginings."[23] He is even somewhat mollified by the revelation, in "A Packet for Ezra Pound," of the biographical circumstances that attended *A Vision*. We learn that the book came about through the mediation of Yeats's wife who, four days after their marriage began to receive messages in the form of automatic writing. Their express intent was, as the messages themselves declared to Yeats, "to give you metaphors for poetry."[24]

In another passage Wilson touches so delicately, so lightly on another aspect of the psychological background of Yeats's mysticism we are almost given the false impression that he means to attribute it to a distinctly un-Freudian instinct – a "fear of philosophy." But, upon closer examination, it develops that Wilson wishes to suggest a "fear of the Father" as the unconscious culprit, for he quotes Yeats as saying something of the kind: "Apart from two or three of the principal Platonic Dialogues I knew no philosophy. Arguments with my father . . . had destroyed my confidence and driven me from speculation to the direct experience of the Mystics."[25]

Wilson here reveals the reticence he feels about being plainer in any psychoanalytic comments over a living subject: "Into the personal situation suggested by Yeats's account of his revelations," he says, "it is inappropriate and unnecessary to go: the psychological situation seems plain."[26] In fact, it is far from plain, Wilson's delicacy having prevented us from having any very clear idea what he might be hinting at. What follows does seem to imply, however, that in his view *A Vision* is the manifestation of a deep need on Yeats's part to dwell "with part of his mind – or with his mind for part of the time – in a world of pure imagination."

This need, he suggests, had been thwarted when Yeats withdrew from fairyland as being unhealthily seductive and deliberately set about re-creating his style so as to make it "solid, homely and exact."[27] Out of this repressed need, Wilson implies, came the mystic system of the Great Wheel.

This part of the essay concludes with another instance of Wilson withdrawing to his comparative method, this time comparing and contrasting the work and the life of Yeats with that of his so-different countryman, George Bernard Shaw:

> Here we can see unmistakably the differences between the kind of literature which was fashionable before the War and the kind which has been fashionable since. Shaw and Yeats, both coming as young men to London from eighteenth-century Dublin, followed diametrically opposed courses, Shaw shouldered the whole unwieldy load of contemporary sociology, politics, economics, biology, medicine, and journalism, while Yeats, convinced that the world of science and politics was somehow fatal to the poet's vision, as resolutely turned away.[28]

Of their respective literary testaments, Yeats's *A Vision* and Shaw's "Guide to Socialism and Capitalism," works published almost at the same time, Wilson has this to say: [they] mark the extreme points of their divergence: Shaw bases all human hope and happiness on an equal distribution of income . . . while Yeats . . . has in 'A Vision' made the life of humanity contingent on the movements of the stars."[29]

Leaving this case of starkly contrasting world views without further comment, and thus allowing it to fall rather flat, Wilson goes on to the fourth and final part of the essay. This consists of a short but unusually intense and passionate identification with Yeats's work in the period of his long poetic sequence, "The Tower," begun when Yeats was sixty-three.

Referring to this period as "a sort of third phase," Wilson goes on to characterize it as one "in which he is closer to the common world than at any previous period. In 'The Tower' (1928) he writes more loosely . . . he has become more plainspoken, more humorous. . . . He is much occupied with politics and society, with general reflections on human life – but with the experience of a lifetime, he is passionate even in age."

Recalling Wilson's own humanist bias, we are not surprised to hear approval in his voice as he notes these aspects of Yeats's later work. Nor is it surprising that Wilson, echoing Arnold, should view it as a supreme compliment to Yeats to say that "he writes poems which charge now with the emotion of a great lyric poet that profound and subtle criticism of life of which I have spoken in connection with his prose."[30]

Wilson closes the essay with a commentary on one of the most famous poems from "The Tower" sequence, "Among School Children." The passage reminds us of what Kermode calls Wilson's gift of powerful primary response to poetry as well as of his method of combining this with a more detached appraisal "which does not neglect the primary response."

> A complex subject has been treated in the most concentrated form, and yet without confusion. Perceptions, fancies, feelings and thoughts have all their place in the poet's record. It [i.e., the stanza of the poem that ends with the lines "O body swayed to music, O brightening glance, / How can we know the dancer from the dance?"] is a moment of

human life, masterfully seized and made permanent, in all its nobility and lameness, its mystery and actuality, its direct personal contact and abstraction.[31]

Looking back at the journey we have just made in Wilson's company through Yeats's career we can see that, although it affords some brilliant aperçus about Yeats and some astute and impressive comments on his poetry, the essay as a whole cannot stand as one of Wilson's stronger efforts.

It may be significant, therefore, to note that this essay on Yeats is not only the earliest of Wilson's chapters on individual writers to appear in *Axel's Castle*, it is among the earliest to have been composed. It grows out of a series of articles Wilson wrote for *The New Republic*, the first of which appeared in 1925, and the last of which, a review of *A Vision*, ran in 1929. After the appearance of the latter, Wilson wrote the following in response to a reader's letter: "You were very kind to write me. I was very much surprised and pleased by your having liked my articles to that extant. . . . I have found him [i.e., Yeats] a very difficult subject to treat critically. [32] To some degree that difficulty is still evident in the essay itself.

It is not until the very end of *Axel's Castle* that Wilson is able to resolve the grand dialectic movement of the book as a whole, bringing the opposed goods of humanist concern for society and art for art's sake into a synthesis. That synthesis takes the form of Wilson's finding a place for the "abstractions" of Symbolist poetic language in his view of the artist as a creator of meaning and order. Wilson tells us in the final chapter, that, in his suggestive, associational use of language, the Symbolist poet is really performing the same sort of function as the realistic novelist or the technical scientist (that is, setting the chaotic world into some framework of meaning and order):

The only difference between the language of Symbolism and the literary languages to which we are more accustomed is that the former indicates relations which, recently perceived for the first time, cut through or underlie those in terms of which we have been in the habit of thinking; and that it deals with them in terms of what amounts, in comparison with conventional language, to a literary shorthand which *makes complex ideas more manageable*.[33] (my italics)

When we remember that, to Wilson, the function not only of art but of "all our intellectual activity, in whatever field it takes place, is an attempt to give meaning to our experience – that is, to make life more practicable . . . easier to survive and get around" in, then finding in Symbolism a new area of life made articulate *is* an accomplishment of the same order as the discovery of a new scientific formula or the fixing of a new insight in a realistic novel. And with this aesthetic in mind we are in a position to assess more clearly the profundity of Wilson's appreciation for "Among School Children':

> A complex subject has been treated in the most concentrated form, and yet without confusion.

For according to that aesthetic, "With each such victory of the human intellect, we experience a deep satisfaction: we have been cured of some ache of disorder, relieved of some oppressive burden of uncomprehended events."[34]

CHAPTER SIX

"Proust"

*W*ilson's essay on Proust, like nearly everything else he wrote, is full of interest. As a part of *Axel's Castle*, of which it forms the fifth chapter, its structure follows the same pattern of attachment and withdrawal just traced in "W. B. Yeats." Our exploration of Wilson's practice as a critic will proceed further, however, by studying it from another point of view, for this essay on Proust shows Wilson in what Leon Edel calls his most archetypal critical role, "the critic as helpmate, as explicator, as friend, not only of the common reader, but of the artist himself."[1]

Such sympathetic criticism entails, in the case of Proust, befriending an artist misunderstood or shunned by the reading public, assisting readers to see and to sympathize where before they had only been willing to shut their eyes and judge. The model for such a critic has been described by Wilson himself, in symbolic terms, in the figure of Neoptolemus, the son of Achilles who befriends Philoctetes.

Like Philoctetes, whose festering wound surrounded him with an unpleasant stench, certain facets of Proust's work had rendered him offensive to society; and, like Neoptolemus, Wilson was able to reconcile his audience to his friend's unpleasant qualities by emphasizing the pathos of his situation and describing in glowing terms the contribution he was uniquely empowered to make.

It may be difficult to connect the figure of the beleaguered artist just described with the now much belaurelled and beloved Proust, but we must remember that Wilson was writing this essay at the end of the 1920s.

The whole of *A la Recherche du Temps Perdu* had only just been made available in France and, although it met with increasing critical approbation there (after an initial recoil), finally winning the Prix Goncourt, in this country it was scarcely read. Wilson therefore was endeavoring to bring to the attention of the English reading public a European writer of major importance – one who, if he was known at all, was considered distinctly "foreign."

Wilson begins by identifying Proust with the Symbolist movement, which is, of course, the overall subject of *Axel's Castle*. He notes that verbal mannerisms, which in the Symbolist poets had taken the form of "shifting images" and "multiplied associations," are to be found in Proust's novel as similarly handled characters, situations, places, vivid moments, obsessive emotions, and recurrent patterns of behavior.[2]

Having established the link with Symbolism, Wilson launches directly into a synopsis of the novel. This in itself represents a formidable task; the book, after all, ran to 4000 manuscript pages. Wilson manages to accomplish it in 30 pages of print, a feat that earned him some of the few words of praise Stanley Edgar Human was ever to bestow upon him. Hyman says that *"Axel's Castle* . . . probably had an effect in our time, in opening up a whole new area of literature to a wide audience, second only to that of T. S. Eliot's *The Sacred Wood"* and that it is "memorable" for, among other things, "the amazing thirty pages that summarize Proust's giant novel almost scene by scene."[3]

Wilson's method of synopsis is far from being simply a resume of the plot, however. Beginning at the beginning, Wilson quotes the very first sentence, pausing – as he will pause throughout – to note special effects, such as the novel's symphonic movement, and to single out its recurrent themes. Here, he notices the theme of Time itself and, second, the theme of Combray, the world of the narrator's childhood, where the narrator, Marcel, impatiently awaits the departure of the family neighbor, M. Swann, so that his mother may come up to kiss him goodnight.

Acknowledging that Proust's novel, especially in the beginning, seems to a great many people to be a formless mass, Wilson notes that it is anything but that. On the contrary, "in these first pages of his book, [Proust] has succeeded in introducing nearly every important character. And not merely every strand of his plot, but also every philosophic theme."[4]

After giving a bit of background information (i.e., Proust's original titles for the different sections of his book), Wilson goes on to describe the content of the next volume. But his reference to the earlier titles is an example of the kind of thing that makes Wilson seem so knowledgeable about every subject he undertakes, and it is, in fact, impressive testimony to the degree of preparation he brought to his every undertaking.

Volume Two is *A l'Ombre Des Jeunes Filles En Fleur*, or in the English translation, *Within a Budding Grove*. Wilson characterizes it as "one long adolescent revery." It keeps the reader submerged, Wilson suggests "–and for most tastes, . . . submerged far too long" in those adolescent reveries. But he cautions that the reader who allows himself to bog down here will come away with a completely erroneous idea of what Proust is really like. For, as he puts it, "we are now to be violently thrown forward into the life of the world outside."[5] Wilson goes on to show how, in the next two volumes, Proust takes a much more external view, powerfully dramatizing, as he does so, the life of Parisian high society at the close of the nineteenth century.

Wilson notes Proust's structural technique of proceeding in blocks of social episodes (sometimes several hundred pages long), interspersed with introspective commentary. He notes, too, that each of the long social episodes marks a steady progression of the narrator, Marcel, up the social ladder. Thus, we are shown first the salon of the aspiring but lowly Verdurins, then the high-born but despised Mme. de Sainte-Euverte. Next, we meet the rather dubiously situated but glittering Mme. de Villeparisis and–on the highest rungs of all–first the Duchesse de Guermantes and then the Prince and Princess de Guermantes themselves.

As Wilson proceeds with his synopses of the two predominantly social volumes—*Le Cote de Guermantes* (*The Guermantes Way*) and *Sodome et Gomorrhe* (*The Cities of the Plain*)—he emphasizes the moral attitude being set forth in them by the author. This, he shows us, is done through the device of Marcel's grandmother, contrast with whom he points out "serves entirely to discredit the values of the snobs." Wilson links this underlying moral attitude to Proust's Jewish background – Proust was half Jewish on his mother's side – and calls it "really very un-French." For, says Wilson: "it is plain that a certain Jewish family piety, intensity of idealism and implacable moral severity, which never left Proust's habits of self-indulgence and his worldly mentality at peace, were among the fundamental elements of his nature."[6] This sensitivity to the author's cultural background is traceable back to the Marxist influence on Wilson and also, still earlier, to that of Taine.

Having established the novel's moral attitude and noted the way it is sustained throughout the novel by recurrent reference to the influence exercised in Marcel's childhood by his grandmother in Combray, Wilson then goes on to note the variety of other ways in which Proust gives his immense work unity and significant form. He notes, for example, that all of the characters fall into one of two sets: either they are connected to the Guermantes or they are linked to the figures of the hero's childhood in Combray (though oddly, he fails to make it as clear as he might that these sets correspond to the two paths the family used to take after dinner in Combray, the one nearer path being known as "Swann's Way" and the other, the longer way around, as "the Guermantes Way").

Wilson does, however, point out that the characters, without losing their individuality, are made to take on universal significance: "all illustrate general principles and . . . have been carefully selected by Proust to cover the whole of the world that he knows." Thus, Odette (Swann's mistress and later his wife) is "all that is stupid in woman which, at the same time, arouses men's passions and enchants their dreams," Charlus (the Baron de Charlus, a Guermantes) represents "the struggle in one soul between the masculine and feminine," Mme. de Guermantes is "the best that a snob can hope to be without becoming a serious person, etc., etc."[7]

The continuous development of each of these characters into the fullness of their universal as well as individual significance is what Wilson identifies as the unifying principle underneath the apparent discontinuity. Further, he notes that "Proust's method of presenting them . . . so as to show only one aspect at a time is one of his great technical discoveries."

At this point Wilson pauses in his outline of the plot to follow one illustrative character, Mme. de Villeparisis, through the entire course of the novel. Although too long for inclusion here, it stands as a superb example of the key facet of Wilson's skill at synopsis – his power to compress without distortion.

When Wilson takes up the plot once more, the scene shifts away from the world of the salon into the world of lovers and the passions – in *La Prisonniere* (*The Captive*) and *Albertine Disparue* (*The Sweet Cheat Gone*). This world as Proust presents it can only be described, says Wilson, as "an inferno." Marcel's love for Albertine is predicated upon "one of those fatal emotional see-saws" – desire in the beloved's absence, indifference in her presence – that Wilson likens to the affair between Julien Sorel and Mathilde de la Mole in Stendhal.[8] The narrator's jealousy over what he suspects are Albertine's lesbian tendencies and his virtual imprisonment of her drive the girl to the point where, unable to bear her confinement any longer, she makes an early morning break for freedom and returns to her aunt's home in the country.

Wilson points out that the Albertine episode is meant as only the chiefest of many exemplifications of one of Proust's central ideas, "the tragic subjectivity of love."[9] This concept is to be found in the episode of Swann and Odette, in that of the hero and his adolescent fancy, Gilberte, and in instance after instance of inversion. As Wilson points out this last form occurs with increasing prevalence. The most extensive exploration of it revolves around the figure of the sensitive, yet sadistic, Baron de Charlus. Proust's pursuit of the theme of the elusiveness of human satisfaction extends finally to a still more pervasive theme that Wilson describes as permeating the whole book: "the conviction that it is impossible to know, impossible to master, the external world."[10]

Moving on to the final volume of the novel, *Le Temps*

Retrouvé (*The Past Recaptured*), Wilson points out how Proust
has "varied the color, tone and pace of his narrative to correspond to the various periods of the hero's life," from the brightness of childhood to the ghastly light of the grown-old guests at
the last party we attend, in the sumptuous rooms of the Prince
and Princess de Guermantes.[11]

Picking up the thread of his summary once more, Wilson
notes, however, that before entering the party Proust's hero experiences certain sharp memory impressions that place the past
of his childhood vividly before him, and determine him to turn
away from his idle pursuits to take up at last the work he has all
along felt himself destined to attempt. "He will make of his life a
book," says Wilson, and he will base it upon "those enduring
extra-temporal symbols – incidents and personalities as well as
landscapes – which have been precipitated out by the interaction of one's continually changing consciousness with the continual change of the world."

The "plot" of this last volume is, in fact, "simply the genesis
of the book we have just read," says Wilson. He notes that in the
long last sentence the word "Time" again begins to sound, "and
the book closes the symphony as it began it."[12]

Section I ends here, with the outline of the novel's plot having been brought full circle. The synopsis, miracle of condensation though it is, constitutes more than half the bulk of the essay
as a whole. Section II takes up all but a few pages of the remainder. It is devoted to the man, as Section I was devoted to
the work, and the final three pages consist of Wilson's summation of his views on both.

Section II begins, then, with an abrupt pulling away from
the sympathetic immersion in the text to which we have hither-
to been exposed. Wilson suddenly reminds us that the view of
life in which we have been steeped in Proust's long novel may actually be a false one. Is it really true, Wilson inquires, "that one's
relations with other people can never provide a lasting satisfaction?" that "literature and art are the only forms of creative activity which can enable us to meet and master reality?"[13]

Wilson points out that "Proust's lovers are always
suffering" and "his artists are unhappy, too: they have only the
consolations of art." While Wilson does not precisely term the

atmosphere in Proust's novel *sick*, he calls it "one of the gloomiest books ever written." Here, he makes an analogy with Leopardi, a nineteenth-century Italian poet, also well born and also physically handicapped, who was noted for his deep pessimism. Of him, Wilson says, one is forced to conclude that, in spite of his skill he "is a sick man and that . . . all his thinking is sick." And Wilson goes on to remark that as it is with Leopardi, "so with Proust we are forced to recognize that his ideas and imagination are more seriously affected by his physical and psychological ailments than we had at first been willing to suppose."[14]

On the face of it,. this seems a very strange turn of events. Have we, then, come all this way through thirty-some pages of symphonic movements and technical discoveries only to be told that the work to which we have been asked to give such loving attention "falsifies life?"[15] It would certainly seem so. But it soon becomes evident that Wilson himself far from accepts this view. Rather, he has stated it, just as he has voiced certain other reservations, as part of his adherence to the Arnoldian principles of flexibility and disinterestedness in criticism. In this essay his method of attachment and withdrawal assumes the proportions of a rhetorical strategem of persuasion.

Anticipating opposition to certain features of the novel, he sides with the disgruntled reader (*le moyen sensuel*) granting freely the justice of his sense of the novel's sticking places the better to prepare the ground for the reader's sympathetic reception when he comes to present the case for Proust. Wilson has used this strategem on more than one occasion, even in Part I where he is, ostensibly, simply giving the plot. It is worth pausing to look at these occasions and at the way Wilson handles them.

First, we recall that very early in the essay Wilson concedes that "for most tastes" Proust keeps the reader "submerged far too long" in the narrator's childhood, but he urges us to press on, warning us that the price of stopping is to get Proust all wrong, whereas the reward of going on is not only to avoid this distortion but to be presented with a dramatic picture full of humanity and color of *fin de siècle* Parisian society.[16]

On the other side of the two "social" volumes, in the course of discussing *The Captive* (*La Prisonniere*), Wilson stops the action and steps forward once again in his Neoptolemus role; that is, that of the friendly mediator between the reader, whose case he understands and sympathizes with, and the troublesome artist, whose position is also given its due. "This episode with Albertine, upon which Proust put so much labor and which he intended for the climax of his book, has not been one of the most popular sections, and it is certainly one of the most trying to read," concedes Wilson, noting that "it does not supply us with any of the things which we ordinarily expect from love affairs in novels."[17] He then turns to its defense – a defense made up of exactly these objectionable components turned inside out: "But, this is also its peculiar strength . . . it is one of the most original studies of love in fiction and . . . we recognize in it an inescapable truth."

If we should still resist and continue to feel that Proust's truth is too special, too exotic for universal application, Wilson renders it recognizable to all: "The tragedy of Albertine is the tragedy of the little we know and the little we are able to care about those persons whom we know best and for whom we care most."[18]

Undertaking in this way to voice the sentiments of the *le moyen sensuel* and respond to them is not in the least condescension on Wilson's part. He *does* find the long sentences and the extensive repetitions tiresome (just as he was to do with the Valley of the Winds chapter and The Oxen of the Sun chapters in *Ulysses*). But, in line with his humanist training, he uses the discipline of dispassionate reasoning to stand away from his subjective reactions and offers us in their stead the insights to which his trained intelligence – and his own perspicuity – have made him privy.

Wilson uses very much the same technique in reconciling us to the interpolated commentary that persists even throughout the most exteriorized volumes and ends in the ultimate takeover of the introspective voice. In other words, Wilson once again begins by anticipating our objection, then goes on to endorse its validity. The richness and liveliness of Proust's social scenes notwithstanding, says Wilson "in the intermediate sections . . . we feel he has blurred his effects by allowing the outline of the action to become blurred by the hero's reflections on it."[19]

The next step is the reversal overturning the verdict at which he – and we – have jointly arrived. In this case, Wilson argues that the apparently obtrusive running commentary by the novel's narrator has been economical after all. He points out that it has served not one but two purposes for Proust: "It has been made to serve as a device for covering up the calculated ingenuities of his drama and for rendering its sudden peripeties and its moments of passionate eloquence more effective because more unexpected."[20] We may recall this latter point as identical with the argument Wilson uses in the next section for getting us to appreciate the oddities of the love story.

This line of argument (turning it inside out) has always exercised a good deal of appeal for Wilson, and it is easy to see why – it is essentially revelatory in character. Indeed, Wilson thinks well enough of it to use it still another time at the very close of his synopsis. He points out that the brief concluding portion of À la Recherche – the part called Le Temps Retrouvé (The Past Recaptured) – makes no appeal to any of the emotions in which novelists usually deal. Yet, he says of these final pages, "they have a strange dramatic power, and they move us – as Proust is always able to do – just when there seems nothing more to be said."[21]

But, to return to the question of the novel's truth or falsehood: is it possible, Wilson asks, that we have been moved by the pathological intensities of illness rather than truth or art? As we are by now prepared to discover, however, this is in fact another instance of Wilson raising an issue on behalf of the general reader, only to go on and settle it in the artist's favor.

He uses the same strategem very effectively in To the Finland Station when dealing with the historical founders of the communist revolution, Marx and Lenin – he treats his much-bogeyfied subjects biographically, and thus humanizes them. So here we find Wilson turning to Proust's letters and to the memoirs of Proust's friends to tell the story of his illness, never blinking at the unpleasantness but keeping always foremost in our minds that "the elements of an artist's work are the elements of his personality."[22]

One of Wilson's characteristic sources of biographical intelligence – a source used with discretion in Wilson's hands, though it is of course often abused – consists of the early writings of the artist in question. In this case, it consists of the biographical clues to be gleaned from the early short stories of

Proust that were published under the title *Les Plaisirs et les Jours*. Wilson finds in these early stories the seeds of recurrent Proustian themes.

One of the most important themes Wilson identifies as repressed aggression felt toward a parent, which expresses itself in the form of sexual inversion. Another is the presence of an overwhelming sense of guilt such as Marcel expresses over his grandmother in *À La Recherche*, leading him to feel not only that he has disappointed and failed her (by failing to begin his "great work") but that he has actually defiled her.

Just as the biographical aspect of this section is designed to set Proust before us as a flawed but suffering human being, the critical comment Wilson interjects is designed to render justice to a flawed but great work of art.

From these sources we learn of two incidents that wounded Proust, or at least so deeply affected him that Wilson believes them to have had a significant effect on his work. The first involves some fun poked at him by friends who included in their smart Parisian review an irreverent reference to his first published book. Wilson reports that "when Proust saw this scene at a rehearsal, he went away mortally wounded and would not come to any of the performances."[23] The second parallels the incident in *À la Recherche* in which the aging Marcel rather inappropriately and even grossly makes intense conversation with the adolescent daughter of his childhood sweetheart, Gilberte.

As it happens, both of these incidents strike an unpleasant note that Wilson is careful to offset by quoting Proust's friend, Lucien Daudet to the effect that although "There were in Marcel Proust all the elements of a spoiled child," he never actually became one, because of "his genius, his personal dignity and also his sense of humor."[24]

As a further corrective to any unsavoriness, Wilson places the Daudet quote after a scene at Proust's deathbed calculated to arouse our sympathies fully in the artist's behalf. Having "softened us up," so to speak, Wilson undertakes in Section II to answer the question "What is wrong with Proust?" He goes about it by asserting (with biographical and literary illustration of the kind mentioned earlier) that Proust's dependence on his mother, and his consequent Oedipal guilt, led to a concomitant inability to adjust to any nonfilial relation.

All of these biographical indications seem to support Wilson's view that Proust actually clung to his maladjustments – that he seems to have preferred his invalid's cell (and his mother's ministrations) to "the give and take of human intercourse."[25] Wilson further suggests that only his mother's death and Proust's consequent need "to rejoin that world of humanity from which he had allowed himself to become exiled" drove him to undertake his book at last.

In a characteristic linking of life and literature Wilson then goes on from the biographical passages to show us the effect of these neurotic elements on Proust's work. He says that Proust's writing, begun "late in life and with no experience of writing to be read" is susceptible to such self-indulgences as the "unassimilably long sentences and the tiresome repetitious analyses . . . which sometimes make him so exasperating to read." He feels, too, that "Superb as are the qualities of objective dramatic imagination which have gone into it," the novel as a whole "was never quite disengaged from his sickroom."[26]

This is the "wound and the bow" theory to be sure, but in practice it is never reducible to any simple "neurosis generates art" formula. As Wilson shows us here, Proust's neurotic psychological makeup had both positive and negative effects on his work. It may be, as Wilson says, that we owe the novel to it. But, he goes on to argue, "those aspects of his novel which seem ambiguous or distorted are due to Proust's own uncertainty as to whether he is exemplifying universal principals of human conduct or producing by images sometimes monstrous the elements of a personality which he knew to be morbid and special."[27]

In spite of Wilson's evident aversion to these "morbid and special" elements, his sympathetic tolerance is also evident in such passages as this in the beginning of Section III:

> In spite of all the less reassuring or less agreeable aspects of Proust . . . his self-coddling, his chronic complaining, his perversity, his overcultivated sensibility – we get the impression from them, as we do in his novel, of an intellect and imagination vigorous, comprehensive and deep. . . . And in spite of all his parade of weakness, in spite of all his masks and indirections, we remember him as a personality of singular magnanimity, integrity and strength.[28]

It is an integral part of Wilson's humanistic approach that the links between the life and the art should be shown to be intimately intermingled. Over and over again he shows us that the unappealing personal traits of the artist figure we are investigating are offset by instances of courageous self-transcendence. In the last afternoon of his life, for example, Proust is shown to us (having refused all sustenance "except a little iced beer which he had brought in, in a pail, from the Ritz"), insisting upon using the last reserves of his strength to put the finishing touches on a paragraph about the death of Bergotte.[29]

Wilson thought so much of the moral convictions expressed in that paragraph that he used it often, rather like an Arnoldian touchstone. He calls it "perhaps the noblest passage of the book" because it "affirms the reality of those obligations, culminating in the obligation of the writer to do his work as it ought to be done, which seem to be derived from some other world."[30]

Wilson closes his essay on Proust on an elegaic note, elegaic not only in reference to Proust but also to the entire world of which he was a part. It may be, Wilson suggests, "that Proust's strange poetry and brilliance are the last fires of a setting sun – the last flare of the aesthetic idealism of the educated classes of the nineteenth century."[31]

Having found in Wilson's own humanist credo so much that might well be called "aesthetic idealism" one would have to say that, while he is around to write about it at any rate, Wilson's death knell is premature.

Having focused so heavily in this analysis on Wilson's attention to the common reader's reactions to Proust, I conclude with a second glance at Wilson's own reaction to him. This, we recall, was given eloquent voice in his later essay, "The Literary Class War":

> [A] really first-rate book by an agonizing bourgeois may have more human value, more revolutionary power, than second-rate Marxists who attack it. A really great spirit does not lie though its letter killeth. Personally I can testify that the writer who has made me feel most overwhelmingly that bourgeois society was ripe for burial was none of our American Marxist journalists but Proust.[32]

CHAPTER SEVEN

"The Ambiguity of Henry James"

*I*n "The Ambiguity of Henry James," which forms the sixth entry in Wilson's second book of formal criticism, *The Triple Thinkers*, we see Wilson sharpening some of the critical tools that were to emerge so prominently in his subsequent book, *The Wound and the Bow*.[1]

As is the case in his studies of Kipling and Dickens in that work, Wilson is here engaged in the twofold task of·bringing a modern sociological and psychological focus to bear on a figure from the past, and also in the attempt to accomplish a major upgrading of that figure's literary reputation (the James *risorgimento* was just getting underway).

But the key ingredient in this essay – or, at any rate, the one that will be the focus of my interest here – is the flexibility of Wilson's position on the subject of *The Turn of the Screw*. Taking his cue from Christian Gauss, Wilson displays in this essay a remarkable fluidity of thought. We see him adopting a neutral prose style that permits him the widest possible latitude for speculation and follow him as he considers "out loud" first one, then another, solution to the problem of James's intentions regarding the story's "ghosts." We see him entertain one idea through a process of testing, correcting, reversal, and reiteration.

It is, therefore, as an example of disinterested critical inquiry that I mean to study it here. The essay as a whole affords, too, an excellent opportunity to display Wilson in the employment of not only his Freudian critical approach but also of his more broadly humanistic one. Before we can get anything like a clear view of Wilson's essay, "as a whole," however, it will be necessary to recognize and to deal with the fact that the portion of it pertaining to *The Turn of the Screw* has been under heavy fire in the critical journals for some years. Clearing away the smoke from that critical barrage must be our first order of business.

The continuous stream of entries dealing with *The Turn of the Screw* in the *MLA* bibliographies up to the present is ample evidence that each new critical generation finds irresistible the lure and provocation of James's *"jeu d'esprit."* Far and away the most interesting of these modern entries is Shoshana Felman's "Turning the Screw of Interpretation," which not only discusses Wilson's essay extensively but identifies it as the article that, after its appearance, would "henceforth focalize and concretely organize all subsequent critical discussion, all passions and all arguments related to *The Turn of the Screw*"[2]

These arguments (which, as Felman points out, tend always to revolve around the same points, "for or against Wilson, affirming or denying the objectivity or the reality of the ghosts"), she succinctly organizes into "two camps: the 'psychoanalytical' camp, which sees the governess as a clinical neurotic deceived by her own fantasies and destructive of her charges; and the 'metaphysical,' religious or moral camp, which sees the governess as a sane, noble saviour engaged in a heroic moral struggle for the salvation of a world threatened by supernatural Evil."[3]

It is tempting to contemplate engaging in a full-length discussion here of Felman's piquant thesis, which, as I understand it, is the suggestion that the critical reception accorded James's story is itself a recreation of the very text it ostensibly interprets. (It does so, says Felman, by virtue of its diametrically opposed locations of and responses to the locus of its universally recognized "danger.")

To do so, however, would take us beyond the scope of the present study. Fortunately, Wilson himself makes an admirable representative of the first "camp" in the critical battle over James's story. Taken together with two important essays by

Dorothea Krook (a representative from the anti-Freudian side), these will form a very comprehensive picture of the *Screw* "case" and of Wilson's place in it, a place that must be regarded as central, whatever the metaphor in which one casts it.

The Krook articles – "Edmund Wilson and Others on 'The Turn of the Screw'" and "Intentions and Intentions: The Problem of Intention and Henry James's 'The Turn of the Screw'" – take into account all of the theories covered in Gerald Willen's *Casebook on The Turn of the Screw.*[4] What is more, both of the Krook articles single out for special attention the Wilson essay we are looking at here.

So far, the situation seems ideal. As a further auspicious sign, Wayne Booth – a sane critic if ever there was one – takes time out, in the course of his book, *Critical Understanding*, to cite Krook's articles, to commend the account she gives in them of the opposing viewpoints, and to praise hers as "one of the sanest discussions of James's intentions in *The Turn.*"[5] When one looks at the articles themselves, however, dismay quickly sets in, and one can only come away from repeated readings with the distinct impression that, in James studies – in *Turn of the Screw* papers, at any rate – sanity is a highly relative attribute.

In the course of the two essays in which Krook sets out her views on *The Turn of the Screw*, she calls Wilson "irresponsible," personally and professionally, both directly and indirectly a number of times. She characterizes him, personally, as "false," "superficial," and "perverse." His James essay is characterized by her as "sinful," "execrable," "wrong-headed," "reductionist," "harmful," and "fatuous." She complains that his essay has already received too much attention, and she openly campaigns for beating it "to death" and burying it. In her catalogue of its most "glaring flaws," one finds her using such shrill phrases as "really inexcusable" and "completely disregards."[6]

At one point, quoting Rahv's objections to Wilson, she says Wilson "thereby stands condemned, by the pleasantest irony, of a thoroughly unscientific treatment of the story."[7] In another place, on her own authority, she says that Wilson's view shows such "insensibility to the literary evidences before him" that it "may well be taken as a disqualification for the task of interpreting such a work."[8]

The extraordinary thing is that Krook concedes the importance of much of what Wilson says – and was, virtually the first to say – about *The Turn of the Screw*. She acknowledges, for example, that his account:

> does draw attention to elements of the story that are of vital importance for its understanding
> Mr. Wilson's thesis depends, it will be remembered, on two principal points of interpretation: first, that the story is really "about" the governess, the first-person narrator of the story, not – as the common reader has always supposed – about the children and their relations with the dead servants; and second, that the governess is a classical case of neurotic sex-repression who, having fallen in love with the children's charming uncle at her first and only meeting with him in London, sublimates her frustrated passion for the uncle by the elaborate device of the apparitions and their supposed relations with the children.[9]

What is more, she notes in Wilson's behalf that:

> There are at least three vital elements in the story that previous critics had either completely missed, or at least not seen with the clarity and vividness with which Mr. Wilson evidently saw them; and they had certainly not given them the importance that Mr. Wilson rightly does. I refer, first, to the ambiguity; second, to our persistent impression that the governess is, in some sense, guilty, in particular of little Miles's death at the end; and, third, to the significance of the governess's being the first-person narrator of the whole story.[10]

One may well be puzzled, in the light of these acknowledgments, as to how to account for the harshness of Krook's ultimate judgment upon Wilson. This puzzlement only deepens when we look at her remarks on Harold C. Goddard's essay, "A Pre-Freudian Reading of 'The Turn of the Screw'." It turns out that, in its chief points (i.e., regarding the hallucinatory nature of the ghosts, the governess's guilt, and the presence throughout of Jamesian ambiguity) Goddard's essay, according to Krook, gives "the strongest support to Wilson's," is "very close to, if not identical with, Mr. Wilson's," and that it "more than ever proves the validity of Mr. Wilson's perception." Yet, whereas we remember the words she used to characterize Wilson's effort, of which the kindest, perhaps, was "irresponsible," her terms for Goddard's are "cogent," "conclusive," and "brilliant." She deems it "in many ways a model of the kind of criticism of Henry James's works that is most valuable."[11]

Except for the fact that Goddard is a professor, the difference between his critical approach, as described by Krook, and Wilson's would not appear to be profound enough to justify the very different attitudes she displays toward the two. One explanation might be that she simply vehemently prefers academic criticism over the nonacademic kind Wilson practices. When we look at her concluding remarks on Goddard, however, a more psychological basis for her quarrel with Wilson suggests itself. She says that Goddard's explanation "is in the end as one-sided as Mr. Wilson's; it is only less unjust because he at least is free of Mr. Wilson's violent, almost personal, antipathy to the thwarted Anglo-Saxon spinster."[12]

She refers, of course, to the governess-narrator of *The Turn of the Screw*. The awkward thing is that she produces no evidence of this "violent antipathy." Wilson does use the phrase "thwarted Anglo-Saxon spinster" in describing–quite accurately–James's governess, but in a much less strident way than Krook here suggests.[13] It is part of the blunt style he adopted whenever he discussed sexual matters, presumably in an effort to correct the circumlocutions that were prevalent when his style was formed.

At the close of her first article Krook again suggests that Wilson is unbalanced on the subject of the governess. She takes the occasion there to "summarize the several morals for literary criticism to be drawn from Mr. Wilson's errors":

A preliminary moral, admittedly Rymeresque, is that an excessive preoccupation with sexual neurosis in general and an excessive (perhaps neurotic?) antipathy to Anglo-Saxon spinsters in particular may subvert a man's powers of judgment in disastrous ways. *Could* Mr. Wilson (one asks) have ignored, or mentally explained away the testimony to the governess's sanity, intelligence and moral probity set out in the prologue if he had not come to the text with certain preconceived notions (and certain strong feelings) about the psychological makeup of the Anglo-Saxon spinster?[14]

One might ask in turn: is the only basis, then, for Krook's quarrel with Wilson her distaste for his use of the phrase "thwarted Anglo-Saxon spinster?" Is it a phrase that causes her so much pain that she wishes to disqualify him from criticism, kill and bury his work? The answer is that, although this may be partly true, it is not only that; for, in addition Krook has, it develops, a fundamentally different reading of the story. A look at the two critics' opposing views may help us to clarify why Krook devotes so much energy to an attempt at destroying Wilson's credibility.

In Krook's reading of *The Turn of the Screw* the Freudian factors are secondary. The "dominant image" is "that of a typically Jamesian savior-figure" "whose principal savior's task it will be to 'keep' the children from the apparitions so that they may not be 'lost'."[15] In her view, a Faustian spiritual pride, taking the form of a greed to "know everything," forms the principal taint on the governess's moral perfection.

She postulates the source of this as stemming in James's mind from "something . . . he himself had written just recently about the Galahad figure in the 'Grail Catalogue' he had helped to prepare for the Guildhall exhibition of his friend E. A. Abbey's Holy Grail frescoes: this to the effect that Sir Galahad's saving mission is defeated 'at the very goal' by a 'single taint of imperfection' in his otherwise saintly nature."[16]

Krook says this savior-governess is fused in the story with the secondary images suggesting a sexually repressed governess. While the governess, in her view, *is* guilty of little Miles's death, it is not from a primarily Freudian cause but from a primarily Faustian cause. This is evidently the distinction Krook has in mind when she says: "Concerning the governess's guilt, I have argued that Mr. Wilson was right – only for quite the wrong reasons."[17]

After all the attention Krook has given to supplanting Wilson's view of the governess with this more benign interpretation of her own, it comes as something of a shock to discover that, in her opinion, the children, not the governess, are the center of the tale. Dismissing the postscript Wilson added to his essay in 1948 as "a good deal too little" in the way of self-correction, Krook goes on:

For what Mr. Wilson still does not admit is that the children, not the governess, are the centre of the story, and that this makes nonsense of his "governess" theory as such even before the validity of the repressed sex hypothesis is considered; and so far from recanting his misguided Freudianism, he reaffirms and further elaborates it . . . drawing upon what he believes to be certain relevant facts of James's personal history and arriving at conclusions which are no longer even perverse but merely fatuous.[18]

Wilson's 1948 postscript will be examined in more detail later on. At this point it will be useful to look at Wilson's actual writing on *The Turn of the Screw* in order to get a clearer picture than Krook has given us of his interpretation of it.

We may begin by noting that, in Wilson's view, the ambiguity of James's tale consists in its offering either of two readings, each very different and each supportable by direct reference to the text throughout. The first is a simple ghost story in which the governess becomes aware of evil spirits who haunt and corrupt the children in her charge. She battles them bravely but is finally defeated, to the point where one child falls ill and is removed from the household and the other is, in fact, "spirited away" – done to death – by one of the ghosts.

The second reading (which Wilson calls "the obverse side of the narrative") is that the governess hallucinates the ghosts. The children are not total innocents in Wilson's view – as Krook several times represents him to believe. Indeed, they are susceptible to the manipulations of the governess *because* they have sexual fears and anxieties that can be played upon. They are put, finally, in psychic danger – and, in the case of Miles, in mortal physical danger – not by outside evils from which the governess tries to protect them, but by evils that, though real enough, are conjured up to haunt and pursue them out of the fevered repressions of the governess's neurotic mind.

It should be noted that, although Wilson clearly finds the "obverse version" the more compelling, he never suggests that the two versions do not continue to exist equally intact at the same time. It is the effect of ambiguity resulting from their coexistence that, for Wilson, clearly provides much of the interest and value of this story, which he calls one of James's masterpieces.[19] Yet Krook, though she several times credits Wilson with recognizing ambiguity as a pervasive characteristic of the James story, suggests—also several times—that he sees only one side of it, and that his is therefore a "boring," "reductionist," and altogether unworthy interpretation, a "sin" of which the wages ought to be death."[20]

As to the vexed question of James's intentions, Krook decides that James both did and did not know whether what he was writing was a ghost story or a serious work of fiction. That is, he knew what he was doing when he started out, but then his intention changed, says Krook. To prove it, she reconstructs the course James's mind would have had to travel in order to come out with her savior-governess in secondary fusion with her pre-Freudian tainted governess.

This journey takes her far afield from the text into guild hall catalogues and medical journals. From this excursion she returns to say: "If this, or something like this, is the creative process by which the governess figure comes into being, it is obvious, I think, how the simplified theories of intention fail to do justice to its complexity.[21] But, ultimately, says Krook in a rather surprising twist at the very end of her second article, intention is the province not of the originator of a work but of the critic. An artist, she concludes, "is only obliged to enact his intention, not to articulate it or even to recognize it."[22]

Wilson does not address the question of authorial intention in anything like as formal a fashion. He merely notes in the 1934 portion of his essay James's propensity to mislead us initially about certain of his sinister characters. This comment, however, shows that, at this point, he believes the ambiguity in *The Turn of the Screw* to be the result of a conscious artistic decision on James's part. And he says, apropos of *The Sacred Fount*: "[We] decide, as we do with *The Turn of the Screw*, that there are two separate stories to be kept distinct: a romance which the narrator is spinning and a reality which we are supposed to divine."[23]

Before going further in this discussion however, a word about another essay, Edna Kenton's, seems in order. For, as true as it is to say that the controversy over interpreting *The Turn of the Screw* gained its initial momentum after the publication (in *Hound and Horn* in 1934) of Wilson's "The Ambiguity of Henry James," we ought not to forget that what prompted *his* interest in the *double entendre* aspect of the story was an article written by Edna Kenton ten years earlier.

Indeed, Wilson's initial concern, in his essay on James, is to credit Kenton with having been the first to write on the idea, regarding *The Turn of the Screw*, that it "perhaps conceals another horror behind the ostensible one." After synopsizing the way the story might, in this second light, be read, Wilson wonders how, having once got hold of this clue to the story's double meaning, it could ever have been missed. He then goes on to say:

> There is a very good reason, however, in the fact that nowhere does James unequivocally give the thing away: almost everything from beginning to end can be read in either of two senses. In the preface to the collected edition, however, as Miss Kenton has pointed out, James does seem to want to give us a hint.[24]

Here is Kenton on the subject:

> It is as if . . . he determined to write, in *The Turn of the Screw*, a story for "the world." He would write it of course primarily for himself and for that reader for whom he must always write – the reader not content to have the author do all of the work – but he would make this particular work a supreme test, of attention and of inattention alike. He would have his own private "fun" in its writing, his own guarded intention, his own famous centre of interest. But he would put about this centre, not only traps set and baited for the least lapse of attention, but lures – delights and terrors mingled – calculated to distract or break off short any amount of alert intentness.[25]

In 1948, the publication of James's notebooks proved to include a note about the *Screw* containing several references to it as a "ghost story." This prompted Wilson to write a chagrined postscript to his James essay. It is quite evident that he did not, first, return to reread the 1924 article by Edna Kenton that had inspired his original position. Had he done so he would have found that James's statements in the notebooks are superseded by those in his preface, which speak of the *Screw* as a *'jeu d'esprit*" and "a trap." As it is, Wilson does his best to acknowledge the "new" evidence, saying in the postscript that the notebooks seem "to make it quite plain that James's conscious intention, in *The Turn of the Screw*, was to write a bona fide ghost story."

But Wilson cannot, even so, ignore the subtext of James; that "obverse narrative" that as he – and Edna Kenton – had discovered, hung together so beautifully. As a consequence, he is forced into an uncharacteristically weak position. He says "One is led to conclude that, in *The Turn of the Screw*, not merely is the governess self-deceived, but that James is self-deceived about her." This, of course, gives Krook and Wilson's other detractors a field day. The only puzzle is why they should have been so happy to see him fall into error and so oblivious to the fact that – albeit eleven years later, in 1959 – he pulled himself out of it.

The occasion was another new James publication – this time of the portion of the New York Edition that contained *The Turn of the Screw*. His discovery that James's own placement of the story for this edition was among his *psychological* tales rather than among stories of the supernatural gives Wilson the final piece of evidence he needs to confirm him in his original view.

The postscript reads: "1959. Since writing the above, I have become convinced that James knew exactly what he was doing and that he intended the governess to be suffering from delusions.[26] And here is the "hint" James himself gives us in his Preface to *The Turn of the Screw*: "It is a piece of ingenuity, pure and simple, of cold artistic calculation, an amusette to catch those not easily caught (the "fun" of the capture of the merely witless being ever but small), the jaded the disillusioned, the fastidious."[27] When we remember the acuity of Kenton's gloss on this passage we can appreciate why Wilson says of her that her "insight into James is profound."[28]

Krook, on the other hand, would seem to be one of the fastidious, one of those not easily caught, but caught nevertheless in the "cold artistic calculation" of James's "amusette."

Turning at last from this one James work as it has been treated by Wilson and others, I wish, briefly, to take note of what Wilson set out to accomplish in his essay as a whole. For it is worthwhile reminding ourselves that, for all the emphasis given to his interpretation of *The Turn of the Screw* by others, Wilson himself set out in "The Ambiguity of Henry James" to give an overview of James's entire life and work.

Taken as a whole, then we may say that Wilson's essay accomplishes two distinguishable things. First, it isolates the principal themes of James's work, themes which were to occupy scholars for many years. It does this by emphasizing the way virtually all of James's fiction takes as its underlying subject the definition of American culture in terms that differentiate its manners and morals from those of Europe. Wilson's essay also notes the way James, setting his work now in Europe, now in America, emerges as a defender of American culture as well as its critic.

Second, in "The Ambiguity of Henry James," Wilson constructs a plausible Freudian basis for James's "wound." It is responsibly founded upon the few biographical and autobiographical documents then available and, in its placement of James's deep discomfiture in the area of sibling rivalry with his brother, William, it is substantially corroborated by Leon Edel's definitive biography.[29]

Those aspects of the essay that concentrate on James as the definer, defender, and critic of American culture reflect Wilson's historical consciousness as well as his Marxist awareness of the interaction between economic base and cultural superstructure.

On James as the defender of American culture, Wilson points to the evidence in his work of his progressive evolution into this role:

> In those earlier novels of James, it had not been always – as in *The Portrait of a Lady* – the Americans who were left with the moral advantage; the Europeans – as in the story with that title – had been sometimes made the more sympathetic. But in these later ones [i.e., *The Ambassadors*, *The Wings of the Dove*, and *The Golden Bowl*] it is always the Americans who command admiration and respect.[30]

He notes a progressive deepening in James's role as critic of American culture as well. According to Wilson, a fresh look at the changes that had come over American life in the period following the Civil War led James to take a more complex view of American values. For example, of James's *The American Scene* (written after a visit to the United States in 1904-1905, his first in a quarter of a century), Wilson says that it provides a "criticism of the national life" that "shows an incisiveness, a comprehensiveness, a success in knowing his way about, a grasp of political and economic factors, that one might not have expected of Henry James returning to Big Business America."[31]

This is merely another instance of Wilson's preoccupation with the connection between literature and life. The experience of James's visit, says Wilson, "stimulates him to something quite new: a kind of nightmare of the American *nouveaux riches*."[32] So Wilson characterizes James's late story, "The Jolly Corner," and his unfinished novel, *The Ivory Tower*.

But the relations of James's art to economic and historical events are not the only factors of interest to Wilson, as we know. In his humanistic view of the organic connections between life and art he is also interested in the psychological factor, in what Sainte-Beuve has called "the secret line of pain" to be discerned in a writer's work. Along the same lines, we remember Frederick Crews's comment to the effect that:

> the literary work which is completely free from its biographical determinants is not to be found, and in many of the greatest works . . . unresolved emotion and latent contradiction are irreducibly involved in the aesthetic effect. To appreciate why there are gaps in the surface we must be prepared to inspect what lies beneath.[33]

It is precisely his sense of the presence of such "gaps" in the artistic surface in certain of James's novels that prompts Wilson "to inspect what lies beneath."

The first such gap Wilson describes is the curious tendency he discerns in James's novels of the late 1880s – *The Bostonians, The Princess Cassimassima*, and *The Tragic Muse* – "to run into the sands." He goes on to say that

> This is most obvious – even startling – in *The Tragic Muse*, the first volume of which, as we read it, makes us think that

it must be James's best novel, so solid and alive does it seem.
. . . Then suddenly, the story stops short: after the arrival of
Miriam in London *The Tragic Muse* is almost a blank. Of the
two young men who have been preoccupied with Miriam,
one renounces her because she will not leave the stage and
the other doesn't, apparently, fall in love with her.[34]

Wilson has earlier characterized James's men as "not precisely neurotic; but they are the masculine counterpart of his
women. They have a way of missing out on emotional experience, either through timidity or prudence or through heroic re-
nunciation."[35] And he has said, when mentioning another case,
"the men are always deciding *not* to marry the women in Henry
James."[36]

Here, going on with his description of the gap he has discovered in *The Tragic Muse*, Wilson says of the remainder of that
work: "the only decisions that are looming are negative ones,
and the author himself seems to lose interest."[37] In an effort to
explain this lapse of artistic interest, Wilson does what Crews
suggests psychoanalytic assumptions can allow a critic to do, he
looks for evidence of "unresolved emotion" in James's life.

But he amasses his first evidence from the work itself, noting that "something insufficient and unexplained about James's
emotional life seems to appear unmistakably from his novels."
And, he points out, up to *The Tragic Muse*, "there have not been
. . . any consummated love affairs in his fiction – that is, none
among the principal characters and while the action of the story
is going on."[38]

Psychological observations of this kind, in Wilson's hands,
tend to take on both biographical and literary significance.
Thus, Wilson notes that "Precisely one trouble with *The Tragic
Muse* is that James does not get inside Miriam Rooth." He suggests that this is "probably due to James's increasing incapacity
for dealing directly with scenes of emotion."

Wilson sees as a significant defense mechanism the recur-
ring complaint in James's notebooks and prefaces that he is unable to do certain things, such as enter into a variety of points of
view in his fictions, because he cannot find the space within his
prescribed limits to do so.

Taking note of other gaps in the surface of James's work,

Wilson says, apropos of what he considers certain defects of style, that:

> Henry James never seems aware of the amount of space he is wasting through the long abstract formulations that do duty for concrete details, the unnecessary circumlocutions . . . the *as it were's* and *as we may say's* and all the rest – all the words in which he pads out his sentences . . . are probably symptomatic of a tendency to stave off problems.[39]

Having thus drawn both literary and biographical inferences from James's work, Wilson proceeds to do the same with reference to available data about James's life. Noting that, with the petering out of *The Tragic Muse* "something snaps" in James; Wilson tells us that he swears off the novel form altogether during this period and spends the next five years doing little more than make repeated unsuccessful attempts to succeed on the stage.

Applying his Freudian critical approach, Wilson says:

> One feels about the episode of his playwriting that it was an effort to put himself over, an effort to make himself felt, as he had never succeeded in doing. His brother William James wrote home in the summer of 1889, at the beginning of his playwriting period, that Henry, beneath the ". . . barnacles and things" of ". . . alien manners and customs" with which he had covered himself like a "marine crustacean," remained the "same dear old, good, innocent" and "at bottom very powerless-feeling Harry."

Continuing to search in the facts of James's life for a better understanding of his work, Wilson writes of James's last play, *Guy Domville*, which opened in 1895, that "At the first night . . . he ran afoul of a gallery of hooligans, who hissed and booed him . . . and this was the final blow." It was to be the end of James's playwriting and, says Wilson, "When he recovers from his disappointment, he is seen to have passed through a crisis.[40]

Wilson describes the psychological atmosphere of James's work in this period – he is writing novels once more – as thickening and filling up "the structure of the novel . . . with the fumes of the Jamesian gas." Wilson agrees with an observation, which he attributes to Ford Madox Ford, to the effect that "With *What Maisie Knew* James's style . . . first becomes a little gamey. He gets rid of some of his old formality and softens his mechanical hardness; and in spite of the element of abstraction which somewhat dilutes and dims his writing at all periods, his language becomes positively poetic."

It is characteristic of the complex view Wilson takes of artistic genesis that he finds both positive and negative literary results growing out of James's unresolved – or even in his partially resolved – neurotic conflicts. Now, after the crisis of disappointment over the failure of his playwriting career has passed, Wilson tells us that James

> enters upon a new phase, of which the most obvious feature is a subsidence back into himself. And now sex *does* appear in his work – even becoming an obsession in a queer and left-handed way. We have *The Turn of the Screw* and *The Sacred Fount; What Maisie Knew* and *In the Cage.* There are plenty of love affairs now and plenty of irregular relationships, but there are always thick screens between them and us; illicit appetites, maleficent passions now provide the chief interest, but they are invariably seen from a distance.[41]

These "thick screens," we know, Wilson feels to be "symptomatic," "a part of the swathing process with which he makes his embarrassing subjects always seem to present smooth contours."[42]

In the absence of more available data on James's life, Wilson turns to another of the devices listed by Crews as possibilities open to the psychoanalytic critical approach: he draws "biographical inferences on the basis of certain recurrent themes" in James's work, some of which, Wilson postulates, the author hadn't consciously meant to display.[43]

It is of course the question of the degree to which James was conscious of, in control of, his authorial intentions in these works – especially in *The Turn of the Screw* – that leads Wilson to append, in 1948, a nine-page postscript to his original essay (including a one and one-half page footnote summarizing a paper by psychoanalyst Saul Rosenzweig on the theme of impotence in James's work.)[44] The main weakness of this postscript is that it is unnecessarily defensive about *The Turn of the*

Screw. As I stated earlier, James's remarks about the deliberately misleading character of the story in his preface supersede the notebooks. These remarks were known to both Kenton and Wilson; both refer to them in discussing the *Screw's* ambiguity.

As it is, Wilson puts himself to the trouble of showing that James's *enacted* intention in the *Screw* was consonant with the reading he had given it in 1934, whether or not James had intended it so consciously. (It was this position for which Krook was to take him to task as constituting one of Wilson's "most glaring flaws.")[45]

Scaring up support in James's other work for his 1934 view, Wilson notes that "An earlier story, *The Path of Duty*, published in 1884, is perhaps the most obvious example of James's interest in cases of self-deception and his trick of presenting them from their own points of view."[46]

This is astute enough, but, in his attempt to defend his unhappy conclusion that "in *The Turn of the Screw* not merely is the governess self-deceived but . . . James is self-deceived about her," we find Wilson taking a much weaker stand. On the basis of the James notebooks, Wilson says, "One comes to the conclusion that Henry James, in a special and unusual way, was what is nowadays called an 'extrovert' . . . he did not brood on himself and analyze his own reactions . . . but always dramatized his experience immediately in terms of imaginary people."[47] Not only is this a very strange definition of what it means to be an extrovert, it is a very unconvincing description of James. The further Wilson goes with this line, the worse it seems to get, until he actually finds himself writing that "what we are told is going on in the characters' heads is a sensitive reaction to surfaces which itself seems to take place on the surface. We do not often see them grappling with their problems in terms of concrete ambitions or of intimate relationships."

We can only conclude that Wilson can have had no clear recollection of such James characters as Isabel Archer, Lambert Strether, or Kate Croy in mind when he wrote these words. What he *does* have in mind, almost certainly, is the distancing that is the result of James's style. We have witnessed his distaste for this as "symptomatic," and we may speculate that it violates, too, the humanist conviction he shares with Arnold about the necessity for "full-bloodedness" in art.

When Wilson allows himself to pretend that "James's characters 'are not intimate even with themselves,' " something seems to tell him he has gone too far. He hastens to add, "Not, however, that his sense of life – of personal developments and impacts – is not often profound and sure." But, he is soon attempting to defend his precarious position once more, protesting that his point is merely that "it is not always so." The reason it is not always so, Wilson tells us, is, "the presence, lurking like 'the beast in the jungle,' of other emotional factors with which the author himself does not always appear to have reckoned."[48]

Somehow, this assertion bears more weight, seems more solidly grounded in psychological insight than the rest. And now Wilson launches into an extraordinary couple of pages of "biographical inferences" drawn, in this case, both from James's work and from his autobiography which do, indeed, create a compelling picture.

Wilson uses them to identify certain "recurrent themes" of at least some of which James can hardly have been fully conscious. For example, "I remembered that in all James's work of this period – which extends from *The Other House* through *The Sacred Fount* – the favorite theme is the violation of innocence, with the victim, in every case . . . a young or a little girl."[49] Wilson proceeds to give nine instances of plot lines of this kind in James's work. He then says "We are not in a position to explain, on any basis of early experience, this preoccupation of James with immature girls who are objects of desire or defilement; but it seems clear what symbolic role they played from time to time in his work."

Wilson does not in this instance, as he had in his Yeats essay, leave us in the dark about what he means. The symbolic role of the girl innocents in James's stories, he suggests, was as a surrogate for James himself: "There was always in Henry James an innocent little girl whom he cherished and loved and protected and yet whom he later tried to violate, whom he even tried to kill." Wilson supports his assertion with this picture from James's life:

> He seems early to have "polarized" with his brother William
> in an opposition of feminine and masculine. This appears in
> a significant anecdote which he tells in his autobiography

about Williams' having left him once to go to play, as he said, with "boys that curse and swear"; and in his description of his feeling from the first that William was "occupying a place in the world to which I couldn't at all aspire – to any approach to which in truth I seem to myself ever conscious of having signally forfeited a title."[50]

Now, the materials that Wilson is here uncovering are very sensitive indeed and it becomes easier as we look at them to understand Krook's outrage at having had her Faustian-Galahadian, her savior-figure vision of James and his female characters intruded upon with considerations of this kind.

Yet Wilson is *not* insensitive to the man behind the artist, the genesis of whose work he is probing here so deeply. "He must have felt particularly helpless," says Wilson, "particularly unsuited for the battle with the world, particularly exposed to rude insult, after the failure of his dramatic career."[51] Then, Wilson reminds us – and we now see the connection – James "retreated into his celibate solitude" and began to write the "queer and neurotic stories (some of them, of course – *The Turn of the Screw* and *What Maisie Knew* – among James's masterpieces)."[52]

More sensitively still, Wilson tells us that what he has been inferring about James himself from his fiction and his other writings "is not in the least, on the critic's part, to pretend to reduce the dignity of these stories by reading into them the embarrassments of the author." But, he insists, "They do contain, I believe, a certain subjective element which hardly appears elsewhere in James's mature work." Nevertheless, says Wilson, in them "he has expressed what he had to express – disappointments and dissatisfactions that were poignantly and not ignobly felt – with dramatic intensity and poetic color."[53]

The last characteristic I have to note as a salient feature of this essay is the quality I alluded to in the very beginning as being well exemplified in it – the double quality, actually, of openness and flexibility. We have learned to associate both with humanism and more especially with Matthew Arnold and his prescription for good criticism: to see the object as in itself it really is, and to pursue the truth in the case of literary argument as in any other case, with disinterested fervor.

One instance of Wilson's openness to new critical ideas is in evidence in the very beginning of the essay: the credit he accords and the welcome he gives to Edna Kenton's new view of James's governess in the tale of the *Screw*. There is, of course, a negative aspect to the overreadiness with which Wilson changed his position in the 1948 postscript, and I have already noted the places where a degree of defensiveness on Wilson's part leads him astray. Regardless of the merit of the ground on which he did so, however, Wilson was following the highest standards of critical inquiry by taking note of what he took to be new evidence, especially in view of the fact that it seemed to weaken his case.

Others might have ignored the new evidence or written a new version that made no mention of the fact that it was in some sense a correction of the old. But Wilson's own sense of keeping the record straight compelled him to do it as he did.

The 1948 postscript contains an additional instance of Wilson's openness to new data – the footnote in which he gives a detailed account of Dr. Rosenzweig's paper. In a second postscript, appended in 1959, Wilson does more than give new evidence of his willingness to stand corrected in print. He is also generous in giving credit to scholars bringing forth new data that seems to Wilson to have special interest or merit. He does so whether or not it reinforces his own position. Thus, he notes that Marius Brewley has given a more correct interpretation of James's story, "The Liar," than he. And he is impressed by a conjecture brought forward by John Silver to the effect that the governess may have been able to describe Peter Quint (one of the alleged ghosts) by having heard about him from the people in the village.[54]

Although it is not an integral part of "The Ambiguity of Henry James," I cite as a final instance of Wilson's openness with regard to this essay his Foreword to *The Triple Thinkers*. Written for the 1948 edition, Wilson allowed it to stand in the 1963 Galaxy reprint. In it, he tries his best to respond to complaints and takes himself to task about, among other things, his lapses in preparation for the James essay, confessing that he

did not review . . . the three long later novels that I had read first twenty years before; and it may be that, if I had done so, I should have given a somewhat different account. In looking into them again just now, I seemed sometimes to catch sight of qualities which I had not appreciated in my college days – at an age when James's lack of real "love interest" is likely to prejudice one against him – and to which I feared I might not have done justice.[55]

I conclude with two final notes on the humanist concerns that crop up in the last pages of "The Ambiguity of Henry James" and that continue to permeate Wilson's work. First, it is characteristic of him to be both pleased about the new lease on life James's work had received in the time intervening between its first publication and the time of his 1948 postscript and, at the same time, to be concerned about the social implications of a James revival:

> There have contributed to this frantic enthusiasm perhaps a few rather doubtful elements. A novelist whose typical hero invariably decides not to act, who remains merely an intelligent onlooker, appeals for obvious reasons to a period when many intellectuals, formerly romantic egoists or partisans of the political left, have been resigning themselves to the role of observer or of passive participant in activities which cannot possibly command their whole allegiance.[56]

Wilson is never more clearly the humanist, engaged in coopting art as a humanist enterprise than in that passage.

For all his reservations about James's style, however, in the end Wilson shows himself to be a true appreciator. It is instructive to notice though, the terms in which he chooses to praise him:

> yet we do well to be proud of him . . . Henry James stands out today as unique . . . in having devoted wholeheartedly to literature the full span of a long life and brought it to first-rate abilities. . . . Alone among our novelists of the past, Henry James managed to master his art and to practice it on an impressive scale, to stand up to popular pressures so as not to break down or peter out, and to build up what the French call an *oeuvre*.[57]

These are the classical virtues again, couched in modern phrases. Knowing how much each of these attributes was valued by Wilson, we may say that, in effect, he here raises James to a position of residence in his personal pantheon of representative humanists.

CHAPTER EIGHT

"Dickens: The Two Scrooges"

Perhaps nothing he ever wrote better illustrates Wilson's biographical-narrative critical approach or his Freudian and Marxist preoccupations than his pivotal essay, "Dickens: The Two Scrooges." In the following discussion I begin with the essay's publishing history, then move on to a close analysis of the text, a summary of Wilson's basic strategy, and a comment on Wilson's importance to Dickens criticism as a whole.

Composing the opening 104 pages in *The Wound and the Bow*, "Dickens: The Two Scrooges" is the longest single critique Wilson ever devoted to one figure. As usual, he tried to get it printed in as many forms as he could devise. The book version incorporates three shorter essays on Dickens, originally published in five parts as magazine articles – a fact whose significance will become apparent later.[1] Besides various reprintings in the book's hardcover and paperback editions, it also appears in Wilson's 1954 volume called Eight Essays.

In its 1941 form, which remained substantially the final version, the Dickens essay is divided into six sections. They are of unequal length, ranging from six pages in Section I and four in Section II to forty pages in Section V, with the remaining sections falling in between. Reasons can be found for these strangely proportioned divisions of text: roughly, they mark the divisions between Wilson's discussions of Dickens's life and those of his work. But the distinction does not apply uniformly, for Wilson interweaves biographical data and critical observation throughout.

The more probable explanation is that divisions used to break up the text in its magazine form were accidentally retained in some parts and not in others. Unless we assume something of the kind, it is hard to understand Wilson's rationale for just these divisions. The essay could quite easily have been broken up into three more equal parts to bring out the three major chronological periods according to which it is organized. It might, for example, have reflected the way Wilson focuses on the psychological struggles out of which Dickens fashioned his art: first in his childhood, then in his successful middle years, and finally in his unhappy last years. Such divisions would also have thrown into relief one of the essay's strongest achievements: its tracing of a clear, progressive development in Dickens as an artist, from his early work right up to and including his last incomplete novel.

As it is, gaps in logic that attend Wilson's loose linking of the six sections suggest that the divisional apportioning has at least some negative importance to the essay's overall effectiveness. What is clear, in any case, is that the chronological divisions would have been more useful, if only as mnemonic aids.

But the essay as a whole is so complex in its movement and so densely packed with ideas that perhaps the best way to convey a sense of its content it to adopt a technique of Wilson's and attempt a synopsis of the major points as they unfold.

Wilson begins *in medias res* by recounting the traumatic event of Dickens's childhood – his father's imprisonment for debt and his own bitter experience as a child laborer in a blacking factory. Wilson stresses the tensions that must have been felt when Dickens's family struggled to make its way out of the servant class and become, with the aid of aristocratic patrons, members of the *petite bourgeoisie*. He suggests that Dickens's early preoccupation with the social injustices of the debtors' prison and the workhouse was a result of unresolved conflicts over his own early experiences with these institutions.

As Wilson makes clear in a brief statement of intent (which will be looked at in more detail later), his purpose was to overturn the view of Dickens that then prevailed – a view picturing him as primarily a popular writer who happened to possess extraordinary comic gifts. While acknowledging this side of Dickens, Wilson sees him as a serious novelist of the first rank and a social critic whose early reversals in life have had a hand in shaping the themes of his novels into the form of protest. According to Wilson, Dickens's experience led him to fashion and identify with fictional characters who are, even in the guise of children, rebels against society and its institutions.

In pursuit of this purpose, Wilson announces his intention of exempting Dickens's comedy from the discussion altogether. He reasons that it is the one aspect of Dickens that has been adequately dealt with elsewhere. But before leaving the subject, Wilson makes some observations calculated to bring the received view of Dickens's comedy, too, into a more modern – a blacker – light. He calls Dickens's humor "like the laughter of Aristophanes, a real escape from institutions. . . . It leaps free of the prison of life."[2]

Yet, as early as *Pickwick Papers*, Wilson finds that Dickens's laughter "already shows a trace of the hysterical" and that, no matter how gaily or liberatingly it soars, "gloom and soreness must always drag it back."[3] As if to document his point, Wilson goes on to call attention to the grim, often violent nature of the interpolated tales in *Pickwick*. His highlighting causes them to take on the aspect of risings up from the unconscious of Dickens's repressed emotions.

In the early pages of Section I, Wilson manages to present the suffering young Dickens so vividly to our minds that the picture haunts us and seems to inform with significance each of the factors from the novels he chooses to focus on. Wilson has told us that Dickens's father, whom he loved, allowed his son to remain in the blacking factory even after his own release from prison. This seeming betrayal constituted for Dickens ever after an act that he was unable to understand. We are reminded of it when we read Wilson's roll call of Dickens characters who are in some sense victimized or disinherited sons: Oliver Twist, David Copperfield, Barnaby Rudge, Nicholas Nickleby, Martin Chuzzlewit. We are invited, too, to notice the number of wronged sons who exact vengeance from their fathers. (These especially preponderate in the dark interpolations of sunny *Pickwick*.) And of how omnipresent (even, again, in *Pickwick*) are images of debtors' prisons and workhouses, where children are exploited and abused.

Wilson calls our attention also to the precocious grasp Dickens displays of murderous natures such as those of Bill Sykes, Mr. Quilp, the hangman in *Barnaby Rudge*, and Jonas Chuzzlewit.

In fact, making his way chronologically through the novels of the Dickens canon, Wilson constantly stresses the relationship between "the wound and the bow"; that is, between Dickens's childhood humiliation and grief and the way in which his imagination sought to deal with it. Wilson maintains that "the work of Dickens's whole career was an attempt to digest these early shocks and hardships, to explain them to himself, to justify himself in relation to them, to give an intelligible and tolerable picture of a world in which such things could occur."[4]

In addition to its strictly psychological aspects, the essay displays a second focus, equally strong, that is sociological in character. Here Wilson's own early training in Marxian economic theory is evident in the understanding he displays of the complex relation of economic base to cultural superstructure. Along this second axis, Wilson endeavors to trace the progress of Dickens's attitudes toward society and their effect on his work. "Through the whole of this early period," Wilson tells us, "Dickens appears to have regarded himself as a respectable middle-class man."[5] The servants of whom he writes approvingly, from Sam Weller in *Pickwick* to Kit in *The Old Curiosity Shop*, may be outspoken, but they never overstep their place or forget their station.

Wilson notes that Dickens may have had some romantic notions at this time about America as a classless society, but they did not survive his firsthand experience of it. When he visited this country in 1842, Wilson tells us, "Dickens was driven back by what he did find into the attitude of an English gentleman."[6]

In *American Notes* Dickens is capable of a rousing defense of the rights of the working class. (For example, he supports some girls in a piano factory in Lowell, Massachusetts, in their expressed desire to have piano lessons and subscribe to a circulating library.) Yet, as Wilson points out, during the same period Dickens is also capable of making the main theme of *Nicholas Nickleby* revolve around the efforts of Nicholas and his sister to vindicate their position as gentlefolk.

The importance of this ambivalence critically is, in Wilson's view, that the novels of the period suffer because of it. He points out that in *Barnaby Rudge,* for example, the story's principal climax, the burning of the prison, "not only has nothing to do with the climax of the plot, it goes in spirit quite against the attitude which Dickens has begun by announcing. The satisfaction he obviously feels in demolishing the sinister old prison, which, rebuilt, had oppressed him in childhood, completely obliterates the effects of his rightminded references in his preface to 'those shameful tumults'."[7]

But, says Wilson, there is another reason why the political novels of Dickens—he is referring to *Barnaby Rudge, Hard Times,* and *A Tale of Two Cities*—are unclear and unsatisfactory. It is simply that, having formed a contemptuous opinion of government during his days as a reporter covering Parliament, Dickens was fundamentally uninterested in politics.

Here I think Wilson misnames the property he is attempting to isolate. What he describes Dickens as carrying away from his parliamentary experience is not lack of interest, but profound disillusion over the possibility of social redress through political action. Whether Dickens was bored or disillusioned by politics, however, what introduces a damaging ambivalence into these novels, as Wilson rightly suggests, is that at this period Dickens's feelings about authority are still largely in the grip of his unconscious. Wilson points out, too, that Dickens's distrust of politics is very much in keeping with the rebellious aspect of his nature:

> Dickens is almost invariably *against* institutions: in spite of his allegiance to Church and State, in spite of the lip service he occasionally pays them, whenever he comes to deal with Parliament and its laws, the courts and the public officials, the creeds of Protestant dissenters and of Church of England alike, he makes them either ridiculous or cruel, or both at the same time.[8]

With the novels of the middle period—Wilson pinpoints the time very specifically as "after the murder in *Martin Chuzzlewit*"—those characters Dickens means us to see as illustrative of virtue shift from the upper-middle class to the lower-middle class.[9] Wilson evidently takes this as a sign that Dickens is becoming more consciously radical. The ideal is no longer to be found with the likes of Messrs. Pickwick and Brownlow, but in Ruth Pinch and her brother in *Chuzzlewit*, in the bright, homely hearths of the *Christmas Books*, and in the modest home to which Florence Dombey descends when she weds the nephew of a ships' instrument maker.

In *Dombey and Son*, Wilson points out, Dickens shows signs of a heightened awareness of the weaknesses of Victorian society. With this novel he becomes explicit about his feelings of opposition to it for the first time. And, as his anger rises to the conscious level, his insights about the nature of that society deepen immeasurably.

As Wilson sees it, the effect upon the artistry of his novels is also profound. Although Dickens is at this time still struggling under the limitations of the serial form of publication (involving such handicaps as the necessity of having to plan all out before execution and of never being able, as he put it, to "try back" anything once it was down in print), Wilson points out that he is now capable of much tighter plot organization.

Taking the example of *Dombey and Son* to examine and illustrate his point, Wilson shows how in this novel Dickens made the organism of a single company the unifying structure upon which to hinge his story. But, as Wilson appreciates, the advances of *Dombey and Son*, remarkable as they are, are far surpassed in *Bleak House*. He calls it "the masterpiece of the middle period" and suggests that with it Dickens has invented a new literary genre: the novel of the social group.[10]

To Wilson the organizing principle of the chancery suit and the gallery of characters whose lives are intertwined with it stands among the finest things in Dickens. And, in the course of the discussion, he credits Dickens with still another important innovation—combining a detective story with a moral fable. This device, as Wilson sees it, exerts a positive influence on the novel, making for a greater cohesiveness and for a greater profundity as well, because the solution of the mystery now also becomes the moral of the story, its "social message."[11]

As a check against previous Dickens criticism will corroborate, these represent stimulating new insights into *Bleak House*. Wilson goes on to give out others with an almost unseemly plentifulness and ease. Not stopping with what he calls the obvious symbolism of the fog and the chancery – "that hang like emblems over the door" – he delineates the symbolic significance of a dozen or so of the novel's characters as well.[12]

The following is only a fragmentary sampling of his comments on the novel. It is intended to show the ingenious ways Wilson finds to bring out the two aspects of this work (or any work) of literature that must always be of paramount importance at this period: that is, the psychological complexities and the social implications of any fictional situation. He reminds us of what Frederich Engels, visiting London in the early 1840s, had written of the impression made upon him by the people in the streets, noting that "The brutal indifference, the unfeeling isolation of each in his private interest, become the more repellent the more these individuals are herded together within a limited space."[13]

To Wilson this is an immediate echo of the world that Dickens in describing – a world in which

> in general the magnanimous, the simple of heart, the amiable, the loving and the honest are frustrated, subdued, or destroyed. . . . Esther Summerson has been frightened and made submissive by being treated as the respectable middle class thought it proper to treat an illegitimate child . . . Richard Carstone has been demoralized and ruined; Miss Flite has been driven insane."[14]

After mentioning that Esther's plight and Lady Dedlock's, too, are the result of sexual inhibitions socially reenforced – a Freudian view – Wilson goes on to underscore the sense of inevitability that accompanies the novel's denouement – a denouement that he construes in classically Marxist terms: "With this indifference and egoism of the middle class, the social structure must buckle in the end." In the passages cited we see, perhaps too baldly brought into relief by the cutting, Wilson's whole signature as a critic. His humanist moral philosophy is interwoven with the insights of Freud on the one hand and Marx and Engels on the other, the whole made artistic by the prose of a man who himself is a writer of considerable skill.

The key to the brilliance of Wilson's commentary on *Bleak*

House, the stimulus that called forth so rewarding a response, is almost certainly to be found in the excitement Wilson must have felt over the way the book lent itself to his multi-dimensional approach. For Wilson as a critic is ever and always bounded and defined by his gifts of humanist explication.

When he is confronted by works that do not lend themselves to these gifts (works, say, of alienation, on the one hand, or of religious sentiment, on the other) the insights that follow are inclined to be lackluster. As an aesthetic guide, the humanistic principle usually serves Wilson extremely well, but it could, on occasion, make him appear to be somewhat shallow. This is the case when he delivers himself of some unsympathetic views regarding Kafka (in whose work there is a good deal of alienation.) And it would seem to be the case when, at this point in the essay, Wilson deals with *David Copperfield* (in which there is a good deal of religious sentiment), disposing of it in a single paragraph as "not one of Dickens' deepest books." Though he admits that, "in the first half . . . at any rate, Dickens strikes an enchanting vein which he had never quite found before and which he was never to find again," Wilson insists that ultimately, "it is something in the nature of a holiday."[15]

In the same section Wilson dismisses in equally short order *A Tale of Two Cities*, a book that has provided much of the English-speaking world with its most vivid route to an understanding of the French revolution. Unfortunately for Wilson's purposes, it neither displays Dickens as a serious novelist of character and psychological truth nor as an eloquent exposer of the ills of English society.

Of it, Wilson says only that "the conflict is made to seem of less immediate reality by locating it out of England." And he does not fail to note that it contains an implied threat of possible revolution in England – the point being that Wilson seems to feel the need to fit this novel "that deal[s] with a revolutionary subject,"[16] as he calls it, into his own theory of Dickens's conflicts regarding the English governing class.

David Copperfield is a superb romance, but it does not help Wilson to show us Dickens the artist in conflict. One clue to his impatience with it emerges from the arguments he puts forward for denying the book much weight: "David is too candid and simple to represent Dickens himself; and though the blacking warehouse episode is utilized, all the other bitter experiences of Dickens' youth were dropped out when he abandoned the autobiography."[17]

Another emerges when one remembers that Wilson spent a good deal more space discussing *Hard Times*, a book he clearly *likes* less well than *Copperfield*, simply because that novel, with the opportunities it affords for discussions of labor-management relations, lends itself more obviously to Wilson's Marxist preoccupations.

In the case of both these novels Wilson scarcely treats them in terms of their *literary* merits at all, and one could get the impression from passages like those on *Copperfield* and *A Tale of Two Cities* that Wilson's interest is centered exclusively on Dickens the man and his relation to society. (That it is, in other words, not at all fixed on the novels themselves, as literary works to be examined for their own sakes.) But such an impression would be erroneous. It is simply that, as Wilson has said of himself, "writing about literature, for me, has always meant narrative and drama [creating the creators themselves as characters in a larger drama of cultural and social history] as well as the discussions of comparative [i.e., literary] values."[18]

And, to be fair to Wilson, no critic engaged in a massive reclamation project of the kind he is undertaking in this instance, can be expected to dwell on, or even to linger very long, over works that do not contribute to his purposes. One might be justified in noting, however, that, in this essay, Wilson seems prepared to give his serious critical attention to the literary values only of those works that also provide him with opportunities for the application of his biographical and social theories.

The fact that *Little Dorrit* lends itself especially well to these foci explains better than any objective critical scale could the eight pages Wilson devotes to it. As he puts it, *Little Dorrit* is worth our attention because in it: "The treatment of social institutions and the treatment of individual psychology have both taken turns distinctly new."[19] Although Dickens's treatment may be new, the subject, the setting, the chief symbol (all the same) are one of the oldest to be found in his work. Once again we are dealing with the Marshalsea, the prison into which Dickens's father was thrown for debt.

Before going on with his extensive discussion of *Little Dor-*

rit, however (we are at the beginning of Section V), Wilson pauses to take another look at Dickens himself. He makes the point that *Dorrit* marks a new phase in the novelist's work and that "To understand it, we must go back to his life." As Wilson sees it, Dickens was entering what is now referred to as a mid-life crisis. "At forty [he] had won everything that a writer could expect to obtain through his writings: his genius was universally recognized; he was feted wherever he went. . . . Yet from [the summer of 1853] he had shown signs of profound discontent and unappeasable restlessness. . . . He began to fear that his vein was drying up."[20]

Regarding the causes for Dickens's depressed state, Wilson subscribes to those isolated by Dickens's friend and memoirist, John Forster. According to Forster, "There were two things wrong with Dickens: a marriage which exasperated and cramped him and from which he had not been able to find relief, and a social maladjustment which his success had never straightened out."[21]

Apropos of the first "thing wrong," Wilson goes into considerable detail about Dickens's relations with women. He pursues the matter in a number of ways, from Dickens's recurrent absorption in innocent young girls to the painful experience of Dickens's young manhood, when he was rejected by Maria Beadnell.

His ideal woman, Wilson notes, was always prenubile, of the type apotheosized in Little Nell. She was never modeled on Dickens's real wife, Catherine, who seems to have been something of a scold. Wilson writes of her that she "had big blue eyes, a rather receding chin and a sleepy and languorous look." Far from providing a romantic model, according to Wilson, she was more likely to have posed for "Dickens' terrible gallery of shrews who browbeat their husbands."[22]

Although Wilson admits that it is not possible to know much about Dickens's marriage, he feels there is enough evidence to conclude with justice that the two partners were intellectually and temperamentally mismatched. He is sure enough to state that even though they lived together for twenty years and had ten children together, they were probably unhappy with one another.

"And if Dickens was lonely in his household," Wilson goes on, taking up the second "thing wrong," "he was lonely in society also." For he had achieved all his recognition, and all his success in it "without . . . ever really having created for himself a social position in England, that society *par excellence* where everybody had to have a definite one and where there was no rank reserved for the artist." Yet, it appears that this isolation was not all society's doing. It was at least partly a matter of rather stubborn opposition on Dickens's part. As Wilson points out, he consistently sought out for his companions those who were, with the exception of Carlyle, his social inferiors.

At the same time says Wilson, "his behavior toward Society, in the capitalized sense, was rebarbative to the verge of truculence." Describing Dickens's attitude as that of a "middle class 'Radical' opposing feudal precedent and privilege," Wilson sums up, "Dickens is one of a very small group of British intellectuals to whom the opportunity has been offered to be taken up by the governing class and who have actually declined that honor."[23]

On the other hand, "to be caught between two social classes in a society of strict stratifications" can, as Wilson points out, be very useful to a writer. He cites James and Proust, Shakespeare and Dostoevsky as cases in point, explaining that being so situated "enables him to dramatize contrasts and to study interrelations which the dweller in one world cannot know."[24] In this way Wilson prepares us for the discovery that the dark turn of events in Dickens's life, while it also darkens his art, is not necessarily detrimental to it.

Wilson does not make explicit the connection between his report on Dickens's marital unhappiness and his art. He only comments that *Little Dorrit* is "full of the disillusion and discomfort of this period in Dickens' life."[25] The relation to his art of Dickens's social maladjustment is, however, clearer. Wilson sees Dickens's struggle to penetrate the meaning of the Marshalsea as a part of his lifelong sense of humiliation over that childhood blacking incident. He see it as a part, too, of Dickens's unconscious motivation as an artist "to give an intelligible and tolerable picture of a world in which such things could occur."[26]

In choosing the Marshalsea as his subject once more, Dickens appears to have been trying to get the prison out of his system for good. Wilson goes on to suggest that he was also finding the character of John Dorrit a way of getting his father out of his system for good or, at any rate, of coming to terms with him.

> The figure of his father hitherto has always haunted Dickens' novels, but he has never known quite how to handle it. In Micawber, he made him comic and lovable; in Skimpole, he made him comic and unpleasant. . . . But what kind of person, really, had John Dickens been in himself? . . . the old man continued to be a problem up to his death in 1851. . . . Yet Dickens said to Forster after[ward]: "The longer I live, the better man I think him."

In a personal way, Wilson says, Dickens undoubtedly undertook *Little Dorrit* as a kind of search for his father. For Wilson sees the novel as both a study of what bad institutions make of men and as an effort to answer the question, How had the father of Charles Dickens come to be what he was? Dickens's answer, as he works it out in the story of Mr. Dorrit and the Marshalsea is, says Wilson, "something in the nature of a justification of John."[27]

As we have noted, the prison is the main subject of *Little Dorrit*. Before Dickens is done examining it, however, his subject spreads beyond the literal prison to other institutions he saw as "bad" also—to "harsh Calvinism" and "hard business," those "mainstays of the Victorian age."[28]

"Yet," Wilson asserts, "something different from social criticism" is going on in this novel. "Dickens is no longer satisfied to anatomize the organism of society." He cites the short "case" Dickens includes of a woman who is subject to the delusion that she can never be loved. This "case," called *The History of a Self-Tormentor*, Wilson describes as an instance of "remarkable pre-Freudian insight" on Dickens's part. "There is still, to be sure, the social implication that her . . . sense of being slighted [has] been imposed on her by the Victorian attitude toward her illegitimate birth [and here we hear an echo of Esther Summerson]. But her handicap is now simply a thought-pattern, and from that thought-pattern she is never to be liberated."[29]

Wilson is much impressed that the original title for the

novel was to have been *Nobody's Fault*. He emphasizes that the important thing to remember about *Little Dorrit* is that it is about imprisoning states of mind no less than it is about oppressive institutions.

We come now to one of the uncomfortable consequences of Wilson's attempt to blend without obvious division the various parts of what were originally three separate essays. The first, "Dickens and the Marshalsea Prison," ends with this discussion of *Little Dorrit*. The second, having originally borne the title Wilson retains for the essay as a whole, "Dickens: The Two Scrooges," now begins.

It opens with a statement about the dualism that runs through all of Dickens's early novels. Taking Scrooge as the most obvious example of the kind of character in whom good and evil are not intertwined but juxtaposed, Wilson notes that such characters derive from the conventions of melodrama. He then goes back through the Dickens canon citing numerous examples of such one – or shall we say two – dimensional characters. The awkward thing is the absence of any logical transition in the shift from one essay to the other. There is no typographical clue to indicate a break, and the material Wilson *has* inserted, a cursory look at *Great Expectations*, neither completes the point he was attempting to make about *Little Dorrit* nor prepares us for the ensuing discussion of dual personality. In fact, this initial look at *Great Expectations* (Wilson has some better things to say about it later) largely misfires.

Wilson begins by making a great deal out of the greater "psychology" displayed in *Great Expectations*. His examples, however, dwell entirely upon the *social* consequences that devolve upon Pip when wealth comes to him. Wilson notes that Pip's money is criminally derived and therefore socially tainted. The English caste system and everybody's place in it are carefully gone into as well. Yet, of Pip's inner changes from a snob to a compassionate human being under the tutelage of Joe Gargery and others, there is no word.

However, once launched into the "Two Scrooges" essay, the text smooths out into a cohesive flow once more. When Wilson advances his theory that the two irreconcilable sides of Scrooge's nature really represent the dramatization of a manic-depressive split in Dickens's own personality, it becomes clear that he has once again hit his stride. The rationale behind this "essay within an essay" lies in Wilson's conviction that "Scrooge represents a principle (i.e., of duality) fundamental to the dynamics of Dickens' world and derived from his own emotional constitution."

Wilson draws from Kate Perugini's recollections in Gladys Storey's *Dickens and Daughter* as well as from those of another daughter, Mamie, in order to document his case that, "emotionally Dickens *was* unstable."[30] Kate is quoted as saying, after citing many instances of Dickens's irrational outbursts in the presence of his family and friends, "My father was a wicked man – a very wicked man."

Meanwhile, from Mamie, "we hear of his colossal Christmas parties, of the vitality, the imaginative exhilaration, which swept all the guests along." It is, Wilson asserts, for all the world like "Scrooge bursting in on the Crachits. Shall we ask what Scrooge would actually be like . . . when the merriment was over?" The answer, to Wilson at any rate, is that "Unquestionably he would relapse . . . into moroseness, vindictiveness, suspicion. He would, that is to say, reveal himself as the victim of a manic-depressive cycle, and a very uncomfortable person."[31]

For a good part of Dickens's career his powers of characterization were, in Wilson's view, inhibited. Wilson thinks this was due to an inner compulsion on the novelist's part to separate his fictional characters into bad people and good people, comics and characters played straight. "The only complexity of which Dickens is capable, says Wilson of this stage, "is to make one of his noxious characters become wholesome, one of his clowns turn into a serious person." (He is speaking of the reform of Mr. Dombey and, of course, of Scrooge.)

As Wilson sees it, "this was not merely because Dickens's passion for the theater had given him a taste for emotional contrasts; it was rather that the lack of balance between *the opposite impulses of his nature* [my italics] had stimulated an appetite for melodrama."[32]

In an effort to "enter into the central question of the psychology of Dickens' characters" Wilson now takes us still deeper into biographical waters, venturing to follow Dickens in great detail through the trials of his midlife crisis already touched on in the discussion of *Little Dorrit*. It seems that in an attempt to distract himself from his troubles, Dickens embarked on a series of theatricals that "came to look more and more like pretexts for Dickens to indulge his appetite for acting." The measure afforded Dickens only fitful relief, however. In 1857 or 1858, Wilson tells us, he met and became infatuated with Ellen Ternan, the young daughter of a well-known actress. It was an encounter that eventually led to Dickens's making an open break with his wife (rather scandalously using one of his own publications, *Household Words*, to air his domestic grievances) and to his setting up Miss Ternan in an establishment of her own.

Like Dickens's marriage and his uneasy social position, the connection between this affair and its effect on Dickens's writing remains implicit, only, in Wilson's treatment. Yet it seems clear that he intends to illustrate, by following Ellen Ternan into several of Dickens's novels, how Dickens used his characters for the relief of his emotions.

Judged in this light, young Ellen can hardly be supposed to have filled for Dickens "that old unhappy loss or want of something"[33] (as he has David Copperfield put it) that he undoubtedly hoped she would. Wilson believes that she turns up in Dickens's last three novels as Estella Provis (the frigid and indifferent torturer of Pip in *Great Expectations*), Bella Wilfer in *Our Mutual Friend* (who was, as Wilson describes her, a girl "equally intent upon money – which was certainly one of the things that Ellen got out of her liaison with Dickens"), and Helena Landless (the Nemesis figure in Dickens's last book). To clinch the latter, Wilson notes that Ellen's middle name is Lawless. The suggestion, of course, is that Dickens relieved his unconscious resentment of his mistress by portraying her thus unflatteringly in the characters of his novels.[34]

It would be a mistake to convey the impression that Wilson is being reductive in his treatment of Dickens's art of characterization. Rather, it becomes, in his handling of it, necessary to our appreciation of Dickens's artistry to see the personal struggles out of which his art is born – and still more important – out of which it continues to develop. For Wilson stresses that, to a large extent, Dickens outgrows his melodramatically conceived heroes and heroines:

> The endings of his early novels, in which the villain is smashingly confounded and the young juvenile got the leading woman, had been the conventional denouements of Drury Lane. . . . The scene in which Edith Dombey turns upon and unmasks Mr. Carker . . . which is one of the worst in Dickens, must be one of the passages in fiction most completely conceived in terms of the stage. In *Bleak House,* he is still theatrical, but he has found out how to make this instinct contribute to the effectiveness of a novel.[35]

Wilson notices that Dickens's prose style, like his handling of scenes, undergoes a development in the course of Dickens's career. It moves away from the theatrical – in this case, away from high-flown declamations and a tendency (which Dickens admitted knowing he had) to fall into blank verse whenever he wished to be particularly serious. Wilson's mention, at this point, of his belief that Dickens "never quite got rid of" either offending tendency is a mark of his scrupulous honesty as a critic. It is, of course, vital to his claim that Dickens is an artist of the first rank (a view not widely shared in 1941) that Wilson establish Dickens's capacity for growth. Yet, he prefers to weaken his case rather than overlook a stylistic flaw.

Having given up some ground, however, it is not surprising to find Wilson taking pains to recover it by demonstrating that Dickens's powers of characterization undergo a process of change and development as well. He says, for example, of Dickens's early works: "His whole art had been a kind of impersonation, in which he had exploited this or that of his impulses by incorporating it in an imaginary person rather than – up to this point, at any rate – exploring his own personality."[36]

Up to now Wilson has been showing us Dickens's personal difficulties in his forties as a struggle to come to terms with the elements of the "two Scrooges" in his own nature. His formulation of Dickens's *artistic* struggles during the same period constitutes a striking parallel. In Wilson's words,

> Dicken's difficulty in his middle period, and indeed more or less to the end, is to get the good and bad together in one

character . . . the real beginnings of psychological interest may be said to appear in *Hard Times*, which, though parts of it have the crudity of a cartoon, is the first novel to trace with any degree of plausibility the processes by which people become what they are.[37]

Wilson goes on to amplify the point with, among other examples, a much brighter observation regarding Pip than any that accompanied his earlier discussion of *Great Expectations*. He notes that, in the course of the novel "we see Pip pass through a whole psychological cycle. At first he is sympathetic, then by a more or less natural process he turns into something unsympathetic, then he becomes sympathetic again. Here the effects of poverty and riches are seen from the inside in one person."[38]

This time we note that, even though Wilson brings in the ideas of class and money, he does so with the recognition that it is how these things are internalized that is of psychological interest in a novel and in a novel's characters. Wilson goes on to say, "This is for Dickens a great advance; and it is a development which, if carried far enough, would end by eliminating the familiar Dickens of the lively but limited stage characters, with their tag lines and their unvarying stage make-ups.[39] But having brought up the question of dualism versus complexity in Dickens's characters, Wilson is again faced with an awkward problem in terms of the organization of his material.

The original "Two Scrooges" essay ends here with a recapitulation of the critical situation in Dickens's personal life. Wilson goes into his physical afflictions while writing *Great Expectations* and maintains that "the creative strain of a lifetime was beginning to tell on Dickens."[40] One would naturally expect Wilson to follow through, with illustrations from the next novel, on how Dickens struggled to bring "the good and the bad together in one character. [And, in fact, this is precisely the tack Wilson takes when he comes to discuss the unfinished last novel, *The Mystery of Edwin Drood*.) It is not, however, what happens at this point in the essay.

Sticking to the precedent he has established so far, of treating Dickens's work in chronological order (with minor instances of anticipation and doubling back), the novel Wilson takes up next is *Our Mutual Friend*. As it happens, the book does not lend itself at all well to a discussion of its characters' psychology. Wilson attempts none. He simply (temporarily) drops the subject. *Our Mutual Friend* is, rather, much more closely related to *Bleak House*, being another of Dickens's brilliant anatomizations of Victorian society (now at a later, more industrialized phase). As such, it is an excellent example of the type of novel Wilson was hailing forty pages before as a new genre, the novel of the social group. Wilson makes no such link, however, and the only hint of the complete transition of subject is the presence of a double space at this point in the printed text.

In an apparent attempt to establish at least a loose connection with the novels on either side of it, Wilson begins by simply telling us that three years passed after *Great Expectations* before Dickens wrote *Our Mutual Friend* and that it "like all these later books . . . is more interesting to us today than it was to Dickens' public."

One supposes that Wilson is referring to the commonly shared pessimism and gloom about Victorian society of the later novels, which caused them to be less popular with that society than Dickens's other works. It is perhaps this gloomy element Wilson is thinking of when he says, "the book shows the weariness, the fears, and the definitive disappointments of this period."[41] Feeling that Dickens's "formulas" have here gone stale, Wilson finds the plot "tiresome and childish" and the comic characters "pretty mechanical and sterile."

But he makes the same point he made with reference to *Little Dorrit* – that the effects of Dickens's struggles upon his art were by no means all negative: "The difficulty that Dickens found in writing *Our Mutual Friend* does not make itself felt as anything in the nature of an intellectual disintegration." In fact, Wilson says that "the book compensates for its shortcomings by the display of an intellectual force which, though present in Dickens' work from the first, here appears in a phase of high tension and a condition of fine muscular training." The idea of Dickens's development is also asserted once more: "It may be said Dickens never really repeats himself: his thought makes a consistent progress, and his art, through the whole thirty-five years of his career, keeps going on to new materials and effects; so that his work has an interest and a meaning as a whole."[42]

Still arguing along developmental lines (that is, if one agrees with Wilson's premise that moving toward socialist views *is* development) Wilson lays out a convincing case for Dickens as a sort of early Marxist. He cites chapter and book to show the progressively unfavorable view Dickens takes of his middle-class characters. The range is from the sympathetic one of the newly arrived Rouncewell in *Bleak House* to the wickedly drawn portrait of the Meagleses in *Little Dorrit*. Of the latter's insularity, smugness, even vulgarity, Wilson says that it "is felt by Dickens as he has never felt it in connection with such people before." Wilson maintains, further, that the still greater ferocity of his depiction of the Veneerings, the Podsnaps and the Lammles demonstrates that, with *Our Mutual Friend*, Dickens "has come at last to despair utterly of the prospering middle class."[43]

Wilson also notes, however, that "If the middle class has here become a monster, the gentry have taken on an aspect more attractive than we have ever known them to wear as a class in any previous novel of Dickens."[44] (The reference is to the sympathetic portrayal of the impoverished lawyers, Eugene Wrayburn and Mortimer Lightwood, and to the old diner-out, Twemlow.)

Suggesting that Dickens has been influenced by the newly formed Workers' International, Wilson says that *Our Mutual Friend* is something of a Marxist cautionary tale. Thus, he says the final implication of the story is – "to state it in Marxist language – that the declassed representatives of the old professional upper classes may unite with the proletariat against the commercial middle class."[45] This is indeed as "Marxist" as Wilson's critical language ever gets.

In order to find out from Wilson what he values in Dickens, and not just in this novel, we need only examine with care one of those densely packed, summarizing paragraphs of evaluation that are one of his trademarks. This time the occasion is support for his assertion that *Our Mutual Friend*, the last novel Dickens was to complete, is "quite worthy of its predecessors." For, says Wilson,

> Dickens has here distilled the mood of his later years,
> dramatized the tragic discrepancies of his character,

delivered his final judgment on the whole Victorian exploit, in a fashion so impressive that we realize how little the distractions of this period had the power to direct him from the prime purpose of his life: the serious exercise of his art.[46]

That last point seems an important one to hold before us whenever we might be tempted to make too crude the nature of what we conceive to be Wilson's idea of the connection between an artist's life and his work.

In retrospect we can see that it was to make just this point that Wilson took us so far into Dickens's domestic situation – to show us that the true artist, however great his personal difficulties, does not allow those difficulties to deflect him from his work. Wilson feels that in order to appreciate the artistic product and to celebrate it properly, we must have some biographical understanding of against what odds it was produced.

Wilson shrewdly ends his discussion of this novel with a note about the one psychologically complex character in it: Bradley Headstone, the sinister schoolmaster who frightens Lizzie Hexam with the uncontrolled intensity of his desire for her. To be sure, Headstone might seem to be yet another of Dickens's old-fashioned villains. (Wilson admits that he probably derives from those early, theatrically conceived ones.) Yet, Wilson maintains, the dark figures of Dickens's later novels finally take on a convincing reality. (We are left to supply for ourselves such likely names as Magwitch and John Jasper, the villain of *Edwin Drood*.) Wilson notes that even of this type Bradley sets a new precedent, however. He is "the first murderer in Dickens who exhibits any complexity of character. And he is the first to present himself as a member of respectable Victorian society."[47]

Section VI introduces the discussion of *The Mystery of Edwin Drood* with the point that the same combination of factors, complexity and respectability, appears in the murderer here. Wilson's commentary on this novel forms the endpiece of his Dickens essay, and he devotes a good portion of it to working out what he calls the "enigma" of its unfinished ending. He says that, once properly understood, it will help to illuminate "the real meaning of Dickens' work."

Wilson explains that earlier critics, even the best of them

like Forster and Shaw, had failed to see the true importance of this novel because their interest was focused on Dickens's social criticism. So they had missed the significance of the fact that, in Drood, "The psychological interest which had been a feature of Dickens' later period is carried further."

Returning to his point about Dickens having found in *Bleak House* a way to combine the elements of a detective story and a moral fable, Wilson states that, "Here as elsewhere, the solution of the mystery was to have said something that Dickens wanted to say."[48] Before we can hope to understand what that "something" was, Wilson implies, we must first unravel the plot, as it was intended to be worked out by Dickens and never finished.

Of all the many who tried to solve in this way the real mystery of *The Mystery of Edwin Drood*, Wilson singles out for praise two American scholars: Howard Duffield and Aubrey Boyd. They, he says, showed sufficient alertness to follow the psychological possibilities suggested by the character of John Jasper and so hit upon the "cardinal secrets" of his personality (Jasper, in spite of the title, is the main character in the book). We sense the relevance here of Wilson's "Scrooge" theory when we learn that Jasper is a sort of Dr. Jeckyll and Mr. Hyde, a man of dual personality, combining in one body a good and evil character.

As Dickens portrays him, one side of John Jasper is a quiet, scholarly choirmaster, seemingly an ascetic, celibate bachelor. He is fond of his nephew, Edwin Drood, and seems to take an avuncular interest in Edwin's engagement to a pretty young girl. This young lady is a student in the seminary school across the cloister from Jasper's cottage, which stands on a secluded corner of the cathedral grounds.

The other side of John Jasper's character, however, is drastically different. He is a smoker of opium, a man of strange visions and sick passions, a voluptuary who, in a quiet way, terrorizes his nephew's intended bride by pressing on her his unwanted attentions.

There is much more to the plot, but the point that concerns us here is that the story breaks off some time after Drood's mysterious disappearance (and suspected murder) and nobody knows for sure how it is to have ended.

Mr. Duffield supplies the clue, however, that Jasper is

evidently a member of an Indian sect known as Thugs. Its members vow to commit murder and get away with it, all for the greater glory of their patroness, the Hindu goddess of destruction, Kali. Mr. Boyd contributes the information that, like Dickens himself, Jasper is a hypnotist. With these clues, and Dickens's notes to Forster about the novel to guide him, Wilson constructs a most ingenious and plausible ending for *Edwin Drood*—one that bears on his major theories about Dickens.

According to Wilson, Jasper practices malicious mesmerism on his nephew, Drood. He manipulates Drood into a situation where he can strangle him according to the ritual procedures of the Thug society (these, done correctly, were supposed to ensure safety from detection and prosecution). But he has slipped up on one element—the victim is supposed to have no gold in his possession and Drood, unknown to Jasper, is carrying a ring for his fiancee at the time of his death.

As Dickens told Forster, the body is to be identified by means of this ring. Wilson suggests that either mesmerism or opium could create in Jasper the two distinct states of consciousness upon which Dickens based the originality of his tale; that is, that "the last chapters were to be written in the condemned cell" and that they were "to consist in the review of the murderer's career by himself . . . its temptations to be dwelt upon as if, not he the culprit, but some other man, were the tempted."[49]

In analyzing this ending, Wilson draws obvious parallels between Dickens's own life at the time he wrote the novel and that of Jasper. We are made, for example, to see a possible connection between Dickens's equivocal position in society regarding his liaison with Miss Ternan and that of the choirmaster, a covert murderer hiding behind his cloak of respectability.

Wilson reminds us of Dickens's fondness for giving public readings of the murder of Nancy by Sykes, a practice that he insisted on pursuing even against his doctor's orders. Wilson says that "He threw himself . . . into the murder scene with a passion that became quite hysterical, as if reading it had become at this point in his life a real means of self-expression." He further tells us that "at the time of these readings" Dickens was given to making "jokes about his 'murderous instincts' " and to saying that he "goes about the streets feeling as if he is 'wanted' by the police."[50] The implication is that the criminal side of Dickens's nature, of which Wilson has spoken in the very beginning of the essay, has taken over:

> For the man of spirit whose childhood has been crushed by the cruelty of organized society, one of two attitudes is natural: that of the criminal or that of the rebel. Charles Dickens, in imagination, was to play the roles of both, and to continue up to his death to put into them all that was most passionate in his feeling.[51]

Now that Dickens has been cut off from society by the scandal of his illicit affair, Wilson sees him as having "discarded the theme of the rebel" and, instead, to be carrying "the theme of the criminal, which has haunted him all his life, to its logical development in his fiction."

Wilson here notices, not for the first time in this essay, the kinship between Dickens and Dostoevsky, an artist who also understood how, in the human psyche, the desire to be loved can be twisted tragically with the desire to destroy and to kill. But, says Wilson, "the English Dickens with his middle class audience would not be able to tell such a story even if he dared to imagine it." And this is why, Wilson suggests, in order to tell the moral fable of *Edwin Drood*, Dickens feels "he must contrive a whole machinery of mystification: of drugs, of telepathic powers, of remote oriental cults."[52]

Evidently Wilson does not, however, hold such "machinery" against *The Mystery of Edwin Drood* for, finally, he is warmer in his praise of this unfinished, relatively obscure work than he has been of almost any other in the canon, with the possible exception of *Bleak House*.

He reopens the door upon the dark turn Dickens's life has taken by reminding us that, though he loved it in childhood and often recalled it fondly in his fiction, what Dickens now sees in Rochester (the Cloisterham of the novel) is the nightmare of John Jasper. However, Wilson refuses to look upon this darkened mood as a weakening force in Dickens's art. On the contrary, Wilson says that

> There is plenty of brightness in *Edwin Drood* and something of the good things in life: Mrs. Chrisparkle's

> spices, jams and jellies, Mr. Tartar's shipshape rooms; but
> this brightness has a quality new and queer. . . . The
> descriptions of Cloisterham are among the best written in
> all his fiction. . . . Dickens has found a new intensity . . . has
> . . . dropped away here all the burden of analyzing society
> [and] so far as we can see, is exclusively concerned with a
> psychological problem. The dualism of high and low, rich
> and poor has . . . completely given place to the dualism of
> good and evil. . . . We are back to the fairy tale again. But
> this fairy tale contains no Mr. Pickwick . . . its realest figure
> is Mr. Jasper; and its most powerful effect is procured by an
> instillation into the greenery, the cathedral, the winter sun,
> the sober and tranquil old town, of the suggestion of moral
> uncertainty, of evil.[53]

Complexity of character (getting the bad and the good
together in one person) has of course all along been one of
Wilson's criteria for the mature fictional artist. In this and in his
praise for a moral atmosphere of "uncertainty" that contains, at
the same time, a consciousness of evil, Wilson is following the
mainstream of both modern critical thought and of secular
humanism.

By his talk of dualism Wilson has already succeeded in reminding us of the "Two Scrooges" essay (first version). Now it
crops up even more vividly, with Wilson's comment that "The
Christmas season itself, of which Dickens has been the laureate,
which he has celebrated so often with warm charity, candid
hopes and hearty cheer, is now the appointed moment for the
murder."[54] So we find that the dropped thread from an earlier
part of the essay that had promised us greater psychological involvement and – in *Our Mutual Friend*, gave us a social analysis
instead – has now been picked up.

Wilson's own sociological bias has not retreated entirely,
however. As he sees it, "In this last moment" of the novelist's
life, "the old hierarchy of England does enjoy a sort of triumph
over the weary and debilitated Dickens, because it has made
him accept its ruling that he is a creature irretrievably tainted."
Wilson goes on to make more explicit the link he means to establish between Dickens and the character of John Jasper: "the Victorian hypocrite in its final fictional transformation as Jasper
has developed an insoluble moral problem which is identified
with Dickens' own. As Jasper is eventually to destroy himself.

. . . So Dickens, in putting his nerves to the torture by enacting the murder of Nancy, has been invoking his own death." As he has put it a bit earlier, "The protest against the age has turned into a protest against self."[55]

Wilson asserts that "Dickens in his moral confusion was never in this last phase of his art to dramatize himself completely, never to succeed in coming quite clear." He points out that Dickens "was to leave *Edwin Drood* half-finished, with Jasper's confession just around the corner." The implication is that the "confession" would, symbolically, have accomplished for Dickens, as well as for his fictional creation, Jasper, a reconciliation at last between the two sides of their natures.

But it was not to be. Wilson follows the struggling artist through the penultimate day of his life with a series of stark statements to the effect that Dickens worked on *Drood* in the afternoon, had a stroke while eating dinner, rose, fell to the floor and never regained consciousness. "He died," Wilson concludes, abruptly, "the next afternoon." And so ends the essay which was to become the fertile ground of Dickens study up to the present day.[56]

I would like to turn now to the short introductory comment that precedes the essay proper. I have left it until now because it deals with the question of Wilson's scope and purpose, a subject it seemed more useful to discuss after examining the essay's actual, realized content.

Wilson opens on a note of straightforward exposition, and with a general air of setting the record straight. He takes, first, the measure of Dickens's undeservedly low reputation (as it was then) among scholars. Then, after surveying Dickens criticism up to the time of his own writing, weighing it in the balance and (with the exception of some qualified praise for Chesterton, Gissing, and Shaw) finding it wanting, Wilson goes on to state that

> It is the purpose of this essay to show that we may find in Dickens' work today a complexity and depth to which even Gissing and Shaw have hardly, it seems to me, done justice – an intellectual and artistic interest which makes Dickens loom very large in the whole perspective of the literature of the West.[57]

Aside from its obviously ambitious character, one of the chief things one notices about this statement of purpose is its prodigious scope. We must remember that Wilson was not a Dickens specialist, nor an academic, nor was his field Victorian history – he was in fact a working journalist whose previous critical interest in general had been exclusively in the field of the moderns.

Yet, here, Wilson sets himself a task that involved him in a comprehensive overview of the entire canon of Dickens's work, among the largest in the field of English literature. And here again we meet one of the trademarks of Wilson's criticism, his willingness to undertake mountains of reading preparatory to producing a comparatively short commentary on it. The Dickens preparation, for example, necessitated a familiarity with the existing body of Dickens criticism – which was considerable if, as Wilson decided, ultimately undistinguished – to say nothing of the formidable volume of Dickens's work itself. There are fourteen completed novels (if one counts the *Christmas Books* a novel) and scarcely one of them is under 900 pages. Wilson mentions them all, at least in passing, together with *Sketches by Boz, Master Humphrey's Clock, Pictures from Italy, American Notes*, and *Household Words*.

It is true that only parts of *Pickwick Papers* and *Barnaby Rudge* among the early novels; *Dombey and Son, Bleak House*, and *Little Dorrit* in the middle period; and *Our Mutual Friend* and the incomplete *Edwin Drood* from the last works are gone into in any depth. Despite the sometimes cursory discussion of the individual novels, however, Wilson comes astonishingly close to succeeding in his announced purpose; that is, he delivers a view of Dickens's life and work as a whole that so deepens and complicates the one prevailing at the time of his writing that he may fairly be acknowledged to have supplanted it.

I have tried, in imitating Wilson's here, to suggest the way his own method emerges. His synopses of the novels he is criticizing become, in effect, a running commentary on the methods, values, and preoccupations, as well as the characteristic style, of the artist under discussion. It remains to call attention to the way Wilson goes about presenting the biographical data he juxtaposes with his critical discussion of Dickens's writings, for he bases his critical insights and his psychological speculations on these data.

The facts he uses are the same facts now routinely included in the biographical sketches in the front or back of the plentiful cheap editions of Dickens currently in print. However, at the time Wilson presented his version of them, certain so-called scandalous facts concerning Dickens's relation to the young actress, Ellen Ternan, were still a matter of dispute. It is well to remember here that Edgar Johnson's monumental biography, now generally regarded as definitive – and powerfully corroborative of Wilson's earlier positions at every point – was not yet in existence.[58] (It was itself an early entry in the 1950s renaissance of Dickens studies.)

What Wilson had to work with were the sources he names, drawing particularly on the Forster memoir and on the reminiscences of Dickens's eldest daughter, Kate Perugina, as reported by Gladys Storey. Starting, then, with an autobiographical fragment by Dickens himself, as quoted by Forster, and such supplemental facts as could be gleaned from these scattered sources, Wilson's procedure was to extract the most telling detail, the highlight, the moment of greatest dramatic intensity. These he sets forth in the third person, but in such a way as to invoke a strong air of suppressed outrage and sympathetic response.

Now, the evocation of a specific emotional mood, ostensibly without the author's intrusion and by means of the exquisite modulation of seemingly random objective materials, is a trick of the novelist. (This is most especially one of the modern novelists' devices. Dickens could always do it, and he did it with increasing skill in his later novels. But he so often alternated this method with the older, more blatant, intrusions of the explicitly editorializing narrative voice that we more frequently associate this noveletic technique with the great *fin de siècle* innovators: James, Proust, and Joyce – all, not surprisingly, among Wilson's subjects of sympathetic scrutiny.)

The mastery of such tricks and their incorporation into criticism is unusual in a critic. One might almost say unique but for the example of Wilson's models, Sainte-Beuve and Matthew

Arnold, Taine and Michelet. In Chapter 11, the argument made (perhaps only mock seriously) by Kazin is alluded to, to the effect that such artistry has no place in serious criticism.

Be that as it may, it is certainly integral to Wilson's style; he uses it to great effect again and again throughout his work. And, to this basically noveletic technique one can ascribe the generally elusive character of the structure of any given Wilson work, the Dickens essay included. (In analyzing the structural aspects here, I do not intend to comment further on the weakness of overall structure occasioned by the imperfect translation of their magazine article form into a cohesive whole, on the grounds that these have been dealt with *in situ*.)

However, before turning away entirely from the biographical elements in the essay, it is worth pointing out that these elements form a running narrative through the essay and, in Wilson's handling of them, take on a particularly compelling interest. In his hands, the story of Dickens's life never ceases to be filled with drama, struggle, and, incredibly – since we think we know "how it turned out" from the beginning – with suspense. Curiously, these were always elements Wilson was able to handle better in his criticism than in his fiction.

The essay's structure, then, is organic. I use the term *organic* to suggest that the progression of topics and ideas in the essay is primarily rhetorical and associative, although, of course, Wilson wished each of them to contribute logically to his overall argument. To be sure, the essay begins with Dickens's early life and ends with Dickens's death; it takes up the novels in roughly the order in which Dickens wrote them. And, such chronology gives a rational structure of sorts, but in practice, the essay's ideas tend to be generated out of the text itself.

As Wilson discusses *Bleak House*, for example, he finds himself thinking about the novel of the social group – Balzac comes into his mind and is dismissed; the combination of detective story and moral fable is noted – and Wilson takes the opportunity to follow the one into the novels of Dickens's friend and rival, Wilkie Collins, and the other into the writers in *that* form: Shaw, Galsworthy, and Wells. This is not so much argument as it is relevant spinning. The point is that Wilson's criticism is not purely logical but has elements of fiction, drama, associative projection, thought-spinning, and direct apperception. The same might with justice be said of most effective criticism. The object is to get at what is going on in the work of art under consideration by whatever means.

For example, Wilson never *says* that when he wrote *Little Dorrit*, Dickens was relieving himself of the feelings of humiliation and grief he had harbored toward society and toward his father ever since the old trauma of the debtor's prison and the blacking factory. He merely gives us instances of Dickens behaving in society like a man with a chip on his shoulder prior to the writing of *Little Dorrit* and then gives us instances of society's getting raked over the coals in *Little Dorrit* immediately after.

Similarly, in the final section of the essay, Wilson never tells us how to relate to the discovery that Dickens's alter-ego, Jasper, is both the good man he pretends to be and an evil-hearted villain, nor how to relate *that* discovery to Wilson's assertion that Dickens hoped to exorcize his private demons by having Jasper confront himself and his own double nature and confess to the crime. Neither does he tell us how all this relates to Dickens's own feelings of being a murderer when he makes the suggestion that Dickens is trying, by acting them out on the stage, to cope with the social and sexual frustrations of the Ternan affair.

No, Wilson makes no plain statement of logic about a causal relationship between any of these things – he merely sets them in parataxical relation and so we are the more plausibly and persuasively led to supply the missing premises. Such restraint is really a quality of tactful style and so, once again, a mark of good critical speculation generally. It is also reminiscent of Matthew Arnold's description of good criticism, which, by letting the mind play freely around an object under observation permits us to see the object "as in itself it really is."

From the point of view of its place in Dickens criticism, perhaps the most remarkable aspect of this essay is the date of its composition. A dedicatory line appearing on the first page reads "To the students of English 354, University of Chicago, Summer, 1939," and the magazine articles of which it is composed first began appearing in March 1940. Considering that Orwell's perhaps equally cogent Dickens essay came out in England a little later the same year, 1940 undoubtedly represents a watershed in Dickens studies.

Dickens critics, both British and American, are in general

agreement about the essay's primary importance in the field. George Ford, for instance, calls it "undoubtedly the most important critical statement on Dickens of the last twenty-five years" and goes on to say that "It has directly stimulated much of the best recent criticism of Dickens."[59] Ada Nisbet in her preface to *Dickens Centennial Essays* says, "The story of the shift in the critical estimate of Charles Dickens in the past fifty years is as melodramatic, irrational, and comic as any of the author's inventions" and adds that "the midwives of this rebirth have been the critics led, significantly, by the anti-academic Edmund Wilson."[60] Martin Price, in his introduction to the Dickens volume in the series *Twentieth Century Views* excuses its absence on the grounds of length and calls Wilson's essay one of the "landmarks" of Dickens criticism.[61]

Denis Donoghue, while joining in the acknowledgement of its preeminence, gives what may be a first hint that the wheel has come full circle and that we are about to witness a counter-revolution:

> It is widely agreed that the account of Dickens which Edmund Wilson gave in *The Wound and the Bow* (1941) has had remarkable success with academic readers. It is hardly too much to say that we think of Dickens very largely in Wilson's terms. . . . *The Wound and the Bow* presents Dickens as a victim, a man of obsession, and for that very reason as a poet, an artist of modern fears and divisions . . . he is of the modern dispensation now, a tragic hero. If this means that he is taken seriously as a major artist, companion of Shakespeare, George Eliot, James, Dostoevsky, and Tolstoy, perhaps it makes a happy conclusion.

"But," continues Donoghue, "it is hard to avoid the impression that there is still something askew in our sense of Dickens' art. We seem to have run from one extreme position to another. If an instance is required, there is our failure with the comedy."[62] (This failure, if it exists, Donoghue can hardly ascribe to Wilson, who specifically exempts the comedy from his discussion.)

Such rumbles notwithstanding, there can scarcely be a better testimony to the abundant harvest of Dickens leads that *have* been garnered from within the compass of Wilson's wide-cast net than this assessment by John Gross:

Of all modern writings on Dickens, Edmund Wilson's essay *The Two Scrooges* (1941) is the most dramatic. Wilson makes a brilliant case for Dickens as Dostoevsky's master, rather than a classic of the nursery, by effecting some simple but basic shifts of emphasis. . . . That there is a dark side to Dickens was in itself nothing new; early writers had pointed the way. . . . Mr. Wilson himself acknowledges a special debt to Bernard Shaw. But *The Two Scrooges* is more satisfying than any previous overall interpretation, and it has proved extraordinarily persuasive: its influence is plain to see on the full-length studies of Edgar Johnson, J. Hillis Miller, Jack Lindsay, K. J. Fielding, and Monroe Engel, not to mention dozens of shorter articles.[63]

In summing up the major significance of the essay, then, we might, with justice, say that it reveals Wilson as the chief architect of twentieth-century Dickens studies, one of the liveliest areas in critical literature.

But less pretentious – and I think more pleasing to Wilson, because it is so American – would be the praise accorded him by his friend, John Dos Passos, in his memoir. He said of Wilson as John Adams said of Jefferson, "He was a great rubber off of dust."[64]

CHAPTER NINE

"Harriet Beecher Stowe"

*I*n the synthesizing last chapter of *Axel's Castle*, Wilson seems to move beyond the more conventional humanist taste in poetry displayed by Arnold to find that even poets employing the techniques of Symbolism could, if their language were understood properly, be seen to be engaged in a criticism of life. That he had never really left his basic humanist position is nowhere more apparent, however, than in his chapter on Harriet Beecher Stowe in the opening pages of *Patriotic Gore: Studies in the Literature of the American Civil War*.

Patriotic Gore illustrates the broad humanist interpretation Wilson, like Arnold, was inclined to give the term *literature*. He evidently believes it to encompass virtually the entire field of humane letters. In addition to chapters on novelists such as Harriet Beecher Stowe, George W. Cable, and Kate Chopin and one on poets of the period such as Sidney Lanier, Wilson includes the theological writings and correspondence of Calvin Stowe, the speeches and letters of Abraham Lincoln and Oliver Wendell Holmes, and the diaries of "Three Confederate Ladies" including that of Mary Chestnut.

In "Harriet Beecher Stowe," we see Wilson practicing in its full maturity criticism of a kind so alien to most contemporary American critical practice that it was difficult for some to recognize it as belonging to the field of criticism at all.[1] It is the kind of criticism that, as described by R. S. Crane, seeks "to replace the works we study in the circumstances and temper of their times and see them as expressions and forces as well as subjects of art."[2]

Indeed, Wilson's first concern, in his discussion of *Uncle Tom's Cabin*, is to show us the scope and intensity of the force Mrs. Stowe's novel exerted upon American history. He tells us that

> This novel by Harriet Beecher Stowe was one of the greatest successes of American publishing history as well as one of the most influential books – immediately influential, at any rate – that have ever appeared in the United States. A year after its publication on March 20, 1852, it had sold 305,000 copies in America and something like two million and a half copies in English and in translation all over the world. As for its influence, it is enough to remember the greeting of Lincoln to Mrs. Stowe when she was taken to call on him at the White House: "So this is the little lady who made this big war."[3]

Noting that the influence of the novel dropped off at the close of the war in as pronounced a fashion as it had formerly been manifested, Wilson's next concern is to disabuse us of the idea "that *Uncle Tom* was a mere propaganda novel which disappeared when it had accomplished its purpose and did not, on its merits, deserve to live."

Pointing out that the novel "continued to be read in Europe" and that it was popular in pre-Revolutionary Russia, Wilson concludes that a more likely explanation of its postwar neglect "has been due to the strained situation between the North and the South":

> The Northerners, embarrassed by the memory of the war and not without feelings of guilt, did not care to be reminded of the issue which had given rise to so much bitterness. In the South, where before the war any public discussion of slavery had by general tacit agreement been banned, nothing afterwards was wanted less than Northern criticism of pre-war conditions.[4]

Before turning to the novel itself, there are other misconceptions regarding *Uncle Tom's Cabin* that Wilson is at pains to set aside. These have mostly to do with the comic and

melodramatic stereotypes for which several of the characters –
Little Eva, Simon Legree, and Uncle Tom among them – have
come to stand in the public mind. He points out that they were
largely the result of "dramatizations in which Mrs. Stowe had no
hand." Although, Wilson says, the stage versions "kept at first
relatively close to the novel" over the next half-century "they
grotesquely departed from it." So much was this the case that

> By the late seventies, *Uncle Tom's Cabin* was half a minstrel
> show and half a circus. . . . The original characters were
> now sometimes doubled: you had two Topsys, two Lawyer
> Markses, two Uncle Toms. Topsy sang comic songs, and Un-
> cle Tom was given minstrel interludes in which he would do
> a shuffle and breakdown.[5]

At the same time that the novel was being travestied in this
way, Wilson tells us, "on account of sectional feeling" the
original work was being read neither in the schools nor at home
"as the New England classics were." He concludes that "by the
early nineteen-hundreds few young people had any at all clear
idea of what *Uncle Tom's Cabin* contained. One could in fact
grow up in the United States without ever having seen a copy."

Having thus prepared the ground by clearing away the
underbrush, much as he had done in the opening pages of his
Dickens essay, Wilson is ready to state his principal thesis
regarding the novel: "It is a much more impressive work than
one has ever been allowed to suspect."[6]

As we follow the argument and note the evidence that
Wilson marshals in support of his thesis, we become more and
more aware that we are in the presence of a critic who can be
understood only in humanist terms. Such a critic attempts to
give us, as Crane says, "insights into the larger moral and
political values of literature." In *Patriotic Gore*, Wilson does this
by displaying the insights Mrs. Stowe's novels give us into the
issue of slavery and into Calvinism as forces in American life.

Crane's description goes on to state that such a critic explores, too, "the other organic relations with human nature and
human experience in which literature is involved."[7] These relations become a key factor in Wilson's aesthetic judgment of the
Stowe novel. For him, the effective rendering of "human
nature" and "human experience" in terms of life-like fictional

characters is of sufficient value to supersede other artistic considerations. It is, from a humanist standpoint, a supreme artistic good.

Here is Wilson on the subject of *Uncle Tom's* characters:

> Out of a background of undistinguished narrative, inelegantly and carelessly written, the characters leap into being with a vitality that is all the more striking for the ineptitude of the prose that presents them. These characters – like those of Dickens . . . in his early phase – express themselves a good deal better than the author expresses herself. The Shelbys and George Harris and Eliza and Aunt Chloe and Uncle Tom project themselves out of the void. They come before us arguing and struggling like real people who cannot be quiet.[8]

Is verisimilitude, then, the only artistic virtue to be found in *Uncle Tom's Cabin?* Not at all, in Wilson's view: "the farther one reads in *Uncle Tom,* the more one becomes aware that a critical mind is at work, which has the complex situation in a very firm grip and which, no matter how vehement the characters become, is controlling and coordinating their interrelations."

Significantly, this virtue, too, is basically humanist. The rendering of order out of chaotic emotions and events is, after all, an aesthetic principle that entered the humanist tradition not with Matthew Arnold but with the early Greeks.

Wilson goes further in the direction of classical humanism when he praises the novel for its "objectivity," its "statesmanship," and for the "universality" of its view, which "has nothing of the partisan mentality."

> the novel is by no means an indictment drawn up by New England against the South. Mrs. Stowe has, on the contrary, been careful to contrive her story in such a way that the Southern states and New England shall be shown as involved to an equal degree in . . . slavery . . . and that the emphasis shall all be laid on the impracticability of slavery as a permanent institution. The author, if anything, leans over backwards in trying to make it plain that the New Englanders are as much to blame as the South and to exhibit the Southerners in a favorable light.[9]

Wilson's enthusiasm for Mrs. Stowe's ability to create life-like characters is again evident in an extensive passage he includes at this point in the essay, which is designed to demonstrate their interest and diversity. In it, he praises the range of tragic and comic effects she can produce through her dramatic portrayal of them. Wilson wants us to appreciate the novel, however, not only for the vividness of its characters but also for its depiction of a specific historical, social, and cultural world:

> There is, in fact, in *Uncle Tom*, as well as in its successor, *Dred*, a whole drama of manners and morals and intellectual points of view which corresponds somewhat to the kind of thing that was then being done by Dickens, and was soon to be continued by Zola, for the relations of the social classes, and which anticipates such later studies of two sharply contrasting peoples uncomfortably involved with one another as . . . *John Bull's Other Island* of Bernard Shaw or E. M. Forster's *A Passage to India.*[10]

That one should be asked to take an interest in literature for what it can teach us about "two sharply contrasting peoples uncomfortably involved with one another" or, indeed, for its picture of manners or morals or the relations between social classes would no doubt strike the strictly textual critic as most odd if not downright heretical.

But Wilson is, of course, being completely traditional in this view. The sort of interest he displays here manifests his implicit belief in the capacity of literature to impart a broad understanding of human life and society. It is an intrinsic aspect not only of Wilson's humanism but of humanism in general, which takes literature to be, as William Phillips puts it, "an instrument, as it were, of social and intellectual liberation." Outside of feminist circles, an interest in the social ramifications of literature is most frequently found today in European Marxist critics, notably Terry Eagleton. This is not surprising when we recall that Marx's own concept of literature shared with humanism the perspective that views society as an intricate interrelated organism.

Eagleton's view is very similar: Having identified

Marxism's story as the story of the struggle "of men and women to free themselves from exploitation and oppression," Eagleton goes on to admit that relevance to that struggle of a Marxist reading of *Paradise Lost* or *Middlemarch* is not immediately apparent. But, he continues, it would be a mistake to confine the study of literature within academic archives, for literature may be viewed (as indeed it *is* viewed by Marxist critics) as having "a significant, if not central, role to play in the transformation of human societies."

> Marxist criticism is part of a larger body of theoretical analysis which aims to understand ideologies – the ideas, values and feelings by which men experience their societies at various times. And certain of these ideas, values and feelings are available to us only in literature. To understand ideologies is to understand both the past and the present more deeply . . .

"And," Eagleton continues, "such understanding contributes to our liberation."[11]

Wilson's own Marxism, and his Freudianism as well, although both still living presences in the mind he brings to bear upon his criticism of Stowe, have become by now (he is in his sixties) so interwoven with his critical outlook as a whole that they must be almost entirely inferred. Yet, both are there.

Before attempting to unravel the Marxist and Freudian threads in "Harriet Beecher Stowe," however, it should be noted that Wilson's historical consciousness and his historical-comparative method are quite obviously present in the essay. The preceding quote is an example. In it, Wilson compares *Uncle Tom's Cabin* to Dickens, Zola, Shaw, and Forster, mixing both genres and nationalities as was his deliberate practice.

Later, he attempts to place it in the historical context of nineteenth-century world literature. Ruling out comparison with Turgenev's *A Sportsman's Sketches* on grounds of the Stowe novel's lack of sophistication, Wilson rejects, too, any close kinship to the novels of the Brontë sisters. (In an aside that sounds sexist today, he points out that the Brontë subjects are "not social problems but passionate feminine daydreams.") Wilson finally decides that *Uncle Tom* is most "closely akin to some such early novel of Dickens as *Oliver Twist*," and he notes that "Dickens, who admired the book, was correct in detecting his own influence."[12]

Continuing in his comparative mode, Wilson suggests that the "series of wanderings" in which Stowe involves her characters "progressively and excitingly reveal, like the visits of Chichikov in Gogol's *Dead Souls*, the traits of a whole society." A critic less interested in "cross-fertilization" might well have chosen to compare them, rather, to the wanderings of Huck Finn. Perhaps realizing that his point might need expansion – to those unfamiliar with Gogol, at any rate – Wilson illustrates it further with synopses of the "wanderings" in *Uncle Tom*. Synopsis, of course, plays an important part in Wilson's critical method. Here, he uses it to display Mrs. Stowe's powers of laying bare the "traits of a whole society": that is, of America under slavery.

This close involvement with the text is followed by a withdrawal in which he makes a critical judgment – a pattern we saw often in his essay on Yeats and that, in fact, constitutes a regular feature in Wilson's work. The judgment he makes in this case, as we would expect from Wilson who, we know, likes to see "a whole society" spread out before him, is favorable: "The creator of this long sequence, with its interconnecting episodes of riverboat, tavern and slave market, was" he says of Mrs. Stowe, "no contemptible novelist."[13]

Wilson follows this pronouncement with roughly twenty pages of what the new critic would surely deem an entirely digressive biographical account of Harriet Beecher Stowe's life in the years immediately preceding *Uncle Tom's Cabin*. However infrequently practiced among "new" or current academic critics, we may recognize it, nevertheless, as one of the legitimate forms of critical exploration described by Crane: an exploration, that is, of the "temper and circumstances" out of which the Stowe novel was born.

Wilson makes use of his intellectual and artistic skills to bring before us in these pages a diverse combination of factors and to do so in a manner which compels our interest. Among the subjects he covers are these: the religious philosophy of Calvinism, the political motivations of the abolitionists, the social situa-

tion of Cincinnati, Ohio, in the 1840s, the domestic relations between Harriet Stowe and her preacher-husband in that period of
their marriage when they had often to be apart, the inter-
denominational conflict taking place on theological grounds between rival factions of the Protestant Church (an aspect of the
larger movement of religious revival in America known as the
Enlightenment) and the economic hardships of the Stowe household, seen in relation to the surrounding environment.

Regarding the latter, Wilson writes:

> A series of cholera epidemics had been added, in the years of
> their residence, to the other nerve-taxing elements of Cin-
> cinnati life; and while Harriet was handling the household
> alone, this series reached a terrible climax. At the peak of
> the new epidemic, a thousand people a week were dying.
> The city was filled with the fumes of the soft coal that was
> burned as a disinfectant, and everything was black with
> soot. There was general demoralization, and many people
> less austere than the Beechers and Stowes did their best to
> stay drunk all the time.[14]

True, we know the link that exists between Wilson and
Sainte-Beuve. We have heard Walter Jackson Bate tell us that it
was a principal tenet of Sainte-Beuve to deem "nothing relating
to the life, experience, and art of the writer" as alien to the critic.
We know of Wilson's enthusiasm for the kind of criticism that,
like Taine's, creates the creators of literature themselves as
characters in a larger social and cultural drama. Yet, the
presence of this paragraph in what purports to be a chapter of
literary criticism will remain inexplicable unless we see in it both
a Marxist and a Freudian dimension.

Only when we look back at Marx's view that consciousness
is formed by life and not life by consciousness and even entertain the possibility delicately suggested here that the remarkable ability apparent in Harriet Stowe's novel to enter into the
black experience may have been aided by her having been projected for a time quite literally into a black world—only then
does Wilson's probable reason for including such a paragraph
become understandable.

He saw the way Stowe's imagination could have been
worked on in such a situation, how, in the modern parlance, her

consciousness could have been raised by a state of emergency in which external differences were obliterated. What is certain is that he pays meticulous attention to the litany of Harriet Stowe's hardships:

> The Stowe children's pet dog died; then their old colored laundress died – the twins helped to make her a shroud. Then Harriet's most recent baby began to have convulsions, and in four days it, too, was dead. Harriet herself was attacked by cramps, and the doctor assumed she was dying; but her father . . . was back now to give her support. The indomitable old preacher . . . gave Harriet a dose of brandy, which at first made her delirious, but he seems to think it pulled her through.[15]

Certainly the insights into the human mind afforded by Marx and Freud lend support to Wilson's suggestion here and in related passages that the stoicism of Calvinist households under such circumstances bore analogies to black experience that proved useful to Stowe as a novelist. Among these analogies were the necessity of suffering the pain of separation of one family member from another, a pain suffered by so many black families under slavery, and the necessity of suffering oppression in a silence dictated by one's class. In the case of the black servants in Stowe's novel, silence was dictated by slavery; in Stowe's own case, it came from a rigid religious upbringing. Wilson states the parallel in these terms: "in the first sixteen years of her marriage, poor Harriet was suffering from miseries that must have been as little avowed . . . as the ever-rankling anxieties of slavery."

He suggests that the threats, the harassing persecutions, the outbreaks of violence, and the sudden bereavements that are all prominent elements in *Uncle Tom's Cabin* "had been lived in the Beecher home, where the trials and tribulations, as they used to be called, of the small family world inside were involved with, were merged in the travail of the nation to which it belonged."[16]

Although Wilson suggests that these awful domestic experiences "energized" her famous novel, he notes that something more was needed to bring Harriet Stowe to the point of actually taking up her pen. That required both a more comfortable economic situation (Calvin Stowe received a professorship at

Bowdoin College, which resulted in the family's removal to a better life in Maine) and the historical stimulus of the Fugitive Slave Bill, enacted in 1850. Under the bill, Wilson notes, "Non-Southerners were now held responsible for Negroes who had fled from the South." The result was that the entire Beecher and Stowe families were drawn still more actively into the abolitionist cause. Harriet's brother, Henry Ward Beecher, says Wilson, preached abolition "from his pulpit in Plymouth Church, Brooklyn," and both he and her sister-in-law urged Harriet Stowe to "write something that will make this whole nation feel what an accursed thing slavery is."[17]

All of this, one notes, is distinctly less "inward" than the terms in which we are accustomed to learning about the artistic genesis of a literary work. Wilson himself acknowledges this and quotes a statement by Henry James on the subject. He refers to James as "that expert professional" and recalls that, although James had felt "obliged" to pay Stowe his tribute, he had described *Uncle Tom's Cabin* as a novel that "constitutes a perhaps unique case of a book which has made its impression without the author's having concerned herself with literary problems at all."[18]

The immediate factor precipitating the writing of the novel was, as Wilson records it, Harriet Stowe's meeting at the house of her brother "a Negro preacher who had once been a slave and both of whose arms had been crippled by flogging, but who had succeeded in escaping to Canada and getting himself an education."

"Shortly afterward," Wilson goes on, "When she had just taken communion, the death of Uncle Tom was revealed to her 'almost as a tangible vision.' . . . She went home and . . . the rest of Uncle Tom's story 'rushed upon her with a vividness and importunity that would not be denied.'"[19]

After giving a resume of the publishing history of *Uncle Tom's Cabin* and citing the economic gains it brought to the Stowe household, Wilson is moved to comment that "all of her subsequent books were written in comfort and security and in relative tranquillity of spirit, and none of them – perhaps for this reason – approaches the power of *Uncle Tom*."[20] Evidently, he still subscribes to the idea contained in his essay on Philoctetes,

"The Wound and the Bow," written fourteen years before: the idea that art grows out of suffering. This, in turn, is probably a remnant of the classical humanist view that wisdom grows out of suffering.

His estimate of their diminished power notwithstanding, Wilson goes on to give dutiful attention to the later books of Harriet Stowe. First, though, he quotes the explanation given by one of her closest friends of their "astonishing slackness of narrative line" and their "failure in dramatic imagination." According to the friend, Mrs. James Fields,

> The truth was that Mrs. Stowe had in a sense no real interest in literature. Books as a medium of the ideas of the age, as the promulgators of morals and religion, were of course like the breath of her life, but a study of the literature of the past as the only true foundation for literature of the present was outside the pale of her occupations, and for the larger portion of her life outside of her interest.[21]

With nearly all biographical evidence tending in this way to lead us outside the range of literary concerns, we may expect to get in this essay – and we do get it – a picture of what extraliterary interests Wilson feels may legitimately be brought to bear upon a work by the humanist critic. Before we pursue him in this course, however, it will be well to note that he does not altogether discount an artistic dimension in his author.

On the artistic side, Wilson has this to say for her:

> Though it is true that Harriet Beecher Stowe was not really interested in literature, in Mrs. Field's high Bostonian sense, her literary gift was real. She can make us see a person and hear him talk, and she can render a scene or a landscape by a process that can only be likened to a flinging out of handfuls of words which succeed in conveying impressions with a precision that is rather surprising in view of the looseness of her language, of her having no sense whatever of the construction of a sentence or a paragraph, and hardly even of syntax.[22]

Outside of the humanist critical tradition Wilson represents, it is difficult to imagine the practitioner of any of today's critical approaches, with the possible exception of the feminist critic, writing the following words with any similar sense of approbation: "It is as if she were communicating directly – that is, without the artist's deliberate skill – the perceptions of a sensitive woman . . . she will not thrill you as a teller of tales, but she does throw a good deal of light on certain aspects of American society."[23]

As the foregoing suggests and as the balance of his essay confirms, Wilson is of the opinion that some things that literature does supersede considerations of surface polish. Stowe's artlessly effective showers of words and her natural mimetic gift seem to exhaust Wilson's catalogue of her literary merits, yet the historical value of her work becomes, in his expanded humanist frame, a reason for retaining even her lesser works in the canon.

Wilson goes on in warm praise of Stowe's contribution, in the form of her fiction, of "a chronicle of religious history." And when he says "if you want to know what life was like in a parsonage at the beginning of the nineteenth century, at a time when the Puritan clergy were losing their old power . . . these novels will take you there," we can almost hear the note of gratification in his voice.

He has mastered another area of experience, cleared up a puzzlement over the background of America's transformation from Puritanism to Capitalism – a background of which, thanks to Harriet Stowe, he can now "get the hang." Wilson notes that "Her unique, her invaluable picture of American clerical life extends from the end of the eighteenth century . . . when Newport . . . is the home of [the] Jonathan Edwards follower . . . and the doctrine of Predestination hangs over the pious world, to the seventies . . . when Newport has become a playground for the conspicuous-wasters of New York."[24]

In view of the harmony one senses, in this part of the essay, between Mrs. Stowe's religious sympathies and Wilson's Marxist ones, it begins to seem possible that the humanist umbrella can spread over a broad range of proletarian, patrician, and ecclesiastical lineages, both Christian and secular in character. The unifying principle, at least in this instance, is provided by a common condemnation of the mercantile spirit. We have seen

Wilson identify with the same sentiments when he finds them in Dickens and Henry James.

The degree to which Wilson in this essay goes in for psychological interpretations of his author is not very marked. However, the last phase of Stowe's work affords him an opening for some Freudian account of her makeup. It centers on an episode in Harriet Stowe's life that brought her into contact with Byron and led her to write a controversial book about him, or rather about Byron, his sister-in-law, and his wife, entitled *Lady Byron Vindicated.*

As we have seen him do in his essay on Dickens, Wilson makes only an implied connection between Stowe and the characters in her books. He says:

> The truth is that this sort of character – sophisticated and fearless – rather piques and excites Mrs. Stowe. . . . We . . . feel it . . . in her writings on the Byron affair. Lady Byron, whom she had known in England, had told her the then horrifying story of the poet's relations with his halfsister and had convinced her that Byron . . . had treated his wife brutally and had afterwards worked systematically to present her in an odious light and himself as the injured party.[25]

Noting that the book Mrs. Stowe wrote about these matters raised an outcry from Byron's admirers, Wilson nevertheless wishes to put it on record that "her handling of the Byron affair is not in the least hysterical: she shows a good deal of sympathetic insight into both Lady Byron and Byron." And he credits her with what is of course a signal humanist virtue – disinterestedness – when he notes that "Through it all she never lost her admiration for the latter."[26]

The implication – and it remains only an implication, as I have suggested – is that, the child of a clergyman herself, Stowe could empathize with minister's son rebels of the type of Aaron Burr and Lord Byron and even find a vicarious release in their rebellion.

Returning to the chronological account of all of Stowe's work, Wilson dismisses three of her later novels on the grounds that they are as devoid of substance as a squeezed-out "bath sponge." Ever scrupulously fair, however, he notes that, these dismal performances notwithstanding, "at the end of her life, she succeeds in writing another not uninteresting book."

This is *Poganuc People*, and we discover that, in Wilson's view, it owes its comparative success to being the story of Harriet Beecher herself. Touching his characteristic twin poles, Wilson hints there is both psychological and sociological significance in Stowe's departure from autobiographical veracity at the book's end:

> it is curious that Harriet Beecher Stowe, writing in her middle sixties, should have arranged for her heroine a destiny which was really a young girl's dream, which exempted her from all the circumstances that had molded her own personality and given her work its importance – the ordeal of Cincinnati, the lifetime of clerical associations, the responsibilities of a public figure – that, as if with a certain wistfulness, she should have married her "little American princess" to an affluent business man and assigned her to a comfortable position among the "matronage of Boston."[27]

Having watched Wilson expend so much "sympathetic imagination" in his attempt to show us all the reasons why we should take an interest in her work, it comes as something of a surprise to learn from him, in this more intimate look at her, that she was rather a cold person. He speculates that her "life-long habit of detachment made her strength as a social critic but it insulated her somewhat from her fellows."

Still more surprising, in light of his praise for the life and vividness he had found in *Uncle Tom's Cabin*, is Wilson's disclosure that, finally, her work displays "a certain lack of warmth."[28] As it happens, warmth is one of the things Wilson is least willing to do without in a novel. At this point, however, what is of interest is the fact that he is able to muster considerable support for his position: "When we come to read her in bulk, we are obliged to conclude that the tragic deaths she inflicts on so many of her heroines are not merely due to literary fashion. . . . The author, we realize, is happiest when . . . she can irrevocably separate her lovers by arranging to have one of them die."

Wilson attributes Harriet Stowe's tendencies in this maudlin direction to the death of her mother when she was five. And he goes on to note that the posthumous influence of these dead heroines "as a permanently uplifting ideal" is made to hold out "more real benefit to her lover than she could ever have been in the flesh if she had lived to be his earthly bride."[29] However touching the biographical genesis of this trait in her work might be, Wilson tells us, he finds it difficult to sympathize when the result is that we are cut off from the emotions of her characters.

Once again, we note, he has in a sense validated his intrusion into the psychological makeup of his subject by showing us the literary consequences of the psychological situation he is investigating. The chilly idealism that Stowe superimposes upon the emotions her characters are supposed to be feeling "in all their earthly relations," says Wilson, represents a serious flaw in her work. He suggests that it is "probably one of the factors that have kept most of her novels from being much read."[30]

In the final paragraph of his essay, Wilson sums up:

> Mrs. Stowe had got rid of Calvinism; she had dramatized the teaching of Jesus. Yet her God was still a God of Justice rather than a God of love. Her pity runs to sentimentality, which is to say that it is sometimes false, but she is never an obnoxious moralist: her judgment of men is quite sober and her judgment of ideas quite sound.[31]

Wilson here is a critic who, having discovered "the secret line of pain" under the writer's brow, nevertheless strives to display the work of that writer in as full and sympathetic a light as possible and who thinks it worthwhile to value in its social dimension that which reveals "the traits of a whole society" and in its theological one that which promotes moral harmony and moral completeness. In "Harriet Beecher Stowe," then, Wilson employs the humanist approach not only to connect literature with life but to connect both to a significant period in American history. A measure of the success of his effort is attested to by Thomas F. Gossett in his recent book, *Uncle Tom's Cabin and American Culture*. Gossett tells us that "More than anyone else, it was probably Edmund Wilson who led other critics to take another look at the novel, one that was more favorable than traditional views of the past."[32]

CHAPTER TEN

"The Strange Case of Pushkin and Nabokov"

*I*n the pages that follow I propose, first, to give a brief description of Wilson's last published volume of criticism, *A Window on Russia*, and to assess the way it relates to his work as a whole.[1] I will then turn to a more concentrated look at one particular essay, "The Strange Case of Pushkin and Nabokov." This essay consists mainly of Wilson's review of Nabokov's translation of *Eugene Onegin*; it reflects the storm of controversy generated by that review in that, in it, Wilson attempts to answer Nabokov's objections as well as to offer, belatedly and cursorily, his critical evaluation of Nabokov's novels. Our best hope of understanding the literary values posed and counterposed involves moving beyond the text set out in the essay itself to explore the contrasting critical values of the two antagonist-friends, Wilson and Nabokov. Thanks to the publication of their correspondence, that contrast emerges with a new clarity.[2]

Wilson's valedictory critical volume, *A Window on Russia* was published in 1972, the year of his death. It is in many ways a typical Wilson performance, reflecting many traits identified in Part I of this study as part of his critical signature. Like virtually all of his critical output, this volume is a pastiche of writings on various subjects first published in periodical form.

Unlike the others we have looked at here, however, this last volume professes to have no thematic continuity. It is, simply, as

179

Wilson describes it, a collection of "all the pieces on Russian subjects that I have not collected in other volumes." One or two of the pieces included are not on writers at all but are discourses on the Russian language. The others range over the field of Russian letters of the past, from the best-known names such as Chekhov, Tolstoy and Gogol, to the little-known Tyutchev and Sukhovo-Kobylin, and from the work of major modern Russians such as Nabokov and Solzhenitsyn to the memoirs of Stalin's daughter, Svetlana.

It would be misleading, however, to take one's impression of the book from its author's rather self-deprecating estimate; that is, as merely "a handful of disconnected pieces, written at various times" (the dates of composition range from the 1940s to 1971), "anything but comprehensive," and with "no logical coherence."[3] Such a description gives no fair idea of the considerable interest of many of the essays in this volume.

In fact, throughout the book, Wilson *does* follow a theme of sorts: he is interested in broadening and complicating the foreign reader's received ideas about the character of Russian literature. These received ideas he sums up, in the first of the literary essays, as follows:

(1) That the Russians are formless and unkempt;
(2) That they are gloomy;
(3) That they are crudely realistic;
(4) That they are morbid and hysterical;
(5) That they are mystical.[4]

Such notions, says Wilson, are the product of misapplied generalizations. To the extent that there is any truth to them at all, he says, they apply to only one of the major Russian writers – to Dostoevsky. In the essays that follow Wilson repeatedly demonstrates and emphasizes the many and various un-"Russian" traits and influences of which Russian literature is, in fact, made up.

This means that we see him applying the comparative mode often in these pages, sometimes moving not only across national boundaries but across artistic mediums as well. For example, he compares Gogol to Hawthorne and Poe in order to show that Gogol possesses a distinctly gothic strain.[5] To demystify some of the reverence with which Chekhovian comedy is often approached – and to show its more robust and popular side – Wilson draws comparisons between Chekhov and Mark Twain.[6] He even draws upon the other arts for his comparisons, as when he makes an association between the careers of Pushkin and Mozart.[7]

The literary essays in this last critical volume demonstrate that one of the critical preoccupations Wilson still has very much in view is historical consciousness, a sensitivity to the *Zeitgeist* of whatever period he explores.

In this collection, his interest in the connections between literature and life is especially evident in the essays on Gogol and Turgenev. Both are reminiscent of his earlier essay on Dickens in the way they combine Freudian and Marxist insights with his powers of biography to produce compelling portraits of literary personality. Both are redolent, too, with the "sympathetic imagination" Edel speaks of; that is, a compassion for the artists' struggles and an ability to relate those struggles to the art they produced.

This is, of course, Wilson's "wound and bow" theory, and it is particularly apparent in the present collection in "Turgenev and the Life-Giving Drop."[8] In this essay, he first lays before us a harsh and terrible picture of Turgenev's mother and the social turmoil out of which her character was formed. He then notes that

> The content of Ivan's early work is mostly in one way or another a product of his mother's personality. In the stories Turgenev wrote before 1847 . . . there is an alternation of two main themes. The salient one is a force of evil so powerful and so audacious that no resistance is possible – a force that, as long as his mother was living, appeared in masculine form.[9]

The second turns out to be a complimentary preoccupation with timid or inadequate men "who let women down." "Here," Wilson notes, "we find a situation which is to run through all of his work and to have its great development in *Fathers and Sons*."[10]

In addition to employing it to identify Turgenev's two main themes, Wilson finds another literary application for his researches into Turgenev's life. He relates Turgenev's sufferings under his mother's domination to the author's ability to identify sympathetically with Russia's oppressed serfs. "In the case of *Sportsman's Sketches*," he writes, "the whole impact of the book is a protest against the antiquated system of serfholding" that his mother "stood for" (Wilson has portrayed her for us earlier as the "ogreish" mistress of thousands of serfs). He now emphasizes Turgenev's power to bring out this element of protest without introducing into his writing any "explicit sympathy for the serfs or overt condemnation of the masters."

Wilson has already praised a similar trait in Pushkin, one that never fails to elicit his admiration:

> He had been able to learn from Pushkin, whom he took for his master, the trick of evading the censorship by telling a story in such a way as to make it convey its moral without any explicit statement, and he was the first Western writer of fiction to perfect the modern art of implying social criticism through a narrative that is presented objectively, organized economically, and beautifully polished in style. . . . *Madame Bovary* was not begun till 1851 and not published till 1857. *A Sportsman's Sketches* appeared as a book in 1852.[11]

It seems to have been vital to Wilson's acceptance of what he terms Turgenev's "pessimism" – the ingredient in Turgenev's stories that shows the "permanent stamp of an oppressive, a completely hopeless and a permanently harrowing experience" – that he can find in Turgenev's art, nevertheless, this implicit social criticism.[12] The man suffered but he created, as Taine had said, and in what he created there was something that can be seen to provide, for the creator and the reader alike, what Frederick Crews has termed "a sign of victory for the ego, if not in 'happy endings,' then in the triumph of form over chaos, meaning over panic, mediated claims over sheer psychic spillage."[13]

It is time to turn to the essay in this volume called "The Strange Case of Pushkin and Nabokov."[14] Having made the point that many of the entries in *A Window on Russia* are typical of Wilson's critical practice as a whole, it must be noted from the outset that his essay on Nabokov's translation of the Pushkin work is decidedly atypical. For one thing, Wilson's sharp attack and Nabokov's equally sharp counterattack were immediately taken up as a kind of literary *cause célèbre*. This quickly made personalities the key, rendering reasoned discourse about the issues involved extremely difficult, both then and now.

The almost unrelievedly negative nature of Wilson's critical assessments in the review were seldom examined for whatever validity they might have. Yet, even though its tone is decidedly uncharacteristic (no amiable, sympathetic, humane notes are apparent anywhere in it), the review is so far the recognizable product of its author that it supports with textual documentation every point it raises.

Nevertheless, the attention of the gallery was focused upon speculation regarding Wilson's probable motive in reviewing so harshly the work of a man avowed to be his friend. The reason usually settled upon was jealousy (combined with *hubris*). But, as V. S. Pritchett notes in rejecting this view with regard to Wilson's distaste for *Lolita*: "Some have thought that Wilson's distaste for [it] sprang from his envy of the success of Nabokov's book, but Wilson was the least envious, most generous of men, as generous as the forthright Dr. Johnson, more particularly the Johnson of 'Lives of the Poets.'"[15]

Whatever the motive behind Wilson's critical attack, it should be remembered that, in his reply, Nabokov gave as good as he got. No attempt will be made at this stage to declare one or the other the winner. The general impression is abroad, however, that Wilson was bested by Nabokov in the Pushkin affair. Further, that he deserved to be, for his temerity in arguing with a native-born Russian over the fine points of his own language and for presuming to instruct an imaginative writer of Nabokov's stature in matters of artistic interpretation. It is only fair to say that this study proposes to take a somewhat different view of the matter, by no means on the grounds of sympathies reposited in Wilson but strictly on the merits of the case. Actually, it is hoped that justice can be rendered to both writers, as opponents truly worthy of one another, doing battle over issues about which they both cared deeply.

The ostensible bases of their disagreement in the matter of Pushkin's *Eugene Onegin* lay in two main aspects of the

Nabokov connection with it, as translator and as commentator. The first pits Wilson against Nabokov in terms of the view each took of the proper nature and execution of the task of translation, the second pits them against one another in terms of the view each took of the proper nature and execution of the task of criticism.

From one standpoint this particular essay, though atypical, does provide a most fitting last entry in this resume of Wilson's critical practice, because of the critical discussion with Nabokov it generated. The revelations that emerge from the sharp exchanges between the two throw into high relief a number of the features that have been prevalent in Wilson's work from the beginning.

At the same time there are underlying factors in the Nabokov-Wilson quarrel that, as we examine them, will be seen to go to the very heart of what each brings to his view of the nature of reality and the nature of art. It was not so much that Wilson and Nabokov had incompatible views in these important matters, but they approached them from such radically discrete angles and worked them out to such radically discrete ends that, except for their brief contact at the point of the literary text itself, their views seem totally unrelated to each other.

Indeed, so complete is their "communication gap" that tracing the trajectory of their inevitable disagreements is positively painful. Yet, it will be profitable to do so because of the insights it yields into the strengths and weaknesses of the humanist approach.

I have suggested that, in the battle between Wilson and Nabokov over *Onegin*, the two were equally matched adversaries. In some respects, it must be acknowledged, what that comes down to is that they were equally matched in error. Each adopted an untenable position and clung to it, resolutely ignoring any evidence to the contrary in spite of the claims of each to be on a disinterested lookout for the truth – in this case, the "truth" that would do justice in translation to what both acknowledged to be Pushkin's masterpiece.

Nabokov's conception of what constitutes adequate translation is, if not precisely untenable, definitely *outré*. Wilson, on the other hand, is on equally shaky, if not shakier, ground when he undertakes to quarrel with Nabokov over his Russian – a language Wilson learned as an adult – and to correct him on points of Russian grammar and prosody.

His rationale for this is Nabokov's own assertion to the effect that, after years of exile and of writing and working in English, his Russian was getting "rusty"; and he urges the further point that Russians of Nabokov's upper-class background frequently spoke better French, English, and German than Russian because at home they had limited exposure to their native tongue.[16] But this appears to be an almost willful misapprehension of the situation.

Matters only grow worse when, matching arrogance for arrogance, Nabokov responds by undertaking to instruct Wilson in *his* native language, giving him lessons in English grammar and prosody.[17] Not surprisingly, bilingual referees of these bouts have declared that Nabokov is most often right about Russian, Wilson about English.

In two key points in the matter of scholarship there is pretty clearly another draw, with Wilson being in the stronger position on the matter of whether Pushkin knew Byron in the original, whereas Nabokov is pretty clearly on solider ground in the matter of his appendix setting forth a recognizably Russian system of versification, instead of being, as Wilson charges, peculiar to himself.

"The Strange Case of Pushkin and Nabokov" originally ran as a review in the *New York Review of Books* (15 July 1965).[18] It begins with Wilson's statement of his overall reaction to Nabokov's translation of *Onegin*, that he finds it "something of a disappointment." Describing himself as "a personal friend of Mr. Nabokov – for whom he feels a warm affection sometimes chilled by exasperation" he goes on to say that, his friendship with and his admiration for Nabokov notwithstanding, he "does not propose to mask" his disappointment in the ensuing review.

The first matter of importance over which he expresses that disappointment concerns the theory of translation on which Nabokov's whole program in the *Onegin* effort is based.

Note: Here, immediately arises the problem inherent in any attempt to do justice to Wilson's essay and Nabokov's translation: I refer to the necessary prerequisite of expertise in Russian, an expertise I lack. However, it is possible, I think, to come up with something like a comparative evaluation of Wilson's points by setting them alongside those of a commentator on the translation of *Onegin* who *does* possess it. I propose, therefore, to begin by enumerating Wilson's objections to the Nabokov work and to compare them with the evaluations of Alexander Gerschenkron.[19]

The basis of Wilson's first objection to Nabokov's translation – bearing, as it does, on his contention that it lacks readability – could scarcely be more fundamental or sweeping. It means that he quarrels with the very premise upon which Nabokov has determined that he will proceed. And here the fact that Wilson has written on the subject of Pushkin before helps us to understand his attitude and to appreciate that, whatever the defects of his tone in the present instance, the literary basis of his position regarding the nature and possibilities of translating this poet are neither lightly arrived at nor lightly held.

As early as 1936, Wilson was manifesting a good deal of sensitivity to the nature of the problems involved:

> the poetry of Pushkin is particularly difficult to translate. It is difficult for the same reason that Dante is difficult: because it says so much in so few words, so clearly and yet so concisely, and the words themselves and their place in the line have become so much more important than in the case of more facile or rhetorical writers. . . . Furthermore, the Russian language, which is more highly inflected and able to dispense with pronouns and prepositions in many cases where we have to use them and which does without the article altogether [separating modifiers from substantives if need be] . . . renders the problem of translating him closer to translating a highly articulated Latin poet like Horace than any modern poet we know.

Yet Wilson makes it clear that, difficult though he may have estimated it to be, he was far from despairing that it could be done and done with a fair degree of both faithfulness *and* readability. Indeed, he attempts on his own the prose translation of selected passages. In the case of a poetic translation he acknowledges, however, that "It would require a translator himself a poet of the first order to reproduce Pushkin's peculiar combination of intensity, compression and perfect ease."[20]

Nabokov takes an entirely different line. His theory of translation, as he propounds it in the Foreword to his version of *Eugene Onegin* sets a far lower premium on readability.[21] The first poetic accoutrement he dispenses with is rhyme. For, he asks rhetorically, "can a rhymed poem like *Eugene Onegin* be truly translated with the retention of its rhymes? The answer, of course, is no."

It is perfectly true of course, and almost a commonplace among critics and translators that, in any pure sense, Pushkin is beyond translation. Gerschenkron speaks for the majority when he acknowledges that "Pushkin's masterpiece is probably untranslatable" and when he declares that "no one will ever recreate it in all its holistic grandeur."

However, this is not quite Nabokov's position. He maintains that losing the rhyme means only that "the poem loses its bloom" and that a translation conforming to the meter of the original and giving what Nabokov calls a "literal" translation is still possible. Differentiating his term *literal* from "paraphrastic" and "lexical" types of translation, he defines this *literal* form as "rendering, as closely as the associative and syntactical capacities of another language will allow, the exact contextual meaning of the original." "Only this," he adds, "is true translation."

Gerschenkron's view of what he calls this "definitional ukase" put forward by Nabokov is that it is "an attractive promise." He goes on to say, however, that while "Truth is a noble word, . . . it should neither disguise the naivete of Nabokov's 'self-advertisement' nor obscure the problem." For, he notes, "Surely the aesthetic truth is a great deal more than correct conveyance of meaning."[22]

But Nabokov has left no doubt about all that he is prepared to forego in quest of that "correct conveyance." In transposing *Eugene Onegin* from Pushkin's Russian into my English," he tells us:

> I have sacrificed to completeness of meaning every formal element including the iambic rhythm, whenever its retention hindered fidelity. To my ideal of literalism I sacrificed

everything (elegance, euphony, clarity, good taste, modern usage, and even grammar) that the dainty mimic prizes higher than truth. Pushkin has likened translators to horses changed at the posthouses of civilization. The greatest reward I can think of is that students may use my work as a pony.[23]

But Gerschenkron reminds us that "what Nabokov sacrifices so lightheartedly and so disdainfully is not his own elegance and clarity, and euphony, but Pushkin's." Indeed, he suggests, the true – and no doubt unconscious – motive underlying Nabokov's method is a deep ambivalence toward Pushkin:

> Vladimir Nabokov's monumental edition of *Eugene Onegin* is the strangest blend, fascinating and exasperating. It has everything: artistic intuition and dogmatic stubbornness; great ingenuity and amazing folly; acute observations and sterile pedantry; unnecessary modesty and inexcusable arrogance. It is a labor of love and a work of hate.[24]

Nabokov did not, as it happened, have the field of Pushkin translation entirely to himself. Both Wilson and Gerschenkron find that, by having attempted more, Walter Arndt – in his rhymed version of *Onegin*, brought out a little before Nabokov's – had, in fact, accomplished more. Arndt's version represents something of a *tour de force*, a translation of the whole of Pushkin's verse novel into the original iambic tetrameter, while preserving the original intricate stanza form.

Gerschenkron says that "while Nabokov tells us with great precision what *Eugene Onegin* is all about, it is from Arndt's and some of his predecessors' passages that one can hope to get at least an inkling of what it is really like.[25] Wilson pronounces Arndt's attempt "heroic" and goes on to say that

> though Arndt is no great poet and . . . his effort to stick to the rhyme scheme sometimes leads him to a certain far-fetchedness, his version is, in general, much closer to *Onegin* than any of the others I have sampled and is likely to give the reader a better idea of what the poem sounds like in Russian than Nabokov's so tortured version.[26]

The question at issue here is the degree of importance one places upon readability. To a humanistic critic like Wilson, it is, of course, of the essence. To Nabokov, who is described by Harry Levin as an "artist mandarin" it is a quality worthy only of scorn: "Readable," he says, "readable indeed! A schoolboy's boner mocks the ancient masterpiece less than does its commercial poetization, and it is when the translator sets out to render the 'spirit,' and not the mere sense of the text that he begins to traduce his author."[27]

With such different ends in view, from the first there could have been no way for Wilson to find Nabokov's translation anything but what he did find it: "disappointing." In addition to characterizing it as "tortured', as he does in the comparison with Arndt's, he deems the translation "uneven and sometimes banal" and says that Nabokov in his attempt to preserve the iambic base "sometimes jolts into prose," and finally, by implication, he concludes that it does an injustice to Pushkin.[28] We have already heard Gerschenkron render much the same evaluation.

Citing Gerschenkron's conclusion that Nabokov's translation "can and should be studied, but . . . it cannot be read," Harry Levin says that "Thus he lent authority to the judgment that Wilson was, in any case, fully qualified to make for himself on the question of the poem's readability."[29]

Faced with such a clear obstacle to any sympathetic appreciation of his friend's monumental effort – and it is, as Gerschenkron suggests, monumental: the 1850 page, four-volume work, consisting of one volume of translation and three volumes of commentary occupied Nabokov for many years – it is hard to see how Wilson could ever have supposed he would be able to overcome his bias against its premise sufficiently to render it critical justice. Perhaps, the knowledge that he had done so, in the case of Yeats and many others – that is, rendered critical justice to artistic efforts that were in some sense at odds with his own convictions – prompted Wilson to attempt it. And, perhaps, he would have found it a different matter if he had felt free to proceed out of his accustomed humanist approach.

But his approach in "The Strange Case of Pushkin and Nabokov" is very different. He proceeds in this review to raise objection after objection – pausing at one point three-quarters of the way through, to note in an aside that he is doing so from a desire "to get all my negatives out of the way at once." However, even after he has announced that he is turning to the–

much briefer – positive side, he digresses to interject two more complaints.[30]

Instead of following his habitual pattern of passionate identification, followed by withdrawal for historical inference and appraisal, instead of any sympathetic immersion in the artist's (or, in this case, the translator's) struggles, Wilson simply begins with his barrage of negatives and permits them to dominate the review. Through it all, one looks in vain for any classical ideal of amiability or magnanimity of spirit.

Some attempt will be made to discover the springs of this deviation on Wilson's part from his critical norm. At the moment, it will be of interest to our examination of his critical practice to register the objective grounds of his comments, mainly negative as I have said. Throughout the review Wilson continues to compare Nabokov's work unfavorably to Arndt's. Remembering a reference on Nabokov's part to "infelicities" in Arndt's translation, Wilson says that "Nabokov's aberrations in this line are a good deal more objectionable than anything I have found in Arndt. He gives us, for example, *rememorating, producement, curvate, habitude, rummers, familistic, gloam, dit, shippon,* and *scrab.* All these can be found in the OED, but they are all entirely dictionary words, usually labelled 'dialect,' 'archaic,' or 'obsolete.'"[31]

Pursuing the matter into Nabokov's "actual errors of English," Wilson goes on to add "loaden," "dwelled" (instead of dwelt), and "remind one about me." And he again incorporates into his comment a rebuke to Nabokov for his criticism of Arndt, saying: "If it is a question of picking on Germanisms in Arndt, it is not difficult to find Russianisms in Nabokov." These involve, according to Wilson, such "Russian" constructions as "listen the sound of the sea" and "Byanov, my mettlesome cousin, toward our hero leads Tatiana with Olga."[32] Such criticisms might have been urged with justice, even by a critic prepared to accept the translator's "given" of eschewing polish in favor of adherence to the principle of "literal" meaning. But, to echo an old humanist objection of Sainte-Beuve, it is difficult to see the necessity for Wilson's doing so "in that tone or on that note."

There is also apparent in this portion of the review a peculiar deafness to Nabokov's disclaimers. Wilson acknowledges them, at least to the point of reporting that Nabokov has made them, but he proceeds to object to their every practical consequence. Wilson even goes so far as to turn a prominent instance of Nabokovian modesty, his hope that it will be used by students, into a cause for complaint. He maintains that Nabokov's use of so many "rare and unfamiliar" English words is "entirely inappropriate" "in view of his declared intention to stick so close to the text that his version may be used as a trot."[33]

What seems to have happened in this instance is that Wilson allowed himself to be drawn into composing the review as if it were an extension of one of the literary quarrels he and Nabokov had been conducting, in their personal get-togethers and through their correspondence, for years. Regarding the whole tenor of this correspondence, John Updike notes:

> Both men took pride in being frank about what mattered, and nearly from the start the friendliness of their letters has to surmount such abrasive opening lines as "I am going to steal an hour from Gogol and thrash out this matter of Russian versification, because you are wrong as can be" (Nabokov) and "I was rather disappointed in *Bend Sinister*, about which I had had some doubts when I was reading the parts you showed me, and I will give you my opinion for what it is worth" (Wilson).[34]

This raises the possibility that the displays of bad feeling evident to some extent in Wilson's initial review and increasingly prominent in the exchanges that follow Nabokov's reply are playful intellectual poses and ought not to be taken too seriously. There is some evidence that Wilson, at least, was proceeding on that assumption. On an earlier occasion, his candid advice to Max Eastman—a participant in another celebrated literary skirmish, in his case, with Hemingway—seems to suggest a tongue-in-cheek attitude even as it gives a clue to Wilson's strategy in such affairs:

> The critic must remain invulnerable. For the fighter, the worker in the field of ideas, to be seen to have had one's feelings hurt is detrimental—it may even prove fatal to the effectiveness of one's case. He should assume a note not of peevishness but indignation, with a background of scorn.[35]

And, in *Upstate,* Wilson chooses to put it on record that, in his view, the literary disagreements he was long accustomed to having with Nabokov were "really intellectual romps, sometimes accompanied by mauling."[36] Along the same lines, V. S. Pritchett writes that "when one looks up the full text of Wilson's attack in The New York Review of Books and . . . Nabokov's reply in Encounter and 'Strong Opinions' the whole thing seems more like a display of fireworks than an attempt to draw blood."[37]

But the fact is that this quarrel did draw blood, if only on Nabokov's side. It was at one point briefly and extremely tenuously patched up, only to be reopened. This time the result was a rift that prevailed at the time of Wilson's death and seems to have continued giving Nabokov pain up to the time of *his* death a few years later.

In his first response to Wilson's review, the so-called *Encounter* reply, Nabokov gives clear signs of having had his feeling hurt by Wilson long before the *Onegin* affair, not by what Wilson had written but by what he had failed to write:

> I fully reciprocate "the warm affection sometimes chilled by exasperation" that he says he feels for me. When I first came to America a quarter of a century ago, he wrote to me, and called on me, and was most kind to me in various matters, not necessarily pertaining to his profession. I have always been grateful to him for the tact he showed in not reviewing any of my novels while constantly saying flattering things about me in the so-called literary circles where I seldom revolve.[38]

Had he not been writing in the grip of wounded feelings, he might have seen the same facts in the very different light in which they are presented by Simon Karlinsky, the Russian scholar who edited the Nabokov-Wilson correspondence:

> The beginnings of Nabokov's second literary career (as an American author writing in English) can hardly be imagined without Wilson's help, advice and literary contacts . . . it was Wilson, as Nabokov tells us in his introduction to the 1964 edition of the novel, who helped arrange the publication of *Bend Sinister.* With the same impartial generosity, Wilson refrained from reviewing this novel, which he dis-

liked, trying to arrange good reviews for it by other critics; still later, he offered Nabokov his help in finding a producer for a dramatized version.[39]

The quarrel went on, and in a letter to *The New York Times* which was to be his final word on the subject in print, Nabokov shows how personally he, if not Wilson, had been taking it all: "I am aware that my former friend is in poor health but in the struggle between the dictates of compassion and those of personal honor the latter wins."[40]

To return to Wilson's review, there are clear indications in it that Wilson *means* his tone to come across as friendly and teasing – however inappropriately, considering the glare of publicity in which he must have realized his review would be read and the degree of serious importance he must have known the occasion would have for Nabokov. Take, for example, this passage:

> One knows Mr. Nabokov's virtuosity in juggling with the English language, the prettiness and wit of his verbal invention.
> One knows also the perversity of his tricks to startle or stick pins in the reader; and one suspects that his perversity here has been exercised in curbing his cleverness; that – with his sado-masochistic Dostoevskian tendencies so acutely noted by Sartre – he seeks to torture both the reader and himself by flattening Pushkin out and denying to his own powers the scope of their full play.[41]

Even so, there is something not so much friendly as mischievous about his own pin pricks here. When he accuses Nabokov of displaying "sado-masochistic Dostoevskian tendencies so acutely noted by Sartre," he is twitting his friend with a hated Freudianism as well as finding a resemblance to him in one author he knew Nabokov detested and endorsing the views of another equally despised.

Yet there *are* recurrent instances of unequivocally friendly teasing on Wilson's part, such as his remark that, "Since Mr. Nabokov is the least modest of men, I do not hesitate to urge my own rival claims against him," and a little further on, where, having used the word *obelized*, Wilson hopes parenthetically that Nabokov "has had to look up that word."[42]

But surely there is a distinction to be made between such undefensive, openly competitive statements and the considerably more sour tone discernible in the following passage:

> Mr. Nabokov, before the publication of his own translation of *Evgeni Onegin*, took up a good deal of space in the pages of the *New York Review of Books* to denounce a previous translation by Walter Arndt. This article – which sounded like nothing so much as one of Marx's niggling and nagging attacks on someone who had the temerity to write about economics and to hold different views from Marx's – dwelt especially on what he regarded as Professor Arndt's Germanisms and other infelicities of phrasing, without, apparently, being aware of how vulnerable he himself was.[43]

The thing calculated to make the reader who is conversant with the literary and personal background of the situation uneasy about this passage is the gratuitous analogy Wilson draws in it between Nabokov and Marx. It is one thing to twit him about being like an author he disliked; it is quite another to twit him about being like the figure responsible, however indirectly, for real pain in his friend's life. (The entire Nabokov family was driven into exile, where Vladimir's father was eventually assassinated, by the Marxist revolution.)

Here and repeatedly in this Pushkin review Wilson badly misjudges the effect of what he may have thought was merely mischievous. Wilson admits as much, in his rejoinder to Nabokov's initial letter to the *New York Review of Books* when he says that on rereading his article he felt it sounded "more damaging" than he had meant it to be.[44]

That begins to seem the only explanation for the tone as well as the construction of the whole review. Wilson was simply not consciously in control of his effects. This is not to suggest that, on substantive points with regard to the merits of the translation itself and to the quirky word choice and their awkward rhythms, Wilson is not consistently at least preponderantly right. It is just to register the inescapable fact that, in this critical performance, he is personally, humanly, disastrously wrong.

The irony is that Wilson could well have picked up the bad

habits he displays here from Nabokov himself. It is a facet of Nabokov's work that numerous commentators have taken Nabokov to task for, even in favorable reviews. Wilson, disapproving, describes it as his "instinct to take digs at great reputations."[45]

On this point Gerschenkron is much harder on Nabokov than Wilson is. He says, for example, of Nabokov's three volume *Onegin* commentary, that it is "interspersed with disagreeing and disagreeable remarks about everybody" and that

> If, in reading the Commentary, the feelings of admiration and the sense of gratitude [for what both he and Wilson consider its many fine points] are dulled by growing irritation, the reason must be sought in the author's uncontrolled anger, his lack of generosity, his narrow prejudices, eccentricities, and irrelevancies.[46]

In the same vein elsewhere, he points out that "most of this remarkably foolish abuse is heaped quite gratuitously in that it has no bearing at all on *EO* or Pushkin in general." What is more, says Gerschenkron, "Nabokov is out to cut throats, and there is no literary fair practices act to restrain him."[47]

What Gerschenkron refers to as Nabokov's "nugatory ire" would, he says, be "fully incomprehensible if one did not know so well its antecedents in Russian and German petty and rude polemical habits."[48] And one wonders if one of the sources of the abrasive misunderstanding that pervades the exchanges between Wilson and Nabokov may not lie just here – in Wilson's adherence (in principle at any rate) to humanist French and English critical models, Nabokov's to Russian and German scholastic ones.

A second insight into the sources of their rift comes to us in the form of a detailed account by Simon Karlinsky of the history of their quarrel on Russian prosody. As Karlinsky tells it:

> [their] vehement disagreement on the nature of Russian versification is an instance of an argument in which the participants either talk past one another or talk about two different things. . . . Nabokov did not realize that he was addressing his contrapuntal lesson to a person who had not been told about the pitch and length of various notes. . . .

The result, of course, was that:

> the misunderstanding was consolidated and in their subse-
> quent arguments on metrics it is all too clear that Wilson
> has English prosody in mind when he writes of either
> English or Russian verse, while Nabokov for the most part
> seems to do just the opposite.

Karlinsky's account makes it clear, as he says, that:

> Nabokov's unwitting withholding of essential information,
> based on his apparent failure to perceive some fundamental
> gaps in Wilson's command of Russian, was the obstacle to
> communication in this case. . . . [49]

In the context, then, of the long and utterly frustrating
argument about Russian prosody which ensued, it is easier to
understand Wilson's muted air of triumph when he introduces
what is clearly meant to be a knockout punch: "Mr. Nabokov's
most serious failure, however . . . is one of interpretation. He
has missed a fundamental point in the central situation."[50]

Here, Wilson is on his own ground, for he has himself done
a full-scale interpretation of the poem in the "Evgeni Onegin"
portion of his 1936 essay "In Honor of Pushkin" – an essay which
is included in *The Triple Thinkers*. The main scene the interpretation of which is at issue occurs in Chapter Six of *Eugene
Onegin*, the duel scene.

More illuminating, because more detached, than their exchanges about the interpretation of this scene at the time of
their public quarrel are the divergent approaches Wilson and
Nabokov evidence in their respective commentaries written
when each was oblivious of the other's scrutiny.

In his 1936 Pushkin essay Wilson approached this scene
with his characteristic critical preoccupations in the forefront.
His commentary displays an interest in the Freudian undercur-
rents to be discerned in the situation:

> Evgeni has killed in the most cynical fashion a man whose
> friend he had believed himself to be and whom he had
> thought he did not want to kill. Now at last we are sure of
> what Pushkin, who has always given us Evgeni's version of

his own motives, has only so far in various ways suggested: that, for all Lensky's obtuseness and immaturity, Evgeni has been jealous of him, because Lensky has been able to feel for Olga an all-absorbing emotion whereas Evgeni, loved so passionately by Tatyana, has been unable to feel anything at all.[51]

Wilson displays, too, an interest in the sociological ramifications, the Marxist superstructure, of the relations between the characters in the poem:

> For, after all, the chief disaster of *Evgeni Onegin* is not Evgeni's chagrin or Lensky's death: it is that Tatyana should have been caught up [at poem's end she is the wife of a Russian general and an important, though unhappy figure in the aristocratic society of Moscow] irrevocably by that empty and tyrannical social world from which Evgeni had tried to escape and which she had felt and still feels so alien.[51]

Noting that Pushkin, like the poet Lensky in his verse novel, was killed in a duel "before he was out of his thirties," Wilson, again characteristically, enlarges the scope of his criticism to make a literary point that is both historical and comparative. Setting Pushkin's early death beside those of Byron, Shelley, Keats, Leopardi, Lermontov, and Poe, he says:

> [I]t was as if in that great age of the bourgeois ascendancy – and even in still-feudal Russia – it were impossible for the poet to survive. There was for the man of imagination and moral passion a basic maladjustment to society in which only the student of society – the social philosopher, the historian, the novelist – could find himself and learn to function . . . he had . . . to train himself to write in prose.

Still typically, Wilson concludes by accentuating the contributions Pushkin was nevertheless able to make in the transcendent realm of art:

> Yet Pushkin, who had done for the Russian language what Dante had done for the Italian and who had laid the foundations of Russian fiction, had, in opposing the natural humanity of Tatyana to the social values of Evgeni, set a theme which was to be developed through the whole of Russian art and thought, and to give it its peculiar power.[52]

Nabokov's commentary on the same scene, it soon becomes clear, is true to his life-long distaste for Freud and all of his works and ways. When *he* speaks of an interpretation of dreams, he means no Freudian analyst but rather the more ancient sort of dream interpreter, who was to be found in the courts of old kings, i.e., an "oneirologist.":

> To the oneirologist, Onegin's behavior throughout that morning [the morning of the duel] has an uncanny dreamlike quality, as if he had been infected by Tatiana's recent nightmare. We all know that dream sensation of "lateness," those casual "substitutions" (as here – the valet turned second), those "omissions," that odd discomfort followed by its carefree dismissal. Onegin behaves as he never would have behaved in a normal state of moral awareness.[53]

Wilson, in his 1965 review, seizes on this as the weak point of Nabokov's position:

> He finds himself unable to account for Evgeni Onegin's behavior in first giving offense to Lensky by flirting with Olga at the ball and then, when Lensky challenges him to a duel, instead of managing a reconciliation not merely accepting the challenge, but deliberately shooting first and to kill. Nabokov says that the latter act is "quite out of character. . . .

But, Wilson objects, "There are no out-of-character actions in *Evgeni Onegin*. Nabokov has simply not seen the point."[54]

Nabokov, forced to interpret, though he declares that he does "not believe in *any* kind of interpretation," declares open war on Wilson's humanist approach: "In other words, I do not believe in the old-fashioned, naive, and musty method of human-interest criticism championed by Mr. Wilson. . . ."

Denying that he has in his commentary attempted anything of the kind, Nabokov asserts that his attribution to Onegin's behavior before and during the duel of a "dreamlike" quality was "purely a question of architectonics – not of personal interpretation. My facts are objective and irrefutable. I remain with Pushkin in Pushkin's world. I am not concerned with Onegin's being gentle or cruel, energetic or indolent, kind or unkind. . . ."[54]

And, so saying, he once again puts forth the idea that

Onegin's behavior on the morning of the duel was not in character. He now expands that idea, however, to the point of ascribing it to an oversight on Pushkin's part, made "in the interest of the plot." Rather than ascribe an even remotely Freudian motive to Onegin, Nabokov now sets out to ascribe a purely artistic one to Pushkin: "the author followed wisely the old rule of sparing one's more interesting character while the novel is developing." He does not address the equally old artistic rule of arranging one's character's actions according to the dictates of psychological truth.

Having located the rationale for one character's actions in Pushkin's willingness to overlook proper behavior at the duel in order to get the right character killed, Nabokov now finds the springs of that same character's earlier action at the ball to lie in Onegin's – and Pushkins – scrupulous adherence to *amour propre*. As Nabokov puts it:

> The actual cause of the encounter is . . . quite plausible in Pushkin: upon finding himself at a huge vulgar feast . . . so unlike the informal party promised him by Lenski. . . . Onegin is quite right to be furious with his deceitful or scatterbrained young friend, just as Lenski is quite justified in calling him out for flirting with Olga. . . . Pushkin stresses the fact . . . that *amour propre* is sometimes stronger than friendship.

It was, in other words, a simple social misunderstanding, according to Nabokov. "That is all." And in his view, that is enough. "One should stick to that," he says, "and not try to think up 'deep' variations."[55]

It seems to me this comparison of the critical views of Nabokov and Wilson in the duelling scene shows that, as I have suggested, they are not so much incompatible with one another as indicative of radically discrete approaches directed at radically discrete ends. Even though I am aware that both writers functioned in both fields, it seems to me one gets the best perspective on their "case" by viewing Nabokov as quintessentially an artist and Wilson as quintessentially a critic. One sees the difference here in Nabokov's attention to the specific detail and Wilson's on the larger picture. Thus, when they look at Pushkin, Nabokov concentrates on the "architectonics" and concerns himself with specific details such as the duel and the dance and the weather, whereas Wilson draws large inferences about the moral idealism of Russian literature as a whole and about the historical shift from novels in verse to novels in prose.

One finds the same contrast in their approaches to Kafka's "Metamorphosis."[56] Here we see Wilson drawing analogies between Gregor and Kafka, Kafka and the strangling father relationship, Kafka and the constraints of orthodox Jewish family life, Kafka and artistic temperament thwarted in bourgeois surroundings, Kafka and deep-seated sexual inhibitions, Kafka and membership in an oppressed and somewhat scorned minority, first as a Jew in Czechoslovakia then as a Czech in the Austrian empire and finally as a Central European in an era of Central European defeat.[57]

Nabokov, on the other hand, concerns himself with drawing a picture of just what kind of bug Gregor has turned into and with counting the number of its legs and the number of doors in the Samsa apartment. This is not to suggest that Nabokov is not also capable of tackling the larger ramifications of his subjects or that Wilson is blind to matters of artistic detail, it is a matter of where they locate their habitual focus of attention.

Taking their essays on Pushkin and Kafka as cases in point, I think it is fair to say that Nabokov's focus is on looking at what the artist has made – the process; whereas Wilson's is on what the art has meant – the product. Something of why this should be so can be seen when we compare their statements on what each turns to art for.

Actually, we have already looked at Wilson's statement in "The Historical Interpretation of Literature." In his Kafka essay, Nabokov speaks of what it means to him to take art seriously. He says that it means, in Lear's words, "To take upon us the mystery of things." And he goes on to tell something of what he means by this: "*Beauty plus pity* – that is the closest we can get to a definition of art. Where there is beauty there is pity for the simple reason that beauty must die; beauty always dies, the manner dies with the matter, the world dies with the individual."[58]

Wilson, we know, sees art as a way, not of "Taking upon oneself the mystery of things" but of clearing away life's mystery, its confusion and pain. If we were to put it into a formula akin to Nabokov's it would be *Order plus joy*. My purpose is not to show one approach superior to the other; simply to demonstrate how different they are.

There are reasons why Nabokov's explication of "Metamorphosis" must emerge as the deeper and truer vision – they have to do with the "Metaphysical pathos" of Wilson's situation, the discussion of which must wait until a later chapter. In the instance of *Eugene Onegin*, however – perhaps because it deals with a preabsurd world where he is more at home – I think there can be no doubt that Wilson's critical interpretation shows the greater understanding of the poem. Nabokov really does not seem to understand what Pushkin means to convey in the Lensky-Onegin relationship, whereas Wilson makes a convincing case for the view that it is fraught with the ambivalence that springs from competitiveness.

If this seems a strange assertion to make when one is, after all, choosing a non-Russian's view over that of a native speaker and a scholar on the subject as well, it may become less strange if one adopts my proposition of thinking of each in their quintessential roles. It is in matters of interpretation, after all, that Wilson is on his own most solid footing. His whole expertise as a critic has been based upon his faculty of "sympathetic imagination," that is, of responding "like an artist" to the materials of art; whereas Nabokov, as an essentially imaginative writer, a novelist and poet, is accustomed to working with the materials of his own experience.

In this, perhaps more than in any other instance provided by these essays, we can isolate and differentiate between the skills necessary to be a great critic and those necessary to be a great writer of works of the imagination.

It remains to give some account of Wilson's curious addenda to the original review. If Nabokov had been hurt by Wilson's failure to review his novels earlier, he can scarcely have been less so by the slighting glance Wilson gives them in the last two pages of "The Strange Case of Pushkin and Nabokov." He begins by observing that: "Of his novels written here in English, *Bend Sinister* seems to me the weakest."

He complains that it is pervaded by the quality of *Schaden-*

freude, an untranslatable German word describing a complex emotion that covers a spectrum of intensity ranging from the malicious glee felt in watching someone slip on a banana peel to the out and out sadist's pleasure at the spectacle of another's pain. Wilson seems to place the quality he sees in this novel on the milder side when he notes that in it "Everybody is always being humiliated." But then he goes further to ascribe it, *en passant*, to "the sado-masochism of the author."[59]

Of *Lolita* he says merely that "his panorama of middle-class homes and motels is more vivid and more amusing than his dreary and prosaic German vistas." And though he credits it here with "something . . . like emotion – the ordeals of a torn personality," we know from his letters that he "liked it less than anything you wrote." He has, in fact, found the subject "nasty."

His last fleeting look at Nabokov's fiction is to dismiss *Ada* with the admission that "I could not get through it," and the pronouncement that "its scrambled geography, its polyglot conversations, . . . and its highly intellectualized eroticism, bored me as Nabokov rarely does. This is a brilliance which aims to dazzle, but which cannot be anything but dull."[60]

I conclude this overview of what might well be called "The Strange Case of Wilson and Nabokov," with a note of speculation, which I shall be exploring further in Chapter 12, about what (*other* than jealousy) may have interposed a barrier between Wilson and an ability to respond very warmly to Nabokov's fiction. The persona that characteristically appears as protagonist in Nabokov's novels is far too prey to the same ills Wilson suffers from (being overly cerebral, emotionally repressed) to call forth Wilson's sympathies. It would have been like responding sympathetically to himself – a knack he never quite acquired.

IV.
Evaluations of Wilson's Critical Achievement

CHAPTER ELEVEN

An Examination of Prevailing Opinion

*I*n this chapter I wish to examine certain charges, characterizations, and descriptions of Wilson's work put forward by commentators in the past and to test their validity by setting them against the work itself, drawing upon the analyses just completed. Taking the most full-scale assessment first, I begin with Stanley Edgar Hyman's chapter on Wilson in *The Armed Vision*, called "Edmund Wilson and Translation in Criticism."[1]

Elmer Borklund begins his entry on Hyman in *Contemporary Literary Critics* by referring to the "obvious limitations" of *The Armed Vision*, a remark that seems to indicate that Hyman's reputation is presently in decline, but as Borklund also notes with regard to the Hyman book, "it was widely read and generally admired for a number of years after its appearance" in 1948.[2] Thus, its unfriendly and reductionist view of Wilson as a critic was both influential and damaging.

Hyman characterizes Wilson as "probably our foremost practitioner in this field of interpreting or 'translating' the content of literature." In this way, he focuses on only one aspect of Wilson's criticism, that in which Wilson serves "as a conduit between the obscure or difficult work and the reader."[3] Sherman Paul regards Hyman's choice of the term "translator" as "denigrating," and he is no doubt justified in this, especially in view of the fact that Hyman expands upon it with the still more denigrating terms "introducer" and "popularizer."[4]

However, Paul may somewhat overstate the case when he says that Hyman's "treatment of Wilson in *The Armed Vision*" accounts for his "almost total neglect in the schools."[5] Such an evaluation seems to be in contradiction, for example, to the frequent appearance of Wilson essays in the widely used critical anthology series, *Twentieth Century Views*.[6] Nevertheless, it is certainly true that Wilson's critical reputation in academic circles suffered and may still be suffering because of it.

Actually, Hyman says a good many positive things about Wilson's criticism in the course of his essay: one comes upon such phrases, for example, as that quoted earlier with regard to the effect of *Axel's Castle* (i.e., that it "opened up a whole new area of literature to a wide audience" in a way "second only to that of T. S. Eliot's *The Sacred Wood*").[7] Elsewhere he says that "Sometimes Wilson's exegesis is subtle symbolic analysis," that it is sometimes "remarkably ingenious," that "At all times . . . it continues to be stimulating" and "sometimes it is essential."[8]

When Hyman gets more specific in his appreciative remarks, he notes, for example, that Wilson

> writes clearly and readably and is able to work the most recondite material into simple and comprehensible English sentences. He has a wide reading . . . in a number of the primary fields that filter into literature, including history, philosophy, and psychology, . . . Marxism and psychoanalysis. He has . . . an unusual command of languages, including Latin and Greek . . . , French, and . . . German and Russian.[9]

Hyman goes further, stating that, "In addition to his knowledge . . . Wilson is excellently qualified . . . by a genuine critical shrewdness, an ability to perceive relationships and generalize from them." And he maintains that "The evidences of this ability in his books are far too many to list."[10]

What undercuts the praise I have just singled out, and ultimately negates it, is the fact that Hyman intersperses throughout the essay such qualifying – and reductive – phrases as "to the relatively uninformed reader at least" and "at least a competent lay background." Also, he uses "sometimes" and "probably" (terms that seldom accompany his negatives) until the impression is left that these "formidable qualifications" are effectively set off by "a number of limitations and inadequacies."[11]

Hyman closes the first section of his essay on Wilson with a summation that is worth looking at more closely as it is indicative of the sweeping and often unfounded nature of Hyman's attack. His favored method of proceeding throughout this essay is to take something Wilson has written, quote it out of context, and use it against him. Thus, he makes a remark of Wilson's that comes at the end of *Axel's Castle* stand for a general quality for want of which Hyman then takes him to task.

Wilson has been discussing the new uses of language discovered by the Symbolist movement. (We have seen something of this passage at the conclusion of the chapter on Yeats.)[12] He makes the routine kind of acknowledgment that anyone who wishes to set limits on a topic would make:

> This discussion would, of course lead us, if we pursued it, to the nature of language itself and hence to the mysteries of human psychology and what we mean when we talk about such things as "reason," "emotion," "sensation," and "imagination." And this must be left to the philosophers.[13]

Hyman, however, interprets the remark to stand for a general trait of evasiveness and proof of his assertion that "Wilson either cannot or will not follow things through." The assertion is patently false with regard to Wilson who, by the end of *Axel's Castle*, had tenaciously "followed through" the use of Symbolist technique in the work of six of the major shapers of modern literature.

Furthermore, in his James and Dickens essays and elsewhere, Wilson has certainly shown himself ready to delve into the "mysteries of human psychology." With the exception of Addison's and Coleridge's extensive explorations of the term *imagination*, I would say most critics have, with regard to the rest of the Wilson quote, been quite willing to leave questions on "the nature of language" and definitions of terms such as "reason," "emotion," and "sensation" to the philosophers – and, in the first instance, to linguistic philosophers, in particular.

Without building a further case for his assertion that

"Wilson has never permitted himself to go into these questions," Hyman asserts that they are "the very things which the critic in our time *cannot* leave to the philosophers but must concern himself with to the best of his ability." Furthermore, Hyman asserts, "they constitute the cornerstone of any serious discussion of literature."

Having thus defined the limits of serious critical discussion to his satisfaction, and in such a way as to suggest that Wilson never engaged in it, Hyman goes on to call the "fact" that he never did so "merely another evidence" of the flimsiness of Wilson's critical base. That base, he says, consists of nothing more than "sharp reading and eclecticism" and results only in "flashy insights" and "shoddy popularization."[14]

Other examples of Hyman using Wilson's own words against him are equally crude. He lifts a line from Wilson's last book of verse in which Wilson humorously renounces the career of poet ("I leave that to you who have the tongue") to substantiate a claim that Wilson "seems generally to dislike" poetry. (Wilson's "passionate embrace" of the poetry of Yeats is only one of many proofs one could cite to the contrary.) He takes another line from Wilson's essay "Is Verse a Dying Technique?" to the effect that "poetry is a more primitive and more barbarous technique than prose," a line that is meant to be taken in a purely historical sense, to support his charge that "Wilson has been announcing the obsolescence or death of poetry at least since *Axel's Castle*." Actually, Hyman misinterprets a good deal that Wilson says in both places.

In *Axel's Castle*, for instance, he completely misses the dialectic at work – the Arnoldian play of mind that first embraces then withdraws to make inferences, critical, historical, or otherwise. Hyman even suggests that the book "was meant as an attack" and the rounded view of Symbolism that emerges was an accident of Wilson's "sweetly appreciative" tone.[15] Throughout the preceding analyses of Wilson's work, however, we have seen it to be part and parcel of his humanist critical method. As for "Is Verse a Dying Technique?" Wilson's essay, in fact, only notes the change in society's uses of poetry, announces the historical fact of the decline of the long poem, and speculates that it may have been replaced by the poetic novel.

On what appear to be purely subjective grounds, Hyman uses Wilson's early support of Poe as a major writer and a serious critic as evidence that Wilson "seems to have a genuine weakness of taste." And he cites Wilson's dislike for the work of Gide and Kafka as proof that he "is simply a man who suffers from a defect of sensibility."[16]

At one point, fairly early in his chapter on Wilson, Hyman comes perilously close to accusing him of plagiarism. Although he admits that proving a direct charge of "critical cribbing is a risky business," Hyman suggests Wilson may not have written *Axel's Castle* but may have "cribbed" it. This is on no better evidence than that he, Hyman, had been "many times informed that at least three full-length theses covering much the same material appeared in France the decade before the book's publication." That he is more interested in repeating that "information" than testing it seems plain. Hyman admits that "no one has ever attempted to trace in print Wilson's unacknowledged indebtedness to these works, *if it exists*" [my italics].[17]

Wilson's free display of gratitude to Edna Kenton and various other James scholars in his Henry James essay would seem an effective indication that he had no difficulty acknowledging sources when he used them. The plain truth is that there is a disturbing *ad hominem* quality evident throughout this essay, which may have been a factor in the decision to withhold the entire Wilson chapter from subsequent editions of *The Armed Vision*.

Hyman inserts a long section – two, in fact – in this chapter in which Wilson figures very little except as he is loosely identified with certain traditional critical approaches. The first aligns him with the interpretive, hermaneutic, exegetical line of criticism Hyman traces from Anaxagoras and Glaucon (early critics of Homer) through biblical Dantean and Shakespearean critics (there is a large patch when Hyman gets this branch of criticism confused with allegory) to Dryden, Pound, and Eliot. Second, the historical-biographical antecedents of Wilson's critical tradition are traced by Hyman, much as Wilson himself gives it in "The Historical Interpretation of Literature."

Returning to Wilson, Hyman, in discussing the essay on Proust, warms to the point of giving a somewhat appreciative description of Wilson's incorporation into these traditional critical practices the insights of Marx and Freud. He does so, however, without noticing that this is in conflict with his earlier description of Wilson's method as simple-minded plot summary or "translation" of the 100 great books variety. He says, for example:

> Wilson's own method has always embraced both sociological and psychological factors, with greater emphasis on the sociological in his earlier criticism and proportion gradually shifting in favor of psychological as he developed. Wilson's analyses have been perhaps most successful where he used both criteria at once, translating back and forth between Marx and Freud, as when he discusses Proust's abnormal dependence on his mother and consequent "impulses toward a sterile and infantile perversity," but also as the "Heartbreak House of capitalistic culture"[18]

Hyman takes a curious sideswipe at the Wilsonian habit of stringing loosely related essays together by means of not always very closely related themes. These Wilson usually chose from some literary source, such as Flaubert's line about the artist being a "triple thinker." In the case of *The Shock of Recognition*, Hyman makes the practice into an occasion of near derision. The quote, about genius the world over experiencing a "shock of recognition" when confronted by other works of genius, was clearly intended by Wilson as a mere device, a way to introduce his anthology of American writers' critical comments on one another's work. Hyman elevates it into a "theory of art" on Wilson's part, equivalent in importance to his "wound and bow" theory. Then he proceeds to devote a good deal of space to exposing the inconsistency with which the quote applied to the artists Wilson had chosen. (It is perfectly true that the quote applies better to some entries than to others; what is also true, and what Hyman fails entirely to note, is that the volume constitutes "a seminal anthology," as Harry Levin has called it. At the very least, it remains a useful reference tool in the study of American literature.)

Hyman seems most interested, however, in trying out Wilson's "theory" on Wilson and using it against him. On Wilson's genius as an artist, he notes, the "shock of recognition" failed to take place – a reference to the relative failure of his imaginative writings to win critical acclaim.

On Wilson's genius as a critic, Hyman makes two attacks. He suggests that there were "a vast number" of instances in which Wilson failed to recognize genius in contemporaries. This seems a wholly inexplicable charge to make against Wilson, the man who was so instrumental in bringing recognition to, if not "a vast number," at any rate a significant number of contemporary writers, among them the writers of *Axel's Castle, The Boys in the Back Room,* Hemingway, Fitzgerald, Faulkner, Malraux, Pasternak, Berryman, and so on. In a second attack on Wilson's genius as a critic, Hyman uses the tag of "recognition" to point out, in a footnote, what he considers Wilson's "abnormally inflated reputation" as a critic. A clue to Hyman's bias on this subject is perhaps located in the preference he shows, in the ensuing paragraph, for academic critics over Wilson: "In this country he has been praised and acknowledged by men immeasurably his superiors, like F. O. Matthiessen and R. P. Blackmur." Noting that

> In Britain he seems generally accepted as America's foremost critic; *Axel's Castle* appears to be considered the very model of psychological and social criticism, and a whole poetic generation from Spender . . . to . . . Philip Toynbee, as well as such critics as F. R. Leavis, has praised and acknowledged his work.

Hyman is inclined to attribute this to "the fact that almost all of his books of criticism have been published in England." They admire him, in other words, because he is the only American critic they know. It does occur to him, upon noting that Wilson is "practically the only modern American critic so honored in Britain" that this "phenomenon in its turn requires an explanation." What does not occur to him is that any merit in Wilson's work might account for it. He concludes instead with the comment that "Whatever the reason, it is to be hoped that a state of affairs wherein Edmund Wilson is the living American critic whose work is familiar to English writers, while that of say Kenneth Burke and Blackmur is largely not, will not continue indefinitely."[19]

When Hyman turns his attention to Wilson's "wound and bow" theory, he misreads it, as many people did, along the lines I indicated in Chapter 1; that is, he fails entirely to take the Neoptolemus figure into account, and he confuses the idea of art and neurosis. He says, for example, that Wilson's theory of art

> is expressed in the metaphor of Philoctetes' wound and bow, the theory that artistic talent is the obverse side of some unpleasant disability. . . . What its defenders have never satisfactorily explained . . . is why only a small number of the sick, neurotic, regressive, or inferior-feeling personalities become artists.[20]

Instead of seeing art and neurosis, as Wilson and Crews do, as "at best a useful analogy" with a single genesis in conflict, Hyman has reduced the artist's motivation to wish fulfillment, and he proceeds, on the assumption that "A theory is always to some extent the projection of its creator's special problems and situations," to turn the theory on Wilson's own work.[21] He does this, not with any intent of relating the "wound" he expects to uncover there to Wilson's work, but to record "a few notes for such a study" taken from Wilson's imaginative writings. These, says Hyman, "perhaps because of inadequate artistic fusing, seem always to be markedly autobiographical and sometimes to be embarrassingly personal."[22]

After a rather detailed combing of Wilson's novels and plays for clues, he concludes that

> This fictional man is coldhearted and repelled by human contact, yet exacerbated by rampant sexuality; lacking in creative talent, yet impelled to produce imaginative work; committed to commercialism and admiring only integrity; "democratic" and "socialist" while bitterly chauvinistic, snobbish, and contemptuous of people; almost without humor and addicted to parody and satire; aware of the complex and oversimplifying everything, from literature to human relations in a series of false "either ors"; hating all ties, yet unable to cut the umbilical cord binding him to school; desperate for adulation, yet repelling admirers; skeptically minded and dogmatically mannered; yearning to be Flaubert and ending up as Emma Bovary [though not, Hyman insists, in the sense Flaubert himself did].

Hyman concludes this catalogue of traits with the rather belated caveat that "we cannot, without a good deal more personal evidence, identify" them with Edmund Wilson himself, and "so we are forced to say" only that they seem characteristic of all his first-person protagonists. He ends with a comment that is evidently an attempt, at one stroke, to cut down to size both Wilson and his theory: "If any of this applies to Wilson himself, and if the wound-and-bow theory makes any correlation between the extent of the wound and the power of the bow, we are reduced to wondering why Edmund Wilson is not the foremost artist of our time."

As it happens, Leon Edel provides a more sympathetic example of something of the same operation in his introduction to *The Twenties*. He too looks at Wilson's life and work with the wound-and-bow theory in mind. His results will be looked at in more detail in Chapter 12, but one can already see, I think, that in Hyman's hands, both subject and theory are subjected to disfiguring distortion.

A further distortion should be noted. Once again turning Wilson's own words against him, Hyman cites Wilson's standard form of rejection slip, known as "Edmund Wilson regrets," to various requests for his time. Hyman buttresses this with a quote from Granville Hicks to the effect that Wilson was "almost without exception bitter and destructive" in his remarks about friends and a man who displayed "a basic incapacity for cooperation with any group of human beings."[23]

Quoting Hicks on Wilson is, of course, like quoting Adler on Freud. As a man consistently frustrated in his attempts to get Wilson to align himself with the Marxist critical principles espoused by himself and Gold (see Chapter 1), Hicks is hardly a disinterested reporter on Wilson's character. To put the matter in perspective, one should keep in mind that Wilson's rejection of petty calls upon his time and the harsh remarks of one ideological foe need considerable qualification before they can be taken as definitive. Some portion of truth is discernible in them, as we shall see; but they must be set against numerous other instances of Wilson giving friendly assistance and his tireless efforts in behalf of other writers. Thanks to the publication of Wilson's *Letters on Literature and Politics* and *The Nabokov-Wilson Letters*, his lifetime record of cooperation with other literary people is a matter of documented fact.

A final comment on Hyman and we may move on to other

critical evaluations of Wilson less heavily freighted with rancor. The point I wish to make is an ironic one, a recognition of the change that has come over the literary climate since Hyman wrote in so contemptuous a fashion of the critical function of translation. He seemed to feel, in 1948, that the days when Wilson's brand of criticism could have any importance were well in the past: "In a day when a wide gap exists between serious literature and the reading taste of the public, that part of the critic's function which requires him to serve as a conduit between the obscure or difficult work and the reader attains a great importance."

Today, however, the accessibility to a large reading public of such works as Proust and Joyce, James and Eliot is once again in doubt, and we seem to be moving further and further away from a print culture into an age of technology. As we do so, the trait for which Hyman most belittles Wilson – "the ability to write 'clearly and readably and . . . to work the most recondite material into simple and comprehensible English sentences' and 'thus by his own skill could charm summon strangers to make the acquaintance of a great writer'" – will in future, it is safe to say, become more, not less, important with each passing year.[24]

One of the serious charges of "limitation and inadequacy" raised by Hyman I have deliberately deferred for discussion until now, because it is a point raised originally by Delmore Swartz and dealt with on a deeper level of understanding in his essay than Hyman was able to attain.[25] The objection is this, in Schwartz's words apropos *Axel's Castle* and Wilson's discussion of Symbolism:

> He knows the life in back of the work. But when it becomes a point of describing the technical working, the craftsmanship and the unique forms, which are an essential part of Symbolism, and the authors who were influenced by the Symbolists, Wilson is impatient and hurried. [Schwartz has earlier made the point that "the book is not the kind of criticism which helps to germinate new writing; it is not a book for writers."] He is not actually interested in the formal working which delivers the subject matter to the reader (as the rhyme-scheme of a limerick delivers the wit.) . . . the main thing is the gift inside, the subject-matter, which always turns out to be an intimate life.[26]

Here and elsewhere in his fine essay on Wilson, Schwartz sees with amazing clarity the strength and weaknesses of Wilson's critical approach. The interesting thing is that he does not recognize the historical roots of the approach in the humanist tradition of Arnold and Sainte-Beuve. This, in a curious way, frees him to go straight through, behind, and beneath the surface of Wilson's critical thought to make some penetrating observations. These touch on what I have quoted Murray Krieger as describing by the phrase the "metaphysical pathos" of the human motivations beneath the critical theory.

It is quite true, for instance, that Wilson is "impatient and hurried" in his dealing with certain innovations that Joyce introduced in *Ulysses*. In Chapter 1 we saw him complain that it was Joyce's elaborate schema of "these organs and sciences and Homeric correspondences which sometimes so discouraged our interest."[27] Now Schwartz tells us the meaning of that impatience.

In the part of *Ulysses* that is *not* devoted to Homeric correspondences, Schwartz points out,

> we "possess Dublin seen, smelt, heard, and felt, brooded over, imagined and remembered." So by way of literature, one can break through into the real world. It is life that matters; books are a way of getting into life; we forget the formal character of the book as we forget the door through which we came into the house.

Without quite realizing what he has noticed – as I have said, there is no historical recognition of the Arnoldian strain in all of this in Schwartz – he nevertheless gives a sharp description of the trait Wilson and Arnold share: a propensity to co-opt literature in the service of the humanist thrust toward a better society. As Schwartz puts it:

> *Axel's Castle* concludes by suggesting that, important as the authors in question are, and unique and valuable though their discoveries may be in the future, literature must return to wholesome objectivity – not, however, without remembering and using the discoveries of these authors.[28]

Having seen so penetratingly into the deepest springs of

Wilson's critical motivations, Schwartz earns an assent to his strictures on Wilson's critical practice in a way that Hyman somehow never commands. Perhaps another reason lies in the fact that Schwartz, a poet himself, speaks with the authority of a poet. In his critique of Wilson on Symbolism, for example, he quotes Wilson's statement that "To intimate things rather than to state them plainly was thus one of the primary aims of the Symbolists, 'to compete with the suggestiveness of music,' 'to communicate unique personal feelings by a complicated association of ideas represented by a complicated medley of metaphors'."

This, as Schwartz points out, "is the closest Wilson can come to a literary definition" of Symbolist technique. And he concludes that it is a definition "so general and so loose that it permits the inclusion of authors who are really apart from Symbolism, such as Yeats."[29]

Schwartz sees, however, that, as his "life behind the work" allusion suggested, Wilson is nevertheless "excellent on the social and intellectual background of Symbolism": 'Wilson knows very well and paints with sure strokes the isolation of the artist from the rest of society, which brought about the need to cultivate language in this way" (i.e., to emphasize "the connotative usages of language to an exclusion . . . of the denotative usages").[30]

It is quite stunning to notice how consistently throughout his critical career Wilson clung to the same approach, and with the same strength in social and intellectual background, and the same weakness in coverage of elements of literary form. Take, for example, the essays we looked at in contrasting his method with Nabokov's. The social and intellectual background of the eighteenth century captured Wilson's attention with regard to the poetry of Pushkin, and the social and intellectual background of Central Europe in the period following the First World War occupied him in the case of Kafka.

The question arises again, Does it constitute a defect of critical ability to concentrate on such aspects of a work to the relative exclusion of specific details of formal technique? As I have suggested, the answer depends upon an understanding of the kind of criticism being attempted. One does, after all, operate under some obligation to grant each literary critic the "givens" of the method he or she is working in. In terms of Wilson's "givens," the salient one, surely, is the fact that he is writing literary criticism in the tradition of Matthew Arnold and Sainte-Beuve; that is, as an art form, not academic criticism as a form of scholarship.

There is some evidence, however that – under another set of "givens" – Edmund Wilson might have done very well as a formalist critic. His essay on Housman shows a good deal of technical expertise on the ins and outs of prosody, and we know from his dismay over the loss of all formal elegance in Nabokov's translation how integral an importance he gave such elements in his appreciation of the poem's effect.

From a description provided by a student in the seminar Wilson gave on Sound in Literature at Harvard University in the fall of 1969, we learn how exact Wilson's attention to formal elements could be:

> We began, naturally, with onomatopoeia. . . . The discussions were always long because it turned out the subject was really the relation of Sound to Meaning in Language, that is, to what extent and by what means the sound of a word or a line *itself* contributes to the meaning of that sound or line.
>
> So, from simple onomatopoeia and alliteration, we went on naturally to rhythm.[31]

Curiously, the strongest suggestion we have that Wilson *could*, with complete adequacy, have dealt with formal elements of literature if he had wanted to, comes into the picture from the oblique angle of Hyman's bad-tempered recognition that, in "The Omelet of Archibald MacLeish," he is forced to acknowledge him as "a remarkably successful" parodist.

In a somewhat different vein, we may turn now to the comment Richard Gilman made on Wilson as a critic; I refer to his charge that Wilson was a critic who, in 1963, had "ceased for a very long time to criticise."[32] To this charge, as well as to charges put forward by Leonard Kriegel and Charles Frank that Wilson imposed extraneous (that is, moral) standards of value on works that should be judged by artistic merit alone, I would urge a return to the part on the humanist background of Wilson's critical stance.[33] When one recalls the close connection between the kind of criticism Wilson writes and that written by Matthew Arnold, many questions that have arisen to puzzle these and other commentators on Wilson are cleared up.

He is, for example, quite clearly adopting in his own work not only Arnold's moral idealism but also Arnold's view that criticism is "the endeavor, in all branches of knowledge, theology, philosophy, art, science, to see the object as in itself it really is."[34] To Wilson, therefore, it would seem quite natural to make a critical inquiry into a theological matter like the Dead Sea scrolls, or an anthropological one such as the meaning of Hopi tribal dances that he examines in *Red, Blond, Black and Olive*. Within the broad concerns of humanism, after all, art was only one of the subjects properly engaging the attention of the critic.

In response to Kazin's, perhaps not quite serious, objection to Wilson's criticism that it was "more artistic in itself than criticism ought to be," one could urge a return to the statements of Wilson and Sainte-Beuve to the effect that sensitive criticism of a literary text must always be done with the skill of an artist.[35] I am thinking of Wilson's appreciation of the artistry of Van Wyck Brooks and Taine, and of Sainte-Beuve's remark that his "method" would work "only for those who have a natural vocation and talent for close observation: it would always be an *art*, demanding a skilled artist."[36]

Reviewing the serious charges leveled at Wilson's criticism over the years, one can see that most, if not all, of them result from a failure to understand or recognize the kind of criticism Wilson was, in fact, practicing. This is not to suggest that some of them are not well taken, particularly those of Delmore Schwartz regarding Wilson's weaknesses as a critic of poetry. But all of them must be modified somewhat by the greater understanding this study has sought to bring about regarding Wilson's humanist ties.

This brings us to Warner Berthoff's evaluation of Edmund Wilson for the Minnesota Pamphlet Series.[37] In the Introduction, I referred to this study as revealing but incomplete and, although characterizing it as both more appreciative and more temperate than Hyman's I suggested that it, too, is reductionist in viewing Wilson as more a "journalist" than a critic. Having urged a greater emphasis on Wilson's humanism as the way to put previous commentator's charges in perspective, it is now necessary to note that Berthoff attacks Wilson on this very point. He puts the term in quotes to indicate, I assume, that he has doubts about its applicability in Wilson's case – recalling Wilson's comments on Byron, for example, Berthoff says: "Wilson's 'humanism' involves first of all an attitude toward the intensity and confusion of ordinary human life." Fair enough, but he rather unfairly takes only the Byron essay to develop that attitude, a small enough sample to lend credence to his next pronouncement on the subject:

> This generalized "humanism" as it finds expression in particular critical judgments, is traditional and familiar to a fault. The positivistic Victorian conception of literature as a "criticism of life," basically uplifting in purpose, is still at the core of it; . . . "life" . . . has simply been brought up to date. . . . [H]owever, . . . at odd moments . . . we may find it stated quite baldly, even primly, as if for a moment we were listening not to a free-minded partisan of modernism in art and thought but to one of those moralizing schoolmasters . . . Edmund Wilson claimed to have shaken off in his adolescence.[38]

To the extent that, by his reference to the phrase "criticism of life," Matthew Arnold is implicated in Berthoff's charges here, our earlier examination of Arnold's position in some detail will, I believe, show Berthoff to have misrepresented him. He has, in consequence, it seems to me, misrepresented both Wilson and the modern humanist position. I do not intend to go back over that position now but will allow the extensive discussion of it elsewhere in this study to support that assertion. In the degree to which we have discovered that Wilson viewed literature more as a product than as a process, and this is certainly only very partially true, there is some ground for Berthoff's objection to the entire humanist position. It seems to me, however, that he deals with it in a reductionist manner.

Responding to Wilson's criticism of Kafka, Berthoff oversimplifies to the point of asking: "If a critic's 'humanism' is finally a matter of not wanting to be 'let down' or made to linger in discouraging situations, what virtue is there in it?"[39]

In a summing up of his evaluation of Wilson, Berthoff concludes that Wilson lacks the mark of a great critic because he fails to fulfill two criteria, one or the other of which must be met in order for an individual critic to qualify. Wilson fails, says Berthoff, because he "failed to alter the foundations according to which literary judgments are made" and because he failed to create "new images of creative personality for literary history to advance by."[40]

Without inquiring into the bases upon which Berthoff chose his criteria, we may still find it difficult to accept his conclusions about Wilson. The first point one could grant quite easily – who, outside of Aristotle, Coleridge, and, possibly, Northrop Frye had?

The second point, however must give pause to anyone who has read the preceding analyses of Wilson's practice as a critic. His sympathetic projections of himself and his reader into the artistic personalities of Yeats, Proust, Dickens, and James would certainly seem to be powerful arguments that Wilson, on this point, does qualify. Specifically, one could urge Denis Donoghue's point that "It is hardly too much to say that we think of Dickens very largely in Wilson's terms . . . an artist of modern fears and divisions. . . . [H]e is of the modern dispensation now, a tragic hero. . . . [A] major artist, companion of Shakespeare, George Eliot, James, Dostoevsky, Tolstoy."[41]

My own evaluation of Wilson's critical achievement, although implicit in these responses to earlier commentators, will be stated more fully in the conclusion.

CHAPTER TWELVE

The Two Wilsons

*I*t may be said, I believe, that Wilson's whole stance as a critic is not an accident of tradition but rather a consequence of wedding private and professional needs. In other words, the humanist critical approach – with its emphases on literary personality, literary content over literary form; its pronounced bias toward the life-enhancing, broadly moral aspects of the literary work; and its intolerance of pessimism and certain forms of the absurd found in writers such as Kafka and Nabokov – was the intellectual measure he took to satisfy the deepest conscious and unconscious needs of his personality.

In the pages that follow, in deliberate recollection of "The Two Scrooges," Wilson's essay on Dickens, I intend to adopt something of Wilson's own approach, looking at his work as a critic from a more private angle in order to discern that "metaphysical pathos" Krieger spoke of and, perhaps more pertinent, to assist in making a just final evaluation of his achievement.

This new perspective will necessitate looking at Wilson's life as well as at his criticism. I shall draw my data on his life in large part from Wilson's own letters, diaries, journals, and the extensive autobiographical disclosures he left in a variety of scattered sources; but the interpretation I shall put upon that data will be drawn very largely from the insights of Leon Edel. Edel, as I noted elsewhere, first perceived that the Neoptolemus figure in Wilson's retelling of the Greek myth of Philoctetes, "The Wound and the Bow" essay from which his theory of the psychological

221

genesis of art is derived, is in fact the symbolic representation of Wilson himself as a critic.

The sympathetic Neoptolemus, we recall, fights to wrest from the insensitive Greek forces some understanding of the myth's artist-figure, Philoctetes, and, by his success in that attempt, is instrumental in achieving the Greek victory over Troy. Edel saw that this figure exemplifies Wilson in his stance as a critic. I have tried to present as my contribution in the present study the insight that it also exemplifies the ideals and practices of a definite critical tradition, originating in classical humanism and carried forward by Sainte-Beuve and Matthew Arnold. Further, it can be seen that this tradition is perpetuated in the modern period in Wilson's critical practice.

In attempting to draw this relationship, I depart somewhat in what follows from Edel's idea that the origin of Wilson's "sympathetic imagination" was the hereditary gift of a similar property in Edmund Wilson, Sr. I do not dispute this; I simply find other, to me more compelling, sources for it. These I take to be both literary and personal.

The literary ones I have examined in the portion of Chapter 4, which expounds the humanist critical tradition and Wilson's connections to it. The personal reasons will be the subject of a closer look here.

I begin by quoting a characterization of Edmund Wilson made by Mary McCarthy, who was the third of his four wives. Taken from Doris Grumbach's book, *The Company She Kept*, it indicates that, on an unspecified occasion, speaking directly of Edmund Wilson, Mary McCarthy summed him up as follows: "He was two people. One is this humanistic Princetonian critic and the other is a sort of minotaur, really with his terror and pathos."[1]

Leon Edel, too, touches on the duality in Wilson, referring to what he calls "the problem of Wilson's being cantankerous and uncompromising, and in some ways a 'cold fish' in certain of his personal relations—qualities which melted away the moment he entered the more personal world of his writings. In his prose he invariably was warm, factual, lively, playful and ingratiating—those qualities that seem to have been a source of great attractiveness in him to women. Personal relations were often a chaos; but in his ordered well-arranged critical world, where he could play with his wit and his ideas he was generous, outgoing, searching, deeply perceptive – the well-tempered humanist and critic."[2]

Concentrating for the moment on the better tempered of these "two Wilsons," I wish now to try to isolate the elements of that Princetonian humanism as they evolved in Wilson's personal life. Looking over his writings with this as our focus, we can see, I think, that Wilson's version of humanism as a personal philosophy never takes the form of explicit statement. Yet it is noteworthy that, throughout his work, whatever finds favor in his eyes – whether it is fortitude in the face of adversity, indifference to monetary gain, or lifelong perseverance in one's work, even in the teeth of approaching death – all seems imbued with the spirit of classical humanism.

No example of Wilson's writing is fuller of this spirit than his warm portrait of Alfred Rolfe, teacher of Greek at the Hill School and, in many ways, the youthful Wilson's culture hero:

> Mr. Rolfe was the perfect Hellenist. He made you get everything exactly right, and this meant a good deal of drudgery. But one was also made to feel that there was something worth having there behind the numbered paragraphs . . . something exhilarating in the air of the classroom, human, heroic and shining.[3]

There seems also to have been a strain of humanist tradition throughout Wilson's rather patrician upbringing. One finds evidence of it in his autobiographical references to his forebears' large libraries and their wide travel. This strain was continued and enhanced by his experience at Princeton University. There, he was impressed by the enthusiasm of his friend, T. K. Whipple, for what Wilson called (anticipating Mary McCarthy) "our Princeton humanism"; and there he fell under the direct influence of Christian Gauss.

Gauss, a man steeped both in the general European tradition of humanism and in the critical tradition of Sainte-Beuve, taught Wilson Dante and Flaubert in his courses in Italian and French literature. Just as Taine, James, Arnold, and Sainte-Beuve had provided Wilson with literary models, Gauss provided him with a significant role model in a personal way. He became, to a large extent, Wilson's mentor at Princeton and remained a respected friend.

According to Wilson's dedication to him in *Axel's Castle*, it was from Gauss that he got his idea of "what literary criticism ought to be – a history of man's ideas and imaginings in the setting of the conditions which have shaped them."

Not surprisingly, Wilson's memoir of his old friend, "Christian Gauss as a Teacher of Literature," portrays him as a veritable representative of the humanist type.[4] He describes Gauss's teaching as undogmatic; and he praises his "fluidity of mind," which starts trains of thought but leaves conclusions open. Gauss, says Wilson, possessed a continuity of tone and a neutrality of style that gave to his discourse of a lifetime the impression of one long conversation.

All this, apparently, was combined in Gauss, with extreme flexibility and an enormous range. Wilson tells us that he seemed to be in touch with "what was going on everywhere" and to know everything. These are qualities Wilson admired enormously, and Gauss's example may have inspired a talk he tells of having with his father on the subject of his future:

> After college, before I enlisted, I told him I should like to go to Washington to try my hand at political journalism. "At Princeton," he answered, "you specialized in literature; then you went to Columbia Summer School to study sociology and labor. Now you want to do political journalism. Don't you think you ought to concentrate on something?" "Father," I replied, "what I want to do is to try to get to know something about all the main departments of human thought. . . . "[5]

Wilson's father termed his son's ambition a possible one and told him, if he was really serious, to go ahead with it – a project that once again identifies him with the ideals of humanism.

Of course, these pedagogical, familial, and environmental factors are not the only ones that went into the making of Wilson's mind and his philosophical position. I regard them, however, as *fundamental*. And I think it is worthy of note that the humanistic elements of Wilson's literary models were, if anything, reinforced by these biographical connections.

That Princeton and all the humanistic values it stood for to him continued to exert an almost mystical power over Wilson's thoughts is evident in a glimpse we get of him in the last years of his life, as remembered by his friend and *New Yorker* colleague, Penelope Gilliatt. She tells of returning to the *New Yorker* offices from one of the outings habitual to them during Wilson's infrequent trips to New York. Suddenly, about half-way between Fifth and Sixth Avenues on Forty-third Street, Wilson's face went very gray, his breath came sharply, and he fell against the nearest building clutching his side.

Concerned, Miss Gilliatt reports that she offered to call him an ambulance, to which he replied, "No, don't do that. Just get me to the Princeton Club [a distance of about 50 yards], and I'll be all right."[6]

Allen Tate gives us a picture of the Wilson of the early 1920s; it, too, very much in the vein of the Princeton humanist:

> When I first arrived in New York, in 1924, I went walking on Saturday afternoons in Washington Square where Edmund Wilson had a downstairs apartment in one of the old brownstone houses. He sat at his typewriter by the large window, typing busily or looking down through his pince-nez at the book on his knees. He never looked out of the window. Sometimes I waved to him but there was never any response."[7]

This is the first ominous sign that, behind the Princetonian humanist critic, there might be a minotaur, or at least a 'cold fish.' Edel remarks that

> His modes of verbal aggression were in counterpoint with his verbal amiability. One is prompted to say that this problem, which deprived him of certain empathies, made it difficult for him in criticism to deal with writers of our time, like Kafka, who explored man's troubled dream-existence. It ran counter to Wilson's concreteness, derived from his ability to look at reality without having to feel it.[8]

When the first of several posthumous volumes of Edmund Wilson's notebooks and diaries was published, under the title *The Twenties*, it provided some clues to this mystery and the eventual solution of the problem of the "two Wilsons."

Looked at as literature, *The Twenties* is rather flat. Looked at as an index to Wilson, however, it is a fascinating, revealing, but largely subtextual history of the "wound" that drove Wilson to great successes as a literary critic and cultural historian but that also extracted from him a fearful toll of aborted relationships and, to some extent, failed artistic ambitions. (Wilson's novels, *I Thought of Daisy* and *Memoirs of Hecate County*, like his plays and poetry, never achieved the success of his other work.)

The important insight into Wilson provided by it (and reinforced by the recently published companion volumes, *The Thirties, The Forties,* and *The Fifties*) is that, unlike the primarily *imaginative* writer who uses as the material of his art his direct experience of life, Wilson had early on adopted a primarily *critical* mode of being whereby the material of *his* art consisted in his responding to life, not in direct relation to it but as it was organized and filtered through the screen of art.

That, at any rate, is the serious implication one draws from such entries in the notebooks as the one paraphrased here from February 1924.

Wilson is on a train heading for California. He is reading Sophocles' *Electra* in Greek. There is a little girl on the train: Maxine, age eight, traveling alone from Milwaukee. Wilson takes note of her as she lunches on Zu-Zu gingersnaps, cries from homesickness, laughs at her own jokes, and stalls so she will not have to go to bed in a berth.

After a while, the Greek play begins to have a morbid effect on him. The tension of waiting for the girl's revenge to work itself out in the murder of her mother tells on his mood. He thinks of other gruesome murders closer to home, some real and some fictional ones he has just read about – all Californian.

The last report Wilson gives on the little girl concludes this way: "I am afraid she is going to grow up into a mealy-faced, mole-specked, hard-r'd, pale-green-eyed Middle Western girl, who says 'This Here'."[9]

One can't help but feel that Maxine might have fared better if Wilson had been reading *Antigone* instead. Or, better still, *What Maisie Knew*, a Henry James novel he rather liked that has a child heroine.

There is another demonstration of art affecting Wilson's attitude toward life in the notebook entry he wrote after seeing the film, "Spread Eagle." He was much moved by the guns being transported up to the front to the tune of "and those caissons go rolling along." It prompted him to muse

> How the war – by fettering our activity and our attention to inhuman, uninteresting things, to the deliberate, method-ical relentless machinery of destruction – made us appre-ciate human beings. . . . With what relief, what delight, one turned from the guns . . . to the good nature of a comrade. . . . I never loved humanity so deeply and sincerely before and I never expect to again."[10]

Remembering Wilson's earlier *A Prelude* (the notebooks covering 1908-1919), it is interesting to note that here, in response to the artificial stimulus of a movie, he is writing more expressively and with more emotion about the war than he was able to do under the stimulus of war itself.

In Wilson's account of his relations with women, too, the emotional block is pronounced. Mary Blair, Wilson's first wife (an actress who appeared in many O'Neill plays), is scarcely referred to except as a shadowy figure who shares, for a time, an apartment with Wilson on Washington Square. Of their daughter, Rosalind, there is barely a trace, save for one passage in which Wilson manifests a linguistic interest in the speech habits she has acquired.

Another selection might properly take its place as a key item in the Wilson index. The entry seems to reflect a displace-ment of the emotion and wonder Wilson perhaps felt for his in-fant daughter, registering it instead as a warm appreciation of the cleverness, beauty, and ingenuity he finds in her set of Ger-man blocks.[11]

In contrast to this reticence about the women close to home, many entries contain extensive descriptions of taxicab rides and conversations on couches with an assortment of follies girls, streetwalkers, and sales clerks with whom Wilson seems to have struck up frequent but fleeting acquaintances. There are isolated entries in these notebooks in which Wilson shows that he understands in part the nature of his problem; he speaks deprecatingly of the praise he had, even in the 1920s, already begun to receive for his "sober judgment" in literary matters, saying, "yet, except when I was writing about literature, nobody could have worse judgments and I – I was invariably treating occasions of importance either too casually or too flippantly or extravagantly overdoing other occasions which were intrinsically trivial."[12]

He tells us of his propensity, when in the midst of one of those archetypal 1920s parties, complete with Greenwich Village setting, bad gin, and Bohemian company, to go off to one side and write about it. We learn from his notes Wilson's conviction that "Literature is merely the result of our rude collisions with reality." Again and again, reality is portrayed as the wounder, the conveyer of rude shocks, and human life as a disease against which some (i.e., the critic) may prefer to be immunized by the protective inoculations of art rather than "risk the more serious and *perhaps for him fatal*, infection of life itself" [my italics].[13]

Wilson saw the act of reporting as a way of bringing art to the service of staving off the pains of life, as if by clinging to the external factual world, by observing and setting it down accurately, an outward order could be achieved, a valuable defense to pit against the chaos within. In fact, in this journal, Wilson gives us more than two hundred entries of nature description that represent just such acutely observed pictures of external reality.

In the second half of *The Twenties*, the functions of sex take over the territory formerly occupied by these external landscapes, absorbing a great deal of Wilson's time and nearly all the attention of his notes. The way his working-class girl friends look, feel to the touch, taste, and smell is minutely noticed by Wilson, who seems more than ever enveloped in the pathos of alienation as he resolutely records the pertinent facts about the agitated limbs, the various undergarments, and the personal histories of his plebeian bedmates.

Finally, toward the very end, the notebooks hint at the possibility that, as Edel suggests, an immersion in a certain kind of literature (Wilson was reading the Symbolists at the time, in preparation for *Axel's Castle*) was having a liberating effect on Wilson's life. Wilson was involved at this time with a girl, Anna, in a more than usually lasting, more than usually satisfying affair. Whether or not his intense personal reaction to, say, the lustiness of Joyce helped bring it about, in the greater tenderness Wilson shows for his sexual partner and in his greater air of relaxation before the task of writing about sex, the last entries seem to take on the note of a freer man. Ultimately, Wilson is able to take the reader into his confidence and into his bedroom, even when he is in the presence of one of his wives (actually, a sort of prewedding honeymoon that he shares with Margaret Canby, in Connecticut). The volume ends on a mellow note, with a touching moment of understanding between himself and Mary Blair achieved, poignantly enough, on the occasion of their having been granted a divorce.[14]

I have said that as a guide to the history of Wilson's psychic "wound," the revelations these notebooks have to offer are largely subtextual. Providentially, however, Leon Edel's insightful, frankly psychological introductions, especially to *The Twenties*, provide the necessary key. Edel attempts to see through the flat, often repetitive notes in these notebooks with a double vision, understanding them as the acts of a man for whom making them at all was a gesture of brave defiance in the face of unacknowledged terrors.

The Twenties both painfully exposes Wilson's inadequacies of personal response and gives expression to some triumphant victories over those inadequacies. In its dogged, careful observation of the way things were, it becomes the document of a man *willing* into life a more compassionate nature for himself than the one he really possessed.

An entry from his journal, *Upstate*, suggests that one reason for his delay in bringing out the 1920s notebooks was that Wilson both wanted and did not want to go back over those years:

> I can hardly believe, at my age now [he was 72] and so far away from that period, that I really lived through all that and did all the things that I did. . . . Some wonderful things to look back on, but also some naive and nasty things that I hate to have to remember.[15]

Ultimately, Wilson's devotion to the truth prevailed over both his ambivalence and his procrastination. He made the significant decision, should he not live to bring this volume out personally, to request that it be brought out under the direction of Leon Edel. The choice was not dictated by sentiment: the two men were not very close. It was deliberate, and therefore an implicit endorsement of Edel's psychological orientation. The Edel introduction is, in fact, very similar in approach to the one he has taken in his biography of another American man of letters, Henry James. Wilson must have realized it would be this line of country in which Edel would place him.

True to form, Edel begins his introduction in the form of a biographical note, with some glimpses of the young Wilson "Riding a bicycle at thirteen or fourteen," saying to himself suddenly, "I'll eventually have friends with whom I'll have something in common." Noting that "when he emerged from college," Wilson still felt "he was 'unable to get on with ordinary people,' " Edel goes on to say that:

> He had many friends and the admiration of the world when he died in 1972 at seventy-seven, but there was to the end something aloof and shut-in, as if he were still reaching out from behind obsolete invisible barriers, using the full force of his intellect to establish a truce with mankind.[16]

According to Edel, the story of the psychic "wound" that is the source of Wilson's uncommon devotion to literature and – I would add – the source of his conviction that literature is indispensable to life, begins in his lonely boyhood.

Wilson was brought up in an eminently respectable Calvinist household that held to all the forms of religion but had for several generations lost touch with any real religious spirit. He was the child of an unhappy marriage, in a home where the mother was (perhaps hysterically) deaf and the father, brilliant but neurasthenic, was extremely remote and often absent altogether.

Edel says that "To understand Edmund Wilson's particular talents as writer and critic we must look closely at his father."[17] He tells us that "Edmund Wilson Sr. was a lawyer, and in middle life attorney general of the state of New Jersey"[18] and states that "He practiced law with resource and skill, and had great successes."[19] However, Edel goes on, "He dropped into despondency for long periods," which caused him to withdraw behind the green felt door of a downstairs chamber in his home or, at times, to spend periods in a private sanitorium.[20] He is described as "a handsome man, with fine moustaches, distinctly a 'personality,' and yet something veiled and mysterious, with depths of depression, in his eyes.[21]

Nevertheless, Edel points out, "in his professionalism and commitment, the father set an example the son would always follow." That is, like him, Wilson "worked most of his life . . . distinctly alone and with great concentration and thoroughness" whenever "he became genuinely involved in a project."[22]

Wilson's mother, whom Edel describes as a "motherly presence that was not in the least 'motherly,' " was, according to him, "a woman of limited intelligence, prosaic, self-confident and self-assured." He reports that she was "often openly hostile to her husband" and suggests that "Her deafness may have been partly psychological: She had taken Edmund Sr. to see a great specialist in England; the specialist pronounced him "mad" and the wife during the voyage home suddenly became totally deaf."[23]

Small wonder that the young Edmund described the atmosphere of his home as "oppressive." There was little emotional nourishment in such a household for a bright, imaginative boy, and the indications are that, in the earliest stages of his relationship to it, literature was for Wilson a veritable life-support system.

Out of the bleak necessity of this loveless home came his conviction that literature possessed magical properties for the relief of pain, that it could make life seem full of color and interest and meaning when in his own damped-down experience it contained nothing of the kind.

The one thing the Wilsons—and on Edmund's mother's side, the Kimbals—were prepared to lavish on the young was culture; well-stocked libraries abounded. In handsome sets of Robert Louis Stevenson and Kipling and Sir Walter Scott, Wilson was to find an escape into a world of excitement and feeling he was scarcely prepared for by anything in his well-ordered but dull existence.

Edel says with regard to Wilson's "wound" that "His father's relapses into apathy" and "his mother's deafness . . . were the central facts." Of the latter, he reports that "Edmund Wilson told himself later that even if his mother had been able to hear, he doubted whether they would have had much to say to each other."[24] This is probably true. According to one source quoted by Edel, "Her criterion of success was making money and the status that money gave – which both her husband and her son despised."

Indeed, as Edel portrays her, Wilson's mother was a "woman who would much sooner have had her son be an athlete." He tells us that "even when a very old lady she continued to attend the Princeton football games." On the other hand, "She never read Edmund's writings."

To this apparition of motherhood, Edel credits Wilson's lasting impression of women as beings who "could inspire fear." (Edel goes on to say "Men of course were easier and more accessible" and, he suggests, working-class girls were, too.)[25] Yet, as Edel tells us, for all his adult years Edmund Wilson kept with him one picture of his mother taken "when she was young" (i.e., not deaf) and that he "always kept around him pictures of" her "gardens at Talcottville and Red Bank."[26] And, in spite of his speculation that even if they could have talked they would have had little to say to each other, he seems to have been unable to crush a deep-seated yearning for such an interchange. Edel tells us that "He remembered in his teens making methodical notes on the train home from school – 'notes of topics about which I could communicate to her.'"[27] It seems to me that here, perhaps even more than in the green felt door that shut him off from his father, is the source of Wilson's deepest hurt.

In an article for the *New Republic* announcing the publication of Wilson's notebooks of *The Thirties* (of which he is also the editor) Edel says of one entry, written on the death of Wilson's second wife, Margaret Canby, that it testifies "to Wilson's core difficulty – there were things he could not allow himself to feel." He goes on to make the crucial connection, then, between this "wound" and Wilson's "bow": 'What he could do was to displace emotion from the human scene into his writing."

It was Wilson's curious fate to be both Philoctetes and Neoptolemus, an artist whose wound had incapacitated him for direct emotional response to life. I do not at all mean to say that one is justified in seeing Wilson as an artist *manqué*. The artistry that he achieves as a critic *is* fully achieved. But I think one must see a measure of that "metaphysical pathos" we keep coming back to in the art that can only be wholly successful in the service of other artists' visions. It was, when one thinks of it, no small triumph that Wilson achieved over his "wound." He was, as he knew, "blocked" in his expression of direct emotion: he made of the gift Frank Kermode discerned in him – the gift of "powerful direct response" to literature – a whole new connection. As Edel puts it, there, "At his desk, the world fell into place. He was free to grasp, explain, sympathize, understand Proust's sensitive childhood, experience Dickens' sufferings and Turgenev's struggles with his mother."[28]

He had said of Marx's idea of consciousness that it left men, not rigidly, economically determined but free to deal with circumstances as they found them. Under the circumstances in which he found himself, Edmund Wilson declared early for literature, and he went on declaring for it to his dying day. (According to his daughter, Helen, he had the card table he worked on drawn up close to the side of his bed during his last illness, so that he could go on writing even though he was in an oxygen tent.)

As we look at his notebooks and letters it becomes plain that few have made higher claims for literature – and few have made greater claims upon it – than Edmund Wilson. He expected it to fill areas of his life that most people fill with other things: religion, causes, society, even love. He expected it to wield the kind of power to effect social change for which most people look, if they look for it at all, to government. A good deal of his early humanistic optimism had been disillusioned by the time he wrote, in his sixties, a book called *A Piece of My Mind*. But he was still able to say "I believe in literature."[29]

Perhaps the depth of his feeling for it can only be understood if one grasps that, for Wilson, the substitution worked. He speaks of the feeling he has when he encounters a successful work of literature as, first of all *relief*, then a sense of *power*, then a sense of *joy*.[30] This is strong testimony to the effect that the return Wilson got for his devotion to literature was a satisfying one for him. The joy he finds in it is implicit throughout his criticism, but it is from his letters – now available in part in the volume called *Letters on Literature and Politics* – that one gets the most direct testimony of the value it held for him. Turning to the *Letters* is like turning away from the "terror and pathos" of the private Wilson to encounter once again the first Wilson, and it is in his full professional regalia that I mean to take this last look at him.

The first reaction is surprise – here is all the spontaneity, vitality, and humanity of the personal voice that seemed so unaccountably absent from his journals, especially of *The Twenties*. One checks the letters of that same period and discovers that it is not the period that makes the difference but the genre. When Wilson is talking to his friends and associates on paper, he can display all these things. When he is talking to himself, he permits himself to speak only in a nearly unaccented, impersonal tone. How are we to explain this?

Wilson himself may give the best explanation when he tells us that, for him transforming life into literature is a way to control a chaotic world, to free the "worried intelligence and balked emotions" induced in the sensitive by exposure to that chaos. In his journals of the 1920s, Wilson had not yet learned to turn the entries into literary art, as he was later to do so superbly in *Upstate*. His comparative naturalness and ease in the letters is a reflection of his regard for letter writing as a branch of literature, and he assumes a comfortable literary persona in them almost from the beginning.

Not surprisingly then, the Wilson we find in them is the Princetonian humanist critic. His broadly humanist outlook accounts for the fact that when he is writing about literature Wilson is never very far from writing about politics, and vice versa. The special attention Wilson pays in all his writing to the interstices between literature and life make the selection of letters focusing on just the two subjects, literature and politics, very apt in his case.

There is nothing abstract about the commentary these letters offer on either subject. To F. Scott Fitzgerald, who gratefully acknowledged him as "my literary conscience," Wilson writes a long critique – affectionate but critical – of Fitzgerald's first published novel, *This Side of Paradise*. It is the sort of close scrutiny any first novelist might covet. Wilson's criticism is both particular ("You handicap your story, for one thing, by making your hero go to the war and then completely leaving the war out") and general (as when he says, "I do think the most telling poetry and romance may be achieved by keeping close to life," but advises Fitzgerald to "Cultivate a universal irony and do read something other than contemporary British novelists.")[31] In either case, it is convincing and sound, and it seems to have had a beneficent effect on Fitzgerald's work.

There are letters to his lifelong friend, John Dos Passos, on both subjects. *Adventures of a Young Man* gets the same kind of close, helpful going-over Fitzgerald's novel got.[32] In the 1960s, the political interchange between the two heated up considerably as they took each other's measure in the light of the various social revolutions then dominating the world scene. In 1964, writing from Paris, Wilson tells Dos Passos:

> I have never regarded myself as a liberal, because the word does not mean anything definite. . . . You've been railing against "the liberals" all your life, and my impression is that your conception of them is a projection of some suppressed alter ego that you perpetually feel you have to discredit. You used to assail this myth from the radical side, and now you assail it from the conservative.[33]

To Malcolm Cowley, in 1938, Wilson expresses the depth of his feeling about both literature and politics – and his sense of the necessary distinction between them: "What in God's name has happened to you?" he asks Cowley.

> I was told some time ago that you were circulating a letter asking for endorsements of the last batch of Moscow trials. . . . I liked your poems in *Poetry* and your remarks about the revolutionary symbolists; and I wish you would purge your head of politics – revolutionary and literary alike – and do the kind of valuable work of which you're capable. I think politics is bad for you because it's not real to you: because what you're really practicing is not politics but literature; and it only messes up a job like yours to pretend it's something else.[34]

Some of this ire has been occasioned by Cowley's praise of Hemingway's *To Have and Have Not* on what Wilson suspected were Marxist grounds rather than those of literary merit alone.

The early letters are amazing for the purposefulness they show Wilson displaying about what he wants from life and how he is going to get it. He seems to have known early that he was going to turn out to be Edmund Wilson. "My single aim has been literature," he wrote a school friend, Stanley Dell, from an army outpost in France, when he was only twenty-two.

Yet, he already understood the duty he must pay to the claims of life: that is, remaining *engagé* in the social and political affairs of the world. "How should I remain *au-dessus de la mêlée* when better men have assumed burdens as dismal as any involved in modern warfare," he wrote.[35]

But he was always first and foremost a literary man, and these letters are the record of a professional, toiling endlessly in the service of what was for him an almost religious calling. He is forever urging this one of his correspondents to reprint an old piece too good to let perish, that one to contribute a new translation of this or a fresh introduction to that – all the while urging them, as he urged himself, to "Be Strong." He is always coming up with suggestions for increasing the sum of the world's art. Some of this he got paid for in the course of his various posts as editor at *Vanity Fair*, the *New Republic*, and elsewhere (though, as one learns from his letters of negotiation with his employers, in many cases not well paid by any means). Much of it he did simply because he couldn't help himself.

Wilson's devotion to literature and to professional standards manifests itself in these letters frequently in the passion he shows for accuracy, for getting it right. He will enter the most minute cavil into the most affirmative letter of praise (or, more often, whole pages of corrections into a mixed bag of positive and negative reactions). He did it in the interests of professionalism and critical detachment. When one learns from these pages the universality and indifference with which he applied this rule (it was visited upon Gilbert Highet one day, Vladimir Nabokov the next, and went on for more than fifty years), it even becomes possible to enter into Wilson's point of view about it.

He is genuinely puzzled and surprised that the recipients should take his remarks about their work amiss. Again and again he is obliged to apologize in response to their wounded outcries – saying he'd meant no harm, that what he had said or written should not have been taken personally. In his view, getting it right was all that counted.

In spite of Wilson's emotional blocks, many of these letters do show emotion: the moving letter he wrote to Zelda Fitzgerald on the occasion of Scott's death, for example, or the equally touching, elegaic letter to Dos Passos upon the death of his wife, Katy. There are powerful letters, too, in which Wilson goes to bat for writers he admires who are in trouble: Mary McCarthy when she was at loggerheads with the *Partisan Review*, and Ezra Pound at the time of his incarceration in St. Elizabeth's Hospital.

Mary McCarthy happened to be his wife in that period. Pound, on the other hand, seems always to have irritated Wilson personally. And, though he admired Pound's poetry, Wilson was so little fond of his critical writing that he once asked John Peale Bishop to stop Pound from contributing any more of his ill-written, ill-spelled, "incoherent and all but illegible" articles to the *New Republic*.[36]

Wilson's style serves him admirably for the bulk of the letters included. Even in an instance when the tone required is softer and more intimate than any in Wilson's repertoire, his effort gains in poignance what it loses in ease. I am thinking of his rather halting attempt (as he sailed for Russia on the *Berengaria* in 1935) to tell Louise Bogan that "I want you to know how appreciative of you and how fond of you, my dear, I really am: I have never had this kind of companionship with a woman for any length of time ever before in my life."[37] Who but Edmund Wilson would use a colon (correctly, of course) in a sentence designed to tell someone of his warm feelings?

I have said of the notebooks of *The Twenties* that they give, from one point of view, a picture of a man "Willing into life a more compassionate nature for himself than the one he really possessed." In the *Letters* this impression becomes more vivid. Wilson's personal, stylistic imprint – reason without frills, plainspoken thoroughness of expression – is present and persistent, whatever the individual letter's content and tone; whether we find him offering (at sixteen) to exchange candid opinions on books with his school chum, Alfred Bellinger, or joking with his friend Dos Passos about their mutual cardiac conditions at the age of seventy-five; whether the person he is addressing is a Wellfleet neighbor or T. S. Eliot.

The classical model is Marcus Aurelius, who spells it out as the ideal of being always the same and the same to everyone. Perhaps because the creation of a strong person is so largely a product of the "will" – and because will is a word that has largely been dropped from the modern vocabulary, Wilson's manifestation of it in these letters makes a very powerful impression.

The letters all, of course, bear the imprint of Wilson's orderly mind, and nearly all of them possess enough individual interest so that they may be savored a bit at a time. Nevertheless, they achieve their greatest impact in the aggregate, for here is the record of a lifetime spent in the steadfastness of one pursuit, one set of values, a lifetime that achieves, in the end, something close to heroism.

CONCLUSION

*F*inally, it remains to give my answer to the question raised by Clive James in the *Times Literary Supplement* review: "What does Wilson's effort amount to? In the words of James, "We need to decide whether critical work which has plainly done so much to influence its time vanishes with its time or continues." James indicates that the answer could be positive only if the work could be seen to have "embodied, not just recommended, a permanent literary value."[1]

I have suggested that the permanent value that remains is Wilson's humanism. It seems to me to remain after other views have risen and cancelled each other out. It also seems to me to contain the answer to the question Elmer Borklund says is "perhaps the most important question one can ask" about Wilson's critical thinking: "what is the relationship between historical explanations – and the act of literary evaluation?"[2]

The answer is that it is the link that connects literature to life and life to history – the link that holds the whole chain of Wilson's critical and private preoccupations together. Only when we see the struggles out of which a work of art was made, Wilson believed, and only when we feel the modification of our own sensibilities by the work – some ache of disorder calmed, some area of the meaningless rendered articulate – only then would we be able to draw the just critical judgment.

For that, Wilson himself has given us our cue when he wrote of his teacher of Greek, "Mr. Rolfe":

> He died last June in Concord, and it is hard to imagine him gone: I had thought of him as a permanent element, a kind of human classic, who persisted through the changes at the Hill and the Wars and revolutions of the world . . . and sud-

denly, as I write this memoir, it seems to me that the stream
he was following flowed out of a past that is now remote: . . .
from the days when people went to Germany to hear Wagner
and study Greek; from Matthew Arnold, from Bernard
Shaw – now almost an old-fashioned classic like Arnold. And
I am glad to renew my sense of Alfred Rolfe's contribution to
it, as I realize that I myself have been trying to follow and
feed it at a time when it has been running low.[3]

To follow Wilson, then, as *he* followed and fed the faltering
stream of humanism, and perhaps even to renew our acquaintance with that stream as it found its – less liquid – embodiment
in him as "a permanent element, a kind of human classic" has
been the course attempted here.

NOTES

PREFACE

1. Denis Donoghue, "The English Dickens and *Dombey and Son*," in *Dickens Centennial Essays*, p. 1.

2. Kenneth Burke, *The Philosophy of Literary Form: Studies in Symbolic Action*, p. 21.

3. R. S. Crane, *The Languages of Criticism and the Structure of Poetry*, p. 192.

4. See "A New Look at Lit Crit," *Newsweek* 22 June 1981, pp. 80-83; Madalynne Reuter, "NBCC Bestows Awards, Hears Alfred Kazin, Elects New Officers," *Publisher's Weekly* 12 February 1982, pp. 44-46; and Jacques Barzun, "A Little Matter of Sense," *New York Times Book Review*, 21 June 1987, p. 1 ff.

5. Crane, p. 192.

INTRODUCTION

1. "Edmund Wilson and the End of the American Dream," (unsigned) rev. of *Upstate* by Edmund Wilson, *Times Literary Supplement*, 19 (May 1972), p. 562. Reprinted in Clive James, *First Reactions: Critical Essays 1968-79* (New York: Knopf, 1980, pp. 3-16.

2. Leonard Kriegel, *Edmund Wilson* (Carbondale and Edwardsville: Southern Illinois Univ. Press, 1971); Charles P. Frank, *Edmund Wilson* (New York: Twayne, 1970); Sherman Paul, *Edmund Wilson: A Study of Literary Vocation in Our Time* (Urbana: Univ. of Illinois Press, 1965); and *Edmund Wilson: The Man and His Work*, ed. John Wain (New York: New York University Press, 1978).

3. Richard Costa, *Our Neighbor in Talcottville* (Syracuse: Syracuse Univ. Press, 1980); George H. Douglas, *Edmund Wilson's America* (Lexington: Univ. of Kentucky Press, 1983; Philip French, *Three Honest Men: Edmund Wilson, F. R. Leavis, and Lionel Trilling* (Manchester: Carcanet New Press, 1984); and David Castronovo, *Edmund Wilson* (New York: Frederick Ungar, 1984).

4. Lewis M. Dabney, "Edmund Wilson: The Early Years," Diss. Columbia 1965; James Y. Dayananda, "Marxist Contributions to Edmund Wilson's Literary Criticism," Diss. Temple 1969; Joseph R. Fargnoli, "Edmund Wilson and the Sociology of Literature, "Diss.

Univ. of Rhode Island 1985; Brian Gallagher, "The Historical Consciousness of Edmund Wilson," Diss. Univ. of Pennsylvania 1973; Janet Carol Groth, "The Literary Criticism of Edmund Wilson," Diss. New York Univ. 1982; Kenneth John Kirkpatrick, "Edmund's Castle: A Study of Edmund Wilson's Three Major Works," Diss. Harvard 1986; Paul Kluge, "Wanderers: Three American Writers of the Twenties, Diss. Univ. of Chicago 1967; Louis Menand IV, "The Nineteenth Century in Modernist Criticism: T. S. Eliot, Edmund Wilson, and F. R. Leavis," Diss. Columbia 1980; James Morris Rodgers, "Dynamics of Creation: The Literary Criticism of Edmund Wilson," Diss. University of Rochester, 1967; Melvyn Rosenthal, "The American Writer and His Society: The Response to Estrangement in the Works of Nathaniel Hawthorne, Randolph Bourne, Edmund Wilson, Norman Mailer, Saul Bellow," Diss. Univ. of Connecticut 1968; Mark D. Savin, "More Violent the Contraries: A Study of Edmund Wilson," Diss. Stanford 1976; and Lorraine A. Schlesinger, " Edmund Wilson on American Literature," Diss. Univ. of Maryland 1968.

5. R. J. Kaufman, "The Critic as Custodian of Sanity," *Critical Quarterly*, 1 (Summer 1959), pp. 85-98; Norman Podhoretz, "Edmund Wilson: Then and Now," in his *Doings and undoings*, (New York: Farrar, Straus, & Giroux, 1964); and Frank Kermode, "Edmund Wilson and Mario Praz," in his *Puzzles and Epiphanies* (London: Routledge and Kegan Paul, 1962).

6. Warner Berthoff, *Edmund Wilson*, No. 67 in Univ. of Minnesota Pamphlets on American Writers (Minneapolis: Univ. of Minnesota Press, 1968) p. 9.

7. Berthoff, p. 36.

8. Edmund Wilson, *The Twenties: From Notebooks and Diaries of the Period*, ed. Leon Edel (New York: Farrar, Straus, & Giroux), p. 427; hereafter cited as *TT*.

9. Lionel Trilling, ed., Intro: *The Portable Matthew Arnold* (New York, Viking, 1949), pp. 7-8.

CHAPTER ONE

1. Edmund Wilson, *Axel's Castle: A Study in the Imaginative Literature of 1870-1930*, p. 18; hereafter cited as *AC*.

2. Edmund Wilson, *The Wound and the Bow: Seven Studies in Literature*, pp. 63-64; hereafter cited as *WB*.

3. Edmund Wilson, *Patriotic Gore: Studies in the Literature of the American Civil War*, pp. 12-13; hereafter cited as *PG*.

4. Murray Krieger, *Theory of Criticism: A Tradition and its System*, p. 55.

5. See Chapter 12.

6. R. S. Crane, "Critical and Historical Principles of Literary History," *The Idea of the Humanities and other Essays Critical and Historical*, II, p. 77.

7. *AC*, pp. 21-22 and dedication.

8. Brian Gallagher, "The Historical Consciousness of Edmund Wilson," 7753A.

9. Edmund Wilson, *The Triple Thinkers*, pp. 258-59; hereafter cited as *TTT*.

10. Ibid., p. 259.

11. Edmund Wilson, *The Bit Between My Teeth: A Literary Chronicle of 1950-1965*, p. 1; hereafter cited as *BBT*.

12. Ibid., p. 1.

13. *AC*, pp. 93-94.

14. *BBT*, p. 2.

15. Ibid., p. 2.

16. Karl Marx and Frederich Engels, *Selected Works*, pp. 13-16.

17. Edmund Wilson, *The American Jitters: A Year of the Slump*, p. 305; hereafter cited as *AJ*.

18. Edmund Wilson, "The Literary Class War," p. 321.

19. "Marxism and Literature," *TTT*, p. 205.

20. Ibid., p. 205.

21. "The Literary Class War," p. 323.

22. Ibid., p. 321.

23. *AC*, p. 305.

24. Ibid., p. 311.

25. "The Literary Class War II," p. 348.

26. Ibid., p. 348.

27. *The New Masses*, p. 59.

28. "Novelist Bites Critic," p. 808.

29. James Y. Dayananda, "Marxist Contribution to Edmund Wilson's Criticism," p. 80.

30. Ibid., p. 62.

31. Ibid., p. 103.

32. Ibid., p. 60.

33. Quoted in *TTT*, p. 205.

34. "The Literary Class War II," pp. 347-48.

35. "Is Politics Ruining Art?" p. 83.

36. "Novelist Bites Critic," p. 809.

37. *TTT*, p. 205.

38. Daniel Aaron, *Writers on the Left*, p.269.

39. Herbert J. Muller, *Science and Criticism: The Humanistic Tradition in Contemporary Thought*, pp. 155-56.

40. Frederick Crews, *Out of My System: Psychoanalysis, Ideology, and Critical Method*, p. 168.

41. *TTT*, p. 266.

42. Crews, *Out of My System*, pp. 5-6.

43. Muller, p. 156.

44. Crews, *Out of My System*, p. 6.

45. Ibid., p. 76.

46. Ibid., p. 77.

47. *WB*, p. 283.

48. Ibid., p. 295.

49. Leon Edel, "Introduction," in *TT*, p. xli.

50. Crews, *Out of My System*, p. 5.

51. Ibid., p. 69.

52. Ibid., p. 12.

53. *WB*, p. 9.

54. *TTT*, p. 266.

55. Ibid., p. 267.

56. *AC*, pp. 213-14.

57. *WB*, p. 8.

58. Ibid., p. 16.

59. Ibid., pp. 30-31.

60. *AC*, p. 176.

61. Quoted in Crews, *Out of My System*, p. 11.

62. Peter Brooks, "The Idea of a Psychoanalytic Literary Criticism," in *The Trials of Psychoanalysis*, ed. Francoise Meltzer.

63. Crews, *Out of My System* p. 12.

CHAPTER TWO

1. *BBT*, p. 546.

2. Ibid., p. 549.

3. Edmund Wilson, *The Shores of Light: A Literary Chronicle of the Twenties and Thirties*, pp. 295-96; hereafter cited as *SL*; ibid., pp. 235-36; Edmund Wilson, *A Piece of My Mind: Reflections at Sixty*, p. 161; hereafter cited as *PMM*.

4. *PPM*, p. 85; Lewis M. Dabney, "Edmund Wilson: The Early Years," p. 102.

5. Edmund Wilson, *Classics and Commercials: A Literary Chronicle of the Forties*, pp. 112-13; hereafter cited as *CC*.

6. J. A. Clark, "The Sad Case of Edmund Wilson," pp. 292-95.

7. *CC*, p. 113.

8. Ibid., p. 16.

9. "Justice to Edith Wharton," *WB*, pp. 195-213.

10. *TTT*, pp. 265-66.

11. Ibid., p. 266.

12. Ibid., p. 269.

13. *TT*, p. 427.

14. *TTT*, p. 270.

15. Ibid., p. 270.

16. *BBT*, p. 5.

17. "The Boys in the Back Room," *CC*, pp. 19-56.

18. "W. B. Yeats," *AC*, pp. 26-63.

19. "Thoughts on Being Bibliographed," *CC*, p. 114.

20. *TT*, p. xlvi.

21. Northrop Frye, *Anatomy of Criticism: Four Essays*, p. 8.

22. Warner Berthoff, *Edmund Wilson*, p. 44; Stanley Edgar Hyman, "Edmund Wilson and Translation in Criticism," pp. 19, 21.

23. Charles I. Glicksberg, "Edmund Wilson: Radicalism at the Crossroads," pp. 466-67.

24. Robert Heilman, "The Freudian Reading of *The Turn of the Screw*," pp. 433-45.

25. Donald A. Stauffer, ed. *The Intent of the Critic*, p. 37.

26. Clive James, "The Metropolitan Critic," in *First Reactions: Critical Essays 1968-79*, pp. 3-16; Giles Gunn, *The Culture of Criticism and the Criticism of Culture*, p. 26.

27. Stephen Jay Gould, "Understanding Science Past and Present," review of *The Search for Solutions* by Horace Freeland Judson, p. 7.

28. Clive James, "Edmund Wilson and the End of the American Dream," *TLS* p. 562 reprinted as "The Metropolitan Critic" in his *First Reactions: Critical Essays 1968-79*, pp. 3-16.

CHAPTER THREE

1. Much of this review of the history of humanism is indebted to H. J. Blackham, *Humanism*.

2. Walter J. Ong, S. J., "Educationists and the Tradition of Learning," *Ramus' Method and the Decay of Dialogue*, p. 167.

3. As quoted in R. S. Crane, *The Idea of the Humanities and Other Essays Critical and Historical*, I, 152, a work to which the greater portion of this area of the discussion is indebted.

4. Giles Gunn, *The Criticism of Culture and the Culture of Criticism*.

5. Edmund Wilson, "Religion," *PMM*, p. 8.

6. *AC*, p. 297.

7. *SL* pp. 518-34.

8. Elena Wilson, ed., *Letters on Literature and Politics*, p. 649; hereafter cited as *LLP*.

9. Edmund Wilson, *Upstate: Records and Recollections of Northern New York*, pp. 166-67; hereafter cited as *Upstate*.

10. *CC*, p. 113.

11. Walter Lippman, *A Preface to Morals* [1929]; reprinted (Boston Beacon, 1960).

12. Ibid., p. 223.

13. Edmund Wilson, "Introduction," *A Preface to Morals*, p. 12.

14. Ibid., p. 13.

15. As quoted in Matthew Arnold, "Sainte-Beuve," *The Last Word*, pp. 106-20, an essay to which the review here of Sainte-Beuve's life is greatly indebted.

16. Ibid., p. 115.

17. Ibid., p. 116.

18. Ibid., p. 115. Lionel Trilling, *Matthew Arnold*, p. 191.

19. "Sainte-Beuve," ibid., pp. 115-16.

20. *AC*, pp. 85-87.

21. As quoted in Matthew Arnold, "The Literary Influence of the Academies," *Lectures and Essays in Criticism*, p. 236.

22. *TTT*, p. 206.

23. Charles Augustin Sainte-Beuve, *Causeries du Lundis*, ed. George Saintsbury, p. xvii.

24. *Literary Criticism of Sainte-Beuve*, p. 1.

25. *BBT*, p. 2.

26. Ibid., p. 2.

27. Walter Jackson Bate, "Charles Augustin Sainte-Beuve," *Criticism: The Major Texts*, p. 490.

28. Ibid., p. 490.

29. Ibid., p. 490.

30. *Literary Criticism of Sainte-Beuve*, p. 2.

31. *AC*, p. 297.

32. As quoted in Bate, pp. 501-02.

33. Saintsbury, in *Sainte-Beuve*, p. xvii.

34. *TTT*, pp. 72-73.

35. Edmund Wilson, *To the Finland Station: A Study in the Writing and Acting of History*, p. 57; hereafter cited as *TFS*.

36. *Literary Criticism of Sainte-Beuve*, p. 3.

37. *TTT*, p. 261.

38. *BBT*, p. 2.

39. As quoted in *TFS*, pp. 59-60.

40. Ibid., pp. 488-89.

41. Matthew Arnold, "The Function of Criticism at the Present Time," *Lectures and Essays in Criticism*, p. 258.

42. Ibid., p. 280.

43. Trilling, *Matthew Arnold*, p. 191.

44. *Lectures and Essays*, p. 280.

45. "Introduction," *The Portable Matthew Arnold*, ed. Lionel Trilling, p. 8.

46. Trilling, *Matthew Arnold*, p. 191.

47. *The Last Word*, p. 115.

48. "New Criticism to Structuralism," Proceedings of a Conference on the State of Criticism, *Partisan Review* 3, (1980), p. 377.

49. *English Literature and Irish Politics*, p. 230.

50. *AC*, pp. 164-65.

51. *English Literature and Irish Politics*, p. 234.

52. *SL*, pp. 57-59.

53. Ibid., pp. 66-67.

54. *Portable Matthew Arnold*, p. 14.

55. "Wordsworth," *English Literature and Irish Politics*, p. 46.

56. "The Study of Poetry," ibid., p. 161.

57. *On the Classical Tradition*, pp. 2-3.

58. *TTT*, pp. 269-70.

59. *English Literature and Irish Politics*, p. 46.

60. Ibid., p. 45.

61. Ibid., p. 46.

62. "The Critic Who Does Not Exist," *SL*, p. 372.

63. *AC*, p. 293.

64. Gunn, *The Criticism of Culture*, p. 20.

65. Ibid., p. 21.

66. *TT*, p. 98.

67. *TTT*, pp. 269-70.

68. Gunn, p. 115.

69. *TTT*, pp. 269-70.

70. As quoted in *AC*, p. 187.

CHAPTER FOUR

1. William Robbins, *The Ethical Idealism of Matthew Arnold*, p. 162.

2. Frank Kermode, *Puzzles and Epiphanies*, p. 57. In his reappraisal of *Axel's Castle*, Kermode notes the tension and poise of Wilson's approach and likens it to Arnold's: "In short, he was patient and flexible; he knew how to attach himself and then withdraw; to ascertain and subsequently to comment critically upon the master-spirit of the age." Alfred Kazin in *On Native Grounds* (1942: reprinted New York: Doubleday-Anchor, 1956), p. 347, describes Wilson's attraction to socialism in the 1930s as "based upon a deeply ingrown alienation from the culture and prizes of capitalism; a reaching that was as Arnoldian as Robert Herrick's, and as quick to turn to literature as a record of society and a criticism of life."

3. *BBT*, pp. 2-3.

4. Trilling, Introduction, *The Portable Matthew Arnold*, p. 16; Introduction, *TT*, p. xiv.

5. "The Literary Influence of Academies," *Lectures and Essays in Criticism*, pp. 232-57.

6. "Joubert," *Lectures and Essays in Criticism*. pp. 183-84.

7. *BBT*, pp. 4-5.

8. Walter Jackson Bate, ed. *Criticism: The Major Texts*, p. 547.

9. Kazin, *On Native Grounds*, pp. 220-21.

10. Ibid., p. 222.

11. *The Genteel Tradition: Nine Essays by George Santayana*, ed. Douglas L. Wilson.

12. C. Hartley Grattan, "The New Humanism and the Scientific Attitude," *The Critique of Humanism*.

13. *Criticism*, p. 546.

14. Ibid., p. 438.

15. *SL*, pp. 457-58.

16. Ibid., pp. 459-61.
17. *AC*, p. 298.
18. Gunn, *Criticism of Culture*, p. 23 ff.

CHAPTER FIVE
1. *AC*, p. 1.
2. Frank Kermode, *Puzzles and Epiphanies*, pp. 57-58.
3. *AC*, p. 28.
4. Ibid., p. 19.
5. Ibid., pp. 19-20.
6. Ibid., p. 30.
7. Ibid., p. 31.
8. Ibid., p. 32.
9. Ibid., p. 33.
10. Ibid., pp. 33-34.
11. Ibid., p. 35.
12. Ibid., pp. 36-37.
13. Ibid., pp. 37-38.
14. Ibid., p. 39.
15. "Yeats's Memoirs," pp. 22-23.
16. *Literary Criticism of Sainte-Beuve*, p. 1.
17. *AC*, p. 39.
18. Ibid., p. 40.
19. Walter J. Bate, *Criticism*, p. 490.
20. *AC*, p. 42.
21. Ibid., pp. 45-46.
22. Ibid., p. 48.
23. Ibid., pp. 58-59.
24. Ibid., p. 55.
25. Ibid., p. 56.
26. Ibid., p. 57.
27. Ibid., p. 58.
28. Ibid., p. 59.
29. Ibid., p. 60.
30. Ibid., p. 61.
31. Ibid., pp. 62-63.
32. *LLP*, p. 177.
33. *AC*, p. 296.
34. *TTT*, pp. 269-70.

CHAPTER SIX
1. *TT*, p. xlvi.
2. *AC*, p. 132.
3. Stanley Edgar Hyman, *The Armed Vision: A Study in the Methods of Modern Criticism*, p. 19.
4. *AC*, p. 134.

5. Ibid., p. 136.
6. Ibid., p. 145.
7. Ibid., p. 147.
8. Ibid., p. 150-51.
9. Ibid., p. 154.
10. Ibid., p. 156.
11. Ibid., p. 159.
12. Ibid., pp. 162-63.
13. Ibid., p. 164.
14. Ibid., p. 165.
15. Ibid., p. 164.
16. Ibid., p. 136.
17. Ibid., p. 153.
18. Ibid., pp. 153-54.
19. Ibid., p. 139.
20. ibid., p. 146.
21. Ibid., p. 163.
22. Ibid., p. 176.
23. Ibid., p. 168.
24. Ibid., p. 188.
25. Ibid., p. 184.
26. Ibid., pp. 184-85.
27. Ibid., p. 185.
28. Ibid., pp. 187-88.
29. Ibid., p. 186.
30. Ibid., p. 187.
31. Ibid., p. 189.
32. Edmund Wilson, "The Literary Class War," p. 323.

CHAPTER SEVEN
1. "The Ambiguity of Henry James," *TTT*, pp. 88-132.

Wilson's essay on James first appeared in *Hound and Horn* in 1934. As was his established practice, Wilson later included it in a critical collection. Though he changed the content of the volume several times, the inclusion of the James essay and the title, *The Triple Thinkers*, remain constant from the first [1938] edition. This title is taken from Wilson's "The Politics of Flaubert," one of the essays included. It is intended by Wilson to provide a unifying principle by which to bring together various of his periodical essays on such disparate figures as Paul Elmer More, Pushkin, A. E. Housman, Flaubert, Christian Gauss, James, John Jay Chapman, Shaw, Marx, and Ben Johnson. The concept of triple thinking, however, is not very precisely formulated by Wilson, even in the essay on Flaubert—the only place in which reference to it occurs.

Wilson says of Flaubert that "When he reasons about society . . . his conceptions seem incoherent." This is consistent, though, in

Wilson's view, and compatible with a recognition that Flaubert possessed "certainly one of the great minds of his time." The point is that although "the artist should be triply (to the *n*th degree) a thinker" he or she is, as an imaginative writer, the kind of thinker "who works directly in concrete images and does not deal at all in ideas." By inference, then, we may suppose the essays in *The Triple Thinkers* to be unified in the sense that they are all testing and exploring the relation of the artist to ideas. In a broad way this is true, but the principle of unity is not, finally, a very effective one; and Wilson has been taken to task for it by several of his critics, notably Stanley Edgar Hyman. See Chapter 11.

2. Shoshana Felman, "Turning the Screw of Interpretation," in *Literature and Psychoanalysis: The Question of Reading Otherwise,* pp. 97-98.

3. Ibid., p. 98.

4. Dorothea Krook, "Edmund Wilson and Others on 'The Turn of the Screw'," *Ordeal of Consciousness in Henry James,* pp. 370-81; "Intentions and Intentions: The Problem of Intention and Henry James's 'The Turn of the Screw'," in *The Theory of the Novel: New Essays,* ed. John Halperin, pp. 353-72; Gerald Willen, ed., *A Casebook on Henry James's "The Turn of the Screw'*; hereafter cited as *Ordeal,* "Intentions," and Willen, respectively.

5. Wayne C. Booth, *Critical Understanding: The Powers and Limits of Pluralism,* p. 286 n.

6. *Ordeal,* pp. 370, 373; "Intentions," pp. 365-66.

7. *Ordeal,* pp. 372, 374.

8. Ibid., p. 375.

9. Ibid., p. 371.

10. Ibid., p. 375.

11. Ibid., pp. 385-86.

12. Ibid., p. 387.

13. *TTT,* pp. 94-95.

14. *Ordeal,* pp. 379-80.

15. "Intentions," pp. 368-69.

16. Ibid., p. 369.

17. *Ordeal,* p. 379.

18. Ibid., p. 373 n.

19. *TTT,* pp. 88-95, 113.

20. *Ordeal,* pp. 370 n, 381; "Intentions," p. 365.

21. "Intentions," p. 370.

22. Ibid., p. 371.

23. *TTT,* p. 98.

24. Ibid., pp. 88, 94.

25. Edna Kenton, pp. 245-55.

26. *TTT,* p. 132.

27. As quoted in Willen, p. 102.

28. *TTT*, p. 88.
29. Leon Edel, *Henry James: The Untried Years, 1843-1870*.
30. *TTT*, p. 113.
31. Ibid., p. 116.
32. Ibid., p. 120.
33. Crews, *Out of My System*, p. 12.
34. *TTT*, pp. 106-07.
35. Ibid., p. 96.
36. Ibid., p. 97.
37. Ibid., p. 107.
38. Ibid., p. 108.
39. Ibid., p. 112.
40. Ibid., p. 109.
41. Ibid., pp. 110-11.
42. Ibid., p. 112.
43. Ibid., p. 101.
44. Ibid., pp. 129-31 n.
45. *Ordeal*, pp. 372-73, 373 n; "Intentions," p. 362.
46. *TTT*, p. 124.
47. Ibid., pp. 125-26.
48. Ibid., pp. 126-27.
49. Ibid., p. 127.
50. Ibid., p. 128.
51. Ibid., pp. 128-29.
52. Ibid., p. 113.
53. Ibid., p. 129.
54. Ibid., p. 132.
55. Ibid., p. viii.
56. Ibid., p. 130.
57. Ibid., pp. 131-32.

CHAPTER EIGHT

1. Edmund Wilson, "Dickens and the Marshalsea Prison," *Atlantic Monthly* 165 (April 1940), pp. 473-83; (May 1940), 68191; "Dickens: The Two Scrooges," *New Republic* 102 (4 March 1940), pp. 297-300; (11 March 1940), pp. 339-42; "The Mystery of Edwin Drood," *New Republic* 102 (8 April 1940), pp. 463-67. These articles were brought togeher in the long essay entitled "Dickens: The Two Scrooges" in *WB*, pp. 1-104.

2. *WB*, pp. 13-14.
3. Ibid., p. 14.
4. Ibid., p. 8.
5. Ibid., p. 23.
6. Ibid., pp. 23-24.
7. Ibid., p. 20.
8. Ibid., p. 28.

9. Ibid., p. 29.
10. Ibid., p. 34.
11. Ibid., p. 36.
12. Ibid., p. 38.
13. Ibid., p. 39.
14. Ibid., pp. 40-41.
15. Ibid, p. 43.
16. Ibid., p. 22.
17. Ibid., p. 43.
18. *BBT*, p. 2.
19. *WB*, p. 51.
20. Ibid., p. 44.
21. Ibid., pp. 44-45.
22. Ibid., p. 47.
23. Ibid., pp. 47-48.
24. Ibid., p. 50.
25. Ibid., p. 51.
26. Ibid., p. 8.
27. Ibid., pp. 51-52.
28. Ibid., p. 54.
29. Ibid., p. 57.
30. Ibid., p. 62.
31. Ibid., p. 64.
32. Ibid., p. 62.
33. Ibid., p. 66.
34. Ibid., p. 72.
35. Ibid., pp. 67-68.
36. Ibid., p. 67.
37. Ibid., p. 65.
38. Ibid., p. 65.
39. Ibid., p. 65-66.
40. Ibid., p. 73.
41. Ibid., p. 74.
42. Ibid., p. 74.
43. Ibid., pp. 75-76.
44. Ibid., p. 79.
45. Ibid., p. 81.
46. Ibid., p. 81.
47. Ibid., p. 82.
48. Ibid., p. 84.
49. Ibid., p. 92.
50. Ibid., p. 96.
51. Ibid., p. 15.
52. Ibid., p. 99.
53. Ibid., pp. 100-01.
54. Ibid., p. 101.

55. Ibid., pp. 102-03.

56. Ibid., pp. 103-04.

57. Ibid., p. 3.

58. Edgar Johnson, *Charles Dickens: His Tragedy and Triumph*, II, pp. 659-60. Also pp. 899, 972-94, 982-83, 991, 1038-39, 1041, 1104-05, 1107, 1123, and 1145-46.

59. George Ford, "A Note on Edmund Wilson's 'Dickens: The Two Scrooges'," in *The Dickens Critics*, ed. George Ford and Laurait Lane, Jr. p. 180.

60. Ada Nisbit and Blake Nevins, eds., *Dickens Centennial Essays*, p. vi.

61. Martin Price, Introduction in *Dickens: A Collection of Critical Essays*, p. 15.

62. Denis Donoghue, "The English Dickens and *Dombey and Son*," in *Dickens Centennial Essays*, p. 1.

63. John Gross, "Dickens: Some Recent Approaches," in *Dickens and the Twentieth Century*, ed. John Gross and Gabriel Pearson, pp. lx-x.

64. John dos Passos, *The Best Times: An Informal Memoir*, p. 139.

CHAPTER NINE

1. See Chapter 11.

2. R. S. Crane, *The Languages of Criticism and the Structure of Poetry*, p. 192.

3. *PG*, p. 3.

4. Ibid., pp. 3-4.

5. Ibid., p. 4.

6. Ibid., pp. 4-5.

7. Crane, p. 192.

8. *PG*, pp. 5-6.

9. Ibid., pp. 6-7.

10. Ibid., pp. 7-8.

11. William Phillips, "New Criticism to Structuralism," p. 377; Terry Eagleton, *Marxism and Literary Criticism*, pp. 7-8.

12. *PG*, p. 11.

13. Ibid., pp. 10-11.

14. Ibid., p. 29.

15. Ibid., p. 29.

16. Ibid., p. 30.

17. Ibid., p. 31.

18. Ibid., p. 11.

19. Ibid., p. 32.

20. Ibid., pp. 32-33.

21. Ibid., p. 33.

22. Ibid., pp. 34-35.

23. Ibid., p. 35.

24. Ibid., p. 47.

25. Ibid., p. 50.

26. Ibid., p. 51.

27. Ibid., p. 56.

28. Ibid., p. 57.

29. Ibid., p. 57.

30. Ibid., p. 58.

31. ibid., p. 58.

32. Thomas F. Gossett, *Uncle Tom's Cabin and American Culture*, p. 398; see also Eric J. Sundquist, ed., *New Essays on Uncle Tom's Cabin*, pp. 3-58.

CHAPTER TEN

1. *A Window on Russia: for the Use of Foreign Readers*; hereafter cited as *WR*.

2. *The Nabokov-Wilson Letters: Correspondence between Vladimir Nabokov and Edmund Wilson, 1940-1971*, ed. Simon Karlinsky, hereafter cited as Karlinsky.

3. "Dearest Elena," prefatory material, *WR*.

4. *WR*, p. 15.

5. Ibid., p. 42.

6. Ibid., pp. 53-54.

7. Ibid., p. 16.

8. Ibid., pp. 68-146.

9. Ibid., p. 72.

10. Ibid., p. 73.

11. Ibid., pp. 73-74.

12. Ibid., p. 87.

13. Crews, *Out of My System*, p. 77.

14. *WR*, pp. 209-37.

15. V. S. Pritchett, "Difficult Friends," p. 52.

16. *WR*, pp. 230, 234.

17. Vladimir Nabokov, "Reply to My Critics," *Strong Opinions*, pp. 247-61; hereafter cited as *Opinions*. See also *Nabokov's Congeries*, pp. 300-21.

18. Pp. 3-6. See also *WR*, pp. 209-31.

19. Alexander Gerschenkron, "A Manufactured Monument?", pp. 336-47; hereafter cited as Gerschenkron.

20. *TTT*, pp. 32-33.

21. Vladimir Nabokov, Foreword, Alexander Pushkin, *Eugene Onegin*, trans. Vladimir Nabokov, I, pp. vii-xii; hereafter cited as *Onegin*.

22. Gerschenkron, pp. 336-37.

23. *Onegin*, I, x.

24. Gerschenkron, p. 336.

25. Ibid., p. 341.

26. *WR*, pp. 215-16.

27. *Onegin,* ix.

28. *WR,* p. 210.

29. Harry Levin, "A Contest Between Conjurors," *Memories of the Moderns,* p. 214; hereafter cited as Levin.

30. *WR,* pp. 223-26.

31. Ibid., p. 211.

32. Ibid., p. 212.

33. Ibid., p. 210.

34. John Updike, "The Cuckoo and the Rooster," p. 156.

35. *CC,* p. 60.

36. Edmund Wilson, *Upstate,* p. 161.

37. Pritchett, "Difficult Friends," p. 1.

38. *Opinions,* p. 248.

39. Karlinsky, pp. 4, 22-23.

40. "Letters," *New York Times Book Review* (7 November 1971).

41. *WR,* p. 210.

42. Ibid., pp. 213-14.

43. *WR,* pp. 209-10.

44. As quoted in *Opinions,* p. 266.

45. *WR,* p. 226.

46. Gerschenkron, p. 341.

47. Ibid., p. 342.

48. Ibid., p. 343.

49. Karlinsky, pp. 14-15.

50. *WR,* p. 223.

51. *TTT,* p. 41.

52. Ibid., pp. 46-47.

53. *Onegin,* III, 40.

54. *WR,* pp. 223-24.

55. *Opinions,* pp. 263-64.

56. Vladimir Nabokov, "Franz Kafka," in *Lectures on Literature*; and Edmund Wilson, "A Dissenting Opinion on Kafka," in *CC*; hereafter cited as Nabokov and Wilson, respectively.

57. Wilson, pp. 387-88.

58. Nabokov, p. 251.

59. *WR,* pp. 236-37.

60. Karlinsky, p. 288; *WR,* p. 237.

CHAPTER ELEVEN

1. Stanley Edgar Hyman, "Edmund Wilson and Translation in Criticism," *The Armed Vision,* pp. 19-48; hereafter cited as Hyman.

2. Elmer Borklund, *Contemporary Literary Critics,* p. 280.

3. Hyman., p. 19.

4. Ibid., pp. 20-21.

5. Sherman Paul, *Edmund Wilson: A Study of Literary Vocation in Our Time,* p. 148 n.

6. See Richard David Ramsey, *Edmund Wilson: A Bibliography.*

7. Hyman, p. 19.
8. Ibid., pp. 19-20.
9. Ibid., p. 21.
10. Ibid., p. 22.
11. Ibid., pp. 19-22.
12. See *AC*, pp. 296 ff.
13. *AC*, p. 298.
14. Hyman, p. 25.
15. Ibid., p. 24.
16. Ibid., pp. 24-25.
17. Ibid., pp. 21-22.
18. Ibid., p. 34.
19. Ibid., p. 44.
20. Ibid., p. 35.
21. Ibid., p. 36.
22. Ibid., p. 37.
23. Ibid., pp. 42-43.
24. Ibid., pp. 19-20.
25. Delmore Schwartz, "The Writing of Edmund Wilson"; hereafter cited as Schwartz (pages cited are from the reprint volume).
26. Ibid., p. 642.
27. See p. 26 of this study.
28. Schwartz, p. 644.
29. Ibid., p. 643.
30. Ibid., p. 344.
31. Letter to the author (9 July 1975).
32. Richard Gilman, "Edmund Wilson, Then and Now," p. 23.
33. Leonard Kriegel, *Edmund Wilson*, p. 89; Charles P. Frank, *Edmund Wilson*, p. 183.
34. See p. 82 of this study.
35. Alfred Kazin, "Edmund Wilson: The Critic and His Age," p. 94.
36. See p. 34 and p. 61 of this study.
37. Warner Berthoff, *Edmund Wilson*.
38. Ibid., p. 22-23.
39. Ibid., p. 28.
40. Ibid., p. 30.
41. See p. 160 of this study.

CHAPTER TWELVE
1. Doris Grumbach, *The Company She Kept: A Revealing Portrait of Mary McCarthy*, p. 120.
2. Letter from Leon Edel (18 August 1988).
3. *TTT*, pp. 255-56.
4. *SL*, pp. 3-26.
5. "The Author at Sixty," *PMM*, p. 227.

6. Conversation with Penelope Gilliatt (20 September 1988).

7. Allen Tate, "Edmund Wilson," in *We Moderns: Gotham Book Mart 1920-1940*, p. 71.

8. Leon Edel, "Edmund Wilson in the 1930s," p. 32.

9. *TT*, pp. 155-57.

10. Ibid., pp. 362-63.

11. Ibid., p. 404.

12. Ibid., p. 423.

13. Ibid., pp. 427-28.

14. Ibid., p. 545.

15. *Upstate*, p. 256.

16. Leon Edel, "A Portrait of Edmund Wilson," introduction to Edmund Wilson, *The Twenties*, pp. xvii-xviii.

17. Ibid., p. xxi.

18. Ibid., p. xviii.

19. Ibid., p. xxii.

20. Ibid., p. xxvi.

21. Ibid., p. xxv.

22. Ibid., pp. xxiii-xxiv.

23. Ibid., pp. xxv-xxvi.

24. Ibid., p. xviii.

25. Ibid., pp. xxv-xxvii.

26. Ibid., p. xxv.

27. Ibid., p. xviii.

28. Edel, "Edmund Wilson in the 1930s," p. 32.

29. *PMM*, p. 98.

30. *TTT*, pp. 269-70.

31. *LLP*, p. 46.

32. Ibid., p. 317.

33. Ibid., p. 643.

34. Ibid., p. 310.

35. Ibid., p. 63.

36. Ibid., p. 95.

37. Ibid., p. 295.

CONCLUSION

1. Clive James, "Edmund Wilson and the American Dream," p. 562.

2. Elmer Borklund, *Contemporary Literary Critics*, p. 519.

3. *TTT*, pp. 255-56.

BIBLIOGRAPHY

WORKS BY EDMUND WILSON

The Undertaker's Garland, in collaboration with John Peale Bishop. New York: Alfred A. Knopf, 1922.

Discordant Encounters: Plays and Dialogues. New York: Boni, 1926.

"Yeats's Memoirs," *New Republic* 50 (23 February 1927).

I Thought of Daisy. New York: Charles Scribner's Sons, 1929.

I Thought of Daisy [and] *Galahad*, rev. ed. New York: Farrar, Straus and Giroux, 1967.

Poets, Farewell! New York: Charles Scribner's Sons, 1929.

Axel's Castle: A Study in the Imaginative Literature of 1870-1930. New York: Charles Scribner's Sons, 1931.

The American Jitters: A Year of the Slump. New York: Charles Scribner's Sons, 1932.

"The Literary Class War," *New Republic* (4 May 1932).

"The Literary Class War II," *New Republic* (11 May 1932).

"Is Politics Ruining Art?" *Forum* 40 (August 1933).

"Novelist Bites Critic," *The Nation* 142 (24 June 1936).

Travels in Two Democracies. New York: Harcourt, 1936.

This Room and This Gin and These Sandwiches: Three Plays. New York: New Republic, 1937.

The Triple Thinkers: Ten Essays on Literature [New York: Harcourt, 1938]. Rev. and enlarged ed. as *The Triple Thinkers: Twelve Essays on Literary Subjects*, New York: Oxford University Press, 1948.

To the Finland Station: A Study in the Writing and Acting of History [New York: Harcourt Brace, 1940; Garden City, N.Y. Anchor-Doubleday, 1953]. Rev. ed. New York: Farrar, Straus and Giroux, 1972.

The Boys in the Back Room: Notes on California Novelists. San Francisco: Colt, 1941.

The Wound and the Bow: Seven Studies in Literature. [Boston: Houghton Mifflin, 1941] reissued with corrections, New York: Oxford University Press, 1947.

Note-Books of Night. San Francisco: Colt, 1942.

The Shock of Recognition: The Development of Literature in the United States Recorded by the Men Who Made It. Garden City, N.Y.: Doubleday, 1943.

Memoirs of Hecate County. [Garden City, N.Y.: Doubleday, 1946]. New York: Noonday-Farrar, Straus and Giroux, 1965.

Europe without Baedeker: Sketches among the Ruins of Italy, Greece and England. [Garden City, N.Y.: Doubleday, 1947]. Rev. and enlarged ed. as *Europe without Baedeker: Sketches among the Ruins of Italy, Greece, and England, together with Notes from a European Diary: 1963-1964.* New York: Farrar, Straus and Giroux, 1966.

The Little Blue Light: A Play in Three Acts. New York: Farrar, Straus and Young, 1950.

Classics and Commercials: A Literary Chronicle of the Forties. New York: Farrar, Straus and Young, 1950.

The Shores of Light: A Literary Chronicle of the Twenties and Thirties. New York: Farrar, Straus and Young, 1952.

Night Thoughts. New York: Farrar, Straus and Cudahy, 1953.

Eight Essays. Garden City, N.Y.: Anchor-Doubleday, 1954.

Five Plays. New York: Farrar, Straus and Young, 1954.

The Scrolls from the Dead Sea. [New York: Oxford University Press, 1955]. Rev. ed. as *The Dead Sea Scrolls.* New York: Oxford University Press, 1969.

A Piece of My Mind: Reflections at Sixty. New York: Farrar, Straus and Cudahy, 1956.

Red, Blond, Black and Olive: Studies in Four Civilizations: Zuni, Haiti, Soviet Russia, Israel. New York: Oxford University Press, 1956.

A Literary Chronicle: 1920-1950. Garden City, N.Y.: Doubleday, 1956.

The American Earthquake: A Documentary of the Twenties and Thirties. Garden City, N.Y.: Doubleday, 1958.

Apologies to the Iroquois, with "The Mohawks in High Steel" by Joseph Mitchell. New York: Farrar, Straus and Giroux, 1960.

Patriotic Gore: Studies in the Literature of the American Civil War. New York: Oxford University Press, 1962.

The Cold War and the Income Tax: A Protest. New York: Farrar, Straus and Giroux, 1963.

O Canada: An American's Notes on Canadian Culture. New York: Farrar, Straus and Giroux, 1965.

The Bit Between My Teeth: A Literary Chronicle of 1950-1965. New York: Farrar, Straus, 1965.

A Prelude: Landscapes, Characters and Conversations from the Earlier Years of My Life. New York: Farrar, Straus and Giroux, 1967.

Upstate: Records and Recollections of Northern New York . New York: Farrar, Straus and Giroux, 1971.

The Fruits of the MLA. New York: The New York Review of Books, 1968.

The Duke of Palermo and Other Plays, With an Open Letter to Mike Nichols. New York: Farrar, Straus and Giroux, 1969.

A Window on Russia: For the Use of Foreign Readers. New York: Farrar, Straus and Giroux, 1972.

The Devils and Canon Barham: Ten Essays on Poets, Novelists and Monsters. New York: Farrar, Straus and Giroux, 1973.

The Twenties: From Notebooks and Diaries of the Period, ed. Leon Edel. New York: Farrar, Straus and Giroux, 1975.

The Thirties: From Notebooks and Diaries of the Period, ed. Leon Edel. New York: Farrar, Straus and Giroux, 1980.

The Forties: From Notebooks and Diaries of the Period, ed. Leon Edel. New York: Farrar, Straus and Giroux, 1983.

The Fifties: From Notebooks and Diaries of the Period, ed. Leon Edel. New York: Farrar, Straus and Giroux, 1986.

WORKS CONSULTED

Aaron, Daniel. "Edmund Wilson's War." Review of *Patriotic Gore, Massachusetts Review* 3 (Spring 1962), pp. 555-70.

_____. "The Life and Thought of Edmund Wilson." *Bulletin of the American Academy of Arts and Sciences*, 28 (February 1975), pp. 26-41.

_____. *Writers on the Left: Episodes in American Literary Communism*. New York: Harcourt, Brace and World, 1961.

Adams, Robert M. "Masks and Delays: Edmund Wilson as a Critic." *Sewanee Review* 55 (April 1948), pp. 272-86.

Aldridge, John W. "Wilson's Daybooks." Review of *The Twenties, Saturday Review*, 210 (17 May 1975), pp. 24-26.

Alter, Robert. "Edmund Wilson vs. America." Review of *Letters on Literature and Politics: 1912-1972*, ed. Elena Wilson. *Commentary* (January 1978), pp. 29-35.

Arnold, Matthew. *On the Classic Tradition*. ed. R. H. Super. Ann Arbor: University of Michigan Press, 1960.

_____. *Lectures and Essays in Criticism*, ed. R. H. Super. Ann Arbor: University of Michigan Press, 1962.

_____. *The Last Word*, ed. R. H. Super. Ann Arbor: University of Michigan Press, 1977.

_____. *English Literature and Irish Politics*, ed. R. H. Super. Ann Arbor: University of Michigan Press, 1973.

Bate, Walter Jackson, ed. *Criticism: The Major Texts*. New York: Harcourt, Brace and World, 1952.

Berthoff, Warner. *Edmund Wilson*. University of Minnesota Pamphlets on American Writers, No. 67. Minneapolis: University of Minnesota Press, 1968.

Bishop, John Peale. "The Discipline of Poetry." Review of *Axel's Castle*. Virginia Quarterly Review 14 (Summer 1938), pp. 343-56.

Blackham, H. J. *Humanism*. London: Routledge, 1953.

Blackmur, R. P. Review of *The Triple Thinkers*. Virginia Quarterly Review 14 (Summer 1938), pp. 446-50.

Booth, Wayne C. *Critical Understanding: The Powers and Limits of Pluralism*. Chicago: University of Chicago Press, 1979.

Borklund, Elmer, ed. *Contemporary Literary Critics*. New York: St. Martin's Press, 1979.

Breit, Harvey. "Talk with Edmund Wilson." *New York Times Book Review* (2 November 1952), p. 18.

Brooks, Peter. "The Idea of Psychoanalytic Literary Criticism," in *The Trials of Psychoanalysis*, ed. Francoise Meltzer. Chicago: University of Chicago Press, 1988.

Brown, E. K. "The Method of Edmund Wilson." *University of Toronto Quarterly* 11 (October 1941), pp. 105-11.

Bryer, Jackson, ed. *F. Scott Fitzgerald: The Critical Reception*. New York: Franklin, 1978.

Burke, Kenneth. *The Philosophy of Literary Form: Studies in Symbolic Action*. [Baton Rouge: Louisiana State University Press, 1941]. New York: Vintage-Knopf, 1957.

Castronovo, David. *Edmund Wilson*. New York: Ungar, 1984.

Chase, Richard. "Wilson as Critic." *Partisan Review* 20 (January-February 1953), pp. 112-13.

Chopin, Kate. *The Complete Works of Kate Chopin*, ed. Per Seyersted, foreword by Edmund Wilson. Baton Rouge: Louisiana State University Press, 1969.

Cioffi, Frank. "Intention and Interpretation in Criticism." In *Issues in Contemporary Literary Criticism*, ed. Gregory T. Polletta. Boston: Little Brown and Company, 1973.

Clark, J. A. "The Sad Case of Edmund Wilson." *Commonweal* 28 (8 July 1938), pp. 292-95.

Costa, Richard Hauer. *Edmund Wilson: Our Neighbor in Talcottville*. Syracuse: Syracuse University Press, 1980.

Cowley, Malcolm. *Exile's Return: A Literary Odyssey of the 1920s*. New York: Viking, 1951.

_____. "Hecate Co. Revisited." Review of 1980 reissued *Memoirs of Hecate County* with an afterword by John Updike. *The New York Times Book Review* (Summer Reading Issue, 1980), pp. 11, 32-33.

Crane, R. S. *The Idea of the Humanities and Other Essays Critical and Historical*. 2 vols. Chicago: University of Chicago Press, 1967.

_____. *The Languages of Criticism and the Structure of Poetry*. Toronto: University of Toronto Press, 1953.

Crews, Frederick C. "A Critic and His Time." *Times Literary Supplement* 28777 (19 April 1957), p. 240.

_____. "Lessons of the Master." Review of *The Bit Between My Teeth*. *New York Review of Books* 5 (25 November 1965), pp. 4-5.

_____. "Edmund Wilson and *The Wound and the Bow*." *Southern Review* 91, no. 1 (Winter 1983), (1), pp. 155-165.

Dayananda, James Y. "Marxist Contribution to Edmund Wilson's Literary Criticism." Diss., Temple University, 1969.

Demetz, Peter. *Marx, Engels, and the Poets: Origins of Marxist Criticism*, trans. Jeffrey L. Sammons. Chicago: University of Chicago Press, 1967.

Dickstein, Morris. *Gates of Eden: American Culture in the Sixties*. New York: Basic Books, 1977.

Donoghue, Denis. "The English Dickens and *Dombey and Son*." In *Dickens Centennial Essays*, ed. Ada Nisbet and Blake Nevins. Berkeley: University of California Press, 1971.

Dos Passos, John. *The Best Times: An Informal Memoir*. New York: New American Library, 1966.

Douglas, George H. *Edmund Wilson's America*. Lexington: University Press of Kentucky, 1983.

Dupee, Frederick. "Edmund Wilson's Criticism." Review of *The Triple Thinkers*. *Partisan Review* 4 (May 1938), pp. 48-51.

Edel, Leon. "Am I, Then, in a Pocket of the Past?" Review of *A Piece of My Mind*. *New Republic* 135 (17 December 1956), pp. 25-26.

_____. *Henry James: The Untried years, 1850-1870*. New York: Lippincott, 1953.

_____. "Edmund Wilson in the 1930s," *New Republic*, (3 May 1980).

"Edmund Wilson's Shelf." Editorial. *New York Times* (6 December 1979), Sec. A., p. 30.

"Edmund Wilson and the End of the American Dream." (Unsigned) review of *Upstate*. *Times Literary Supplement*, (19 May 1972), pp. 561-64.

Epstein, Joseph. Review of *The Twenties*. *New York Times Book Review*, (15 June 1975), pp. 1-2.

Exley, Frederick. *Pages From a Cold Island*. New York: Random House, 1974.

Felman, Shoshana, "Turning the Screw of Interpretation." In *Literature and Psychoanalysis: The Literature of Reading Otherwise*, ed. Shoshana Felman. Baltimore: Johns Hopkins University Press, 1982.

Fargnoli, Joseph R. "Edmund Wilson and the Sociology of Literature." Diss., University of Rhode Island 1985.

Fiedler, Leslie. Review of *The Wound and the Bow*. *New Leader*, 30 (13 Dec. 1947), p. 15.

Fiess, Edward. "Edmund Wilson: Art and Ideas." *Antioch Review*, 1 (Sept. 1941), pp. 356-67.

Fitzgerald, F. Scott. *The Crack-Up*, ed. Edmund Wilson. New York: New Directions, 1945.

_____. *The Last Tycoon*, ed. Edmund Wilson. New York: Charles Scribner's Sons, 1941.

Foerster, Norman, ed. *Humanism and America: Essays on the Outlook of Modern Civilization*. New York: Rinehart, 1930.

Ford, George. "A Note on Edmund Wilson's 'Dickens: The Two Scrooges'." In *The Dickens Critics*, ed. George Ford and Laurait Lane, Jr. Ithaca, N.Y.: Cornell University Press, 1961.

Fraiberg, Louis B. "Edmund Wilson and Psychoanalysis in Criticism." *Psychoanalysis and American Literary Criticism*. Detroit: Wayne State University Press, 1960.

Frank, Charles P. *Edmund Wilson*. New York: Twayne, 1970.

Frye, Northrop. *Anatomy of Criticism: Four Essays*. Princeton: Princeton University Press, 1957.

Gallagher, Brian T. "The Historical Consciousness of Edmund Wilson." Diss., University of Pennsylvania 1973.

Gauss, Christian. "Edmund Wilson, the Campus and the Nassau 'Lit'." *Princeton University Literary Chronicle*, 5 (February 1944), pp. 41-50.

_____. *The Papers of Christian Gauss*, ed. Katherine Gauss and Hiram Haydn. New York: Random House, 1957.

Gerschenkron, Alexander. "A Manufactured Monument?" Review of *Eugene Onegin*, by Alexandr Pushkin, trans. Vladimir Nabokov. *Modern Philology*, 4 (May 1966), pp. 336-47.

Gilman, Richard. "The Critic as Taxpayer." Review of *The Cold War and the Income Tax*. *New Republic* 149 (30 November 1963), pp. 25-27.

_____. "Edmund Wilson, Then and Now." Review of *The Bit Between My Teeth*. *New Republic* 155 (2 July 1966), pp. 23-28.

Glicksberg, Charles. "Edmund Wilson: Radicalism at the Crossroads." *South Atlantic Quarterly* 36 (October 1937), pp. 466-77.

Goldhurst, William. *F. Scott Fitzgerald and His Contemporaries*. Cleveland: World, 1963.

Gossett, Thomas F. *Uncle Tom's Cabin and American Culture*. Dallas: Southern Methodist University Press, 1985.

Gould, Stephen Jay. "Understanding Science Past and Present." Review of *The Search for Solutions* by Horace Freeland Judson. *New York Times Book Review (18 May 1980), p. 7.

Grattan, C. Hartley, ed. *The Critique of Humanism*. New York: Brewer, 1930.

Graves, Robert. "Edmund Wilson, A Protestant Abroad." Review of *Red, Blond, Black and Olive. New Republic*, 134 (30 April 1956), pp. 13-16.

Gross, John and Gabriel Pearson, ed. *Dickens and the Twentieth Century*. Toronto: University of Toronto Press, 1962.

Groth, Janet. "Edmund Wilson: The Private Side." Review of *The Twenties. Commonweal* 12 (29 August 1975), pp. 371-73.

_____. "The Literary Criticism of Edmund Wilson." Diss., New

York University 1982.

_____. Review of *The Nabokov-Wilson Letters*, ed. Simon Karlinsky. *Commonweal* 22 (7 December 1979), pp. 695-96.

_____. "Wilson in Deshabille." Review of *The Forties. The American Scholar* 53, (Summer 1984), pp. 421-26.

_____. "The World of Edmund Wilson." Review of *Letters on Literature and Politics: 1912-1972. Commonweal* 10 (12 May 1978), pp. 311-13.

Grumbach, Doris, *The Company She Kept: A Revealing Portrait of Mary McCarthy*. New York: Coward McCann, 1967.

Gunn, Giles. *The Criticism of Culture and the Culture of Criticism.* New York: Oxford University Press, 1987.

Heilman, Robert. "The Freudian Reading of *The Turn of the Screw." Modern Language Notes* 62 (November 1947), pp. 433-35.

Hicks, Granville. "The Failure of Left Criticism." *New Republic* 113 (9 September 1940), pp. 345-47.

_____. "The Intransigence of Edmund Wilson." *Antioch Review* 6 (Winter 1946-47), pp. 550-62.

Hoffman, Daniel. *Poe Poe Poe Poe Poe Poe Poe*. Garden City, N.Y.: Anchor-Doubleday, 1972.

Hoffman, Frederick J. *The Twenties: American Writing in the Postwar Decade*. New York: Viking, 1959.

Holland, Norman D. *The Dynamics of Literary Response*. New York: Norton, 1975.

Howe, Irving. "Edmund Wilson: A Re-examination." *Nation* 167 (16 October 1948), pp. 430-33.

Hyman, Stanley Edgar. "Edmund Wilson and Translation in Criticism." *The Armed Vision: A Study in the Methods of Modern Literary Criticism*. New York: Alfred A. Knopf, 1948. This chapter is deleted in later editions.

James, Clive. "The Metropolitan Critic," *First Reactions: Criticial Essays 1968-1979*. New York: Alfred A. Knopf, 1980.

Johnson, Edgar. *Chalres Dickens: His Tragedy and Triumph*. New York: Simon and Schuster, 1952.

Jones, Howard Mumford. "The Limits of Contemporary Criticism." *Saturday Review* 24 (6 September 1941), pp. 3-4, 17.

Josephson, Matthew. "Encounters with Edmund Wilson." *Southern Review* 11 (1975), pp. 731-65.

Karlinsky, Simon, ed. *The Nabokov-Wilson Letters, Correspondence between Vladimir Nabokov and Edmund Wilson, 1940-1971*. New York: Harper and Row, 1979.

Kazin, Alfred. "Edmund Wilson: The Critic and the Age." *The Inmost Leaf: A Selection of Essays*. New York: Harcourt, Brace and World, 1955.

_____. "Edmund Wilson: His Life and Books." Atlantic Monthly 220 (July 1976), pp. 80-83.

_____. "Edmund Wilson on the Thirties," *Contemporaries*.

New York: Little, Brown and Company, 1962.

_____. *On Native Grounds: An Interpretation of Modern American Prose Literature.* [New York: Harcourt, Brace and World, 1942.] New York: Doubleday-Anchor, 1956.

Kermode, Frank. "Edmund Wilson and Mario Praz." *Puzzles and Epiphanies: Essays and Reviews 1958-1961.* London: Routledge and Kegan Paul, 1962.

_____. "Edmund Wilson's Achievement." *Encounter* 5 (May 1966), pp. 61-66, 68, 70.

Kluge, Paul Frederick. "Wanderers: Three American Writers of the Twenties." Diss., University of Chicago 1967. Treats work of Carl Van Vechten, Harold Edmund Stearns, and Edmund Wilson.

Kriegel, Leonard. *Edmund Wilson.* Carbondale: Southern Illinois University Press, 1971.

Krieger, Murray. *Theory of Criticism: A Tradition and Its System.* Baltimore: Johns Hopkins University Press, 1976.

Krook, Dorothea. "Edmund Wilson and Others on 'The Turn of the Screw'." *Ordeal of Consciousness in Henry James.* Cambridge, England: Cambridge University Press, 1962.

_____. "Intention and Intentions: The Problem of Intention and Henry James's 'The Turn of the Screw'." In *The Theory of the Novel: New Essays*, ed. John Halperin. Toronto: Oxford University Press, 1974.

Leavis, F. R. "A Serious Artist." *Scrutiny* 1 (September 1932), pp. 173-79.

_____. Review of *The Wound and the Bow. Scrutiny* 11 (Summer 1942), pp. 72-73.

Lebowitz, Naomi. *Humanism and the Absurd in the Modern Novel.* Evanston: Northwestern University Press, 1971.

Lehman-Haupt, Christopher. "Books of the Times." Review of *The Nabokov-Wilson Letters. New York Times* 23 May 1979, Sec. A, p. 27.

Levin, Harry. *Memories of the Moderns.* New York: New Directions, 1980.

Limmer, Ruth, ed. *What the Woman Lived: Selected Letters of Louise Bogan, 1920-1970.* New York: Harcourt Brace Jovanovich, 1973.

Littlejohn, David. "To the Wilson Station: Edmund Wilson's Crusade against Cant." *Commonweal* 76 (7 September 1962), pp. 492-94.

MacDougall, Allan Ross, ed. *The Letters of Edna St. Vincent Millay.* New York: Harper and Row, 1952.

Marx, Karl, and Frederick Engels. *Selected Works.* New York: International Publishers, 1968.

Mathewson, Ruth. "Edmund Wilson's Instruction." Review of *Letters on Literature and Politics. New Leader* 5 December 1977, pp. 3-4.

Matthews, T. S. "An American Original." *Saturday Review* 17 May 1975, pp. 19-23.

Matthiessen, F. O. "A Critic of Importance." *Yale Review* 20 (June 1931), pp. 854-56.

McSweeney, Kerry. "Edmund Wilson and a 'Truly Human Culture'." *Canadian Review of American Studies* 4 (1973), pp. 96-106.

Miller, J. Hillis. *Charles Dickens: The World of the Novel.* Cambridge: Harvard University Press, 1958.

Miller, Perry. "Essays and Asides: A Passion for Literature." *Nation* 172 (27 January 1951), pp. 87-88.

Monteiro, George. "Addenda to Ramsey's Edmund Wilson." *Papers of the Bibliographical Society of America* 68 (1974), p. 439.

Muller, Herbert J. *Science and Criticism: The Humanistic Tradition in Contemporary Thought.* New Haven: Yale University Press, 1971.

Nabokov, Dmitri. *Vladimir Nabokov: A Tribute,* ed. Peter Quennell. New York: William Morrow, 1979.

Nabokov, Vladimir. *Lectures on Literature.* Ed. Fredson Bowers. New York: Harcourt Brace Jovanovich, 1980.

_____. *Novokov's Congeries,* selected by Page Stegner. New York: Viking, 1968.

_____. *Strong Opinions.* New York: McGraw-Hill Book Co., 1975.

Nin, Anais. *The Diaries of Anais Nin.* vol. IV. New York: Harcourt Brace Jovanovich, 1971.

Nisbet, Ada and Blake Nevins, ed. *Dickens Centennial Essays.* Berkeley: University of California Press, 1971.

Novack, George. *Humanism and Socialism.* New York: Pathfinder, 1973.

Olson, Elder. "Recent Literary Criticism." *Modern Philology* 40 (February 1943), pp. 275-83.

Ong, Walter, S. J. "Educationists and the Tradition of Learning," *Ramus: Method and the Decay of Dialogue.* Cambridge: Harvard University Press, 1958.

Paul, Sherman. *Edmund Wilson: A Study of Literary Vocation in Our Time.* Urbana: University of Illinois Press, 1965.

Perenyi, Eleanor. "Wilson." *Esquire* 60 (July 1963), pp. 80-85.

Phillips, William. *New Criticism to Structuralism.* Proceedings of a Conference on the State of Criticism. *Partisan Review* 3 (1980), p. 377.

_____. "The Wholeness of Literature: Edmund Wilson's Essays." *American Mercury* 75 (November 1952), pp. 103-07.

Podhoretz, Norman. *Doings and Undoings: The Fifties and After in American Writing.* New York: Farrar, Straus and Giroux, 1964.

Price, Martin, ed. *Dickens: A Collection of Critical Essays.* Englewood Cliffs, N.J.: Prentice-Hall, 1967.

Pritchett, V. S. "A Commitment to Letters and Life." *New York Times Book Review* 2 October 1966, pp. 1, 36.

_____. "Difficult Friends." Review of *The Nabokov-Wilson Let-*

ters. New York Times Book Review (10 June 1979), pp. 1, 52.

Pushkin, Alexander. *Eugene Onegin: A Novel in Verse*, trans. Vladimir Nabokov. Bollingen Series, 72, 4 vols. New York: Random House, 1964.

_____. *Pushkin Threefold: Narrative, Lyric, Polemic, and Ribald Verse*, the originals with linear and metric trans. Walter Arndt. New York: E. P. Dutton, 1972.

Ramsey, Richard David. *Edmund Wilson: A Bibliography*. New York: David Lewis, 1971.

Richler, Mordecai. "Wilson in Canada." Review of *Canada. New York Review of Books* 5 (30 September 1965), pp. 8-9.

Robbins, William. *The Ethical Idealism of Matthew Arnold*. Toronto: University of Toronto Press, 1959.

Rodger, James Morris. Dynamics of Creation: The Literary Criticism of Edmund Wilson." Diss., University of Rochester 1967.

Rosenthal, Melvin. "The American Writer and His Society: The Response to Estrangement in the Works of Nathaniel Hawthorne, Randolph Bourne, Edmund Wilson, Norman Mailer and Saul Bellow." Diss., University of Connecticut, 1968.

Rosenthal, M. L. *Sailing Into the Unknown: Yeats, Pound, and Eliot*. New York: Oxford University Press, 1978.

Rudin, Louis D., Jr. "Canon Fodder." Review of *The Twenties. New Republic* 167 (24 May 1975), pp. 22-23.

Sainte-Beuve, Charles Augustin. *Causeries du Lundi*, ed. George Saintsbury. Oxford, Eng.: Clarendon, 1894.

_____. *Literary Criticism of Sainte-Beuve*, trans. and ed. Emerson R. Marks. Lincoln: University of Nebraska Press, 1971.

Sammons, Jeffrey L. *Literary Sociology and Practical Criticism: An Inquiry*. Bloomington: Indiana University Press, 1977.

Santayana, George. *The Genteel Tradition: Nine Essays* ed. Douglas L. Wilson. Cambridge: Harvard University Press, 1967.

Savin, Mark D. "More Violent the Contraries." Diss., Stanford University, 1976.

Schlesinger, Lorraine Anne. "Edmund Wilson on American Literature." Diss., University of Maryland, 1968.

Schwartz, Delmore. "The Writing of Edmund Wilson," *Accent* 2 (Spring 1942), pp. 177-86. Reprinted as "Criticism of Edmund Wilson." In *Accent Anthology: Selections from Accent, A Quarterly of New Literature, 1940-1945*, ed. Kerker Quinn and Charles Shattuck. New York: Harcourt, 1946, pp. 641-55.

Spiller, Robert E. "The Influence of Edmund Wilson: The Duel Tradition." *The Nation* 186 (22 February 1958), pp. 159-61.

_____. et al, eds. *A Literary History of the United States*, vol. I. New York: MacMillan Publishing Company, 1963.

Stauffer, Donald A., ed. *The Intent of the Critic*. Princeton: Princeton University Press, 1941.

Steiner, George. *Language and Silence: Essays on Language, Literature, and the Inhuman*. New York: Atheneum, 1967.

Stephens, Robert O., ed. *Ernest Hemingway: The Critical Reception*. New York: Burt Franklin, 1977.

Sundquist, Eric J., ed. *New Essays on Uncle Tom's Cabin*. New York: Cambridge University Press, 1986.

Symons, Arthur. *The Symbolist Movement in Literature*, ed. Richard Ellmann. New York: E. P. Dutton, 1958.

Taine, Hippolyte. *A History of English Literature*, 2 vols, trans. H. Van Laun. New York: Grosset and Dunlap, 1908.

Tate, Allen. "Edmund Wilson." *We Moderns: Gotham Book Mart, 1920-1940*. New York: Gotham Book Mart, 1939, p. 71.

_____. "Three Types of Poetry: II." *New Republic* 78 (28 March 1934), pp. 180-82.

_____. "Post-Symbolism" *Hound and Horn* 4 (July-September 1931), pp. 619-24.

Taylor, Mark. "Edmund Wilson and Literature." *Commonweal* 96 (1972), pp. 386-87.

Trilling, Lionel. "Edmund Wilson: A Backward Glance." In his *A Gathering of Fugitives*. New York: Harcourt Brace Jovanovich, 1977, pp. 53-60.

_____. *Matthew Arnold*. [1939] New York: Harourt, 1954.

_____. Introduction, *The Portable Matthew Arnold*. New York: Viking, 1949.

_____. *The Liberal Imagination*. Garden City: Anchor-Doubleday, 1955.

Turnbull, Andrew. "Cool, Crisp, a Little Tart." Review of *A Prelude*. *Harper's* 235 (September 1967), pp. 120-23.

_____, ed. *The Letters of F. Scott Fitzgerald*. New York: Charles Scribner's Sons, 1963.

Updike, John. "The Cuckoo and the Rooster." Review of *The Nabokov-Wilson Letters*. *New Yorker* 11 June 1979, pp. 156-62.

_____. "*Memoirs of Hecate County* by Edmund Wilson." *New Republic* (17 January 1976), pp. 40-41.

Wagenknecht, Edward. Review of *The Wound and the Bow*. *Modern Language Quarterly* 3 (March 1942), pp. 161-64.

Wain, John. "Edmund Wilson: The Critic as Novelist." *New Republic* 142 (18 January 1960), pp. 15-17.

_____, ed. *Edmund Wilson: The Man and His Work*. New York: New York University Press, 1978.

Warren, Robert Penn. "Edmund Wilson's Civil War." Review of *Patriotic Gore*. *Commentary* 34 (August 1962), pp. 151-58.

Wellek, Rene and Austin Warren. *Theory of Literature*. New York: Harcourt, Brace, and World, 1962.

Whitehead, Alfred North. *Science and the Modern World*. New York: Macmillan Publishing Company, 1925.

Willen, Gerald, ed. *A Casebook on Henry James's "The Turn of the Screw."* New York: Crowell, 1960.

Wilson, Elena, ed. *Letters on Literature and Politics: 1912-1972.* Introduction Daniel Aaron, foreword Leon Edel. New York: Farrar, Straus and Giroux, 1977.

Wimsatt, W. K. and Cleanth Brooks. *Literary Criticism: A Short History.* New York: Alfred A. Knopf, 1967.

Yeats, William Butler. *Selected Poems and Two Plays*, ed. M. L. Rosenthal. New York: Macmillan Publishing Company, 1966.

Zabel, Morton D. "The Turn of the Screw," *The Nation*, 153 (11 October 1941), pp. 348-50.

INDEX

271

A Note about the Author

Janet Groth is an Assistant Professor
of English at the State University
of New York, Plattsburgh.